Finding Helen

Tracy Pain

New Generation Publishing

To Helen and all the staff at Medvale – I would never have made it without the love and strength you gave me – Thank you x

Preface

Medvale, the second children's home I was sent to, was a therapeutic home that took a psychodynamic approach to child therapy. The importance of early childhood experiences on children's behaviour was key to understanding where the children were coming from, where they were stuck and what therapeutic input would help them overcome their often self-destructive behaviour. Unconscious behaviours were brought to the fore, to be examined and confronted to enable the children to heal. Emotional defences were identified and broken down, to allow raw emotions to be healed with love. Using Maslow's hierarchy of needs the children's home ensured that the often neglected, basic needs of the children were met first to allow them to grow emotionally and physically. The staff offered empathy, congruence and unconditional love, the three core conditions Carl Rogers believed were essential in enabling a person to reach their potential. Combining these theories, along with known theories of the need for a child to have a primary attachment figure made Medvale a unique children's home. At a time when many children's homes medicated children who displayed extreme behaviours or even resorted to violence to subdue children, the staff at Medvale worked hard to improve the lives of children in care, without the use of repressive interventions.

Medvale was considered a 'Jewel in the Crown' of Kent Social Services and a video was made intending to promote the therapeutic work, to change the practice of other children's homes around Kent. Unfortunately, due to the controversy surrounding the arrest and later conviction of Medvale's Manager, Peter Jaynes in 1990, Medvale was closed. The historic child abuse charges, dated back to the 1970s when Peter Jaynes worked under Frank Beck in Leicestershire. Despite no evidence of abuse at Medvale,

i

the video disappeared and what was once considered the 'Jewel in the Crown', then became the 'home of shame'.

Despite the horrendous abuse suffered by the children of Leicester, some of the practices in those homes were implemented in Medvale, however, used in the way they were intended, with care and compassion and a desire to help the children that were considered, beyond help.

Regression therapy – as it was applied in Medvale – involved allowing the teenagers to regress emotionally and behaviourally to a time before they had been scared and hurt. A time when they felt safe so that they could then 'grow-up' again in a safe, caring home and have a good solid base, which would provide the building blocks for their future.

For this regression to happen, children were read bedtime stories, given baby bottles and dummies, cuddled and held for extended periods of time, bathed and allowed to play/act at a much younger level. I can only speak about how this was for me, others may have experienced this differently to me and I know this was not as therapeutic as it was intended, for some children. Some, I believe, left before they had a chance to grow up again. Some, I believe, fought against it and didn't allow themselves to lose the level of control needed for the process to work. I suppose the reasons for this lie at the heart of all humanity; we are all different. We all have different genes, different experiences and different barriers to overcome. For me, I needed love; it was that plain and simple. Regression for me made me feel loved and safe. For the first time in a very long time I felt loved; I had been re-born into a family that really cared for me and could keep me safe. People that loved me, regardless of the things I had done.

One of the hardest parts of this therapy was letting go of the anger inside of us. Being provoked into explosive rages so that we could be restrained and learn that it was safe for us to be angry and it was okay to let it out, was frightening, painful and at times made me fear for my life. In the overall therapeutic process, this served its purpose and I expect it was this aspect, which made me believe that the staff loved me. To be able to see me at my worst, to watch me lose control and still have respect, love and time for me was something I could never have imagined possible. Finding Helen has been written using my own personal diaries – my life storybook – which I was encouraged to write during my time at Medvale and memories from my time in care. In addition, actual extracts from the staff communication book – which had been transferred to my social services file – have been included. These extracts in themselves show an interesting portrayal of social work in the 1980s and the importance of thorough, honest and heartfelt communication between the staff, to maintain consistent and effective daily care. The contrast to today's factual recording cannot be ignored; gone are the days when social workers can write without fear of litigation. However, it can be seen clearly that the inclusion of personal opinion and emotions leads to a deeper, all round, understanding of the child's position and is not necessarily a negative practice in this type of residential setting.

My father shouted,
My Mother left.
His love I doubted,
For her I wept.
Eight years passed,
I moved again.
Bringing thoughts,
Of sorrow and pain.
I fought for Love,
I fought for Life.
Both battles failed,
And now I die.
They said they'd help,
They said they care.
But the one I needed,
Was not there.
I see her sometimes,
It makes me cry.
I cannot have her,
So I must die.

Tracy Pain Aged 14

Chapter 1

1984 – Aged 14

The Early Months at Medvale: Nightmares

Extract from Staff Communications Book
Date: 5/4/84
Staff: Helen M. (Social Worker / Keyworker)

Judy (co-keyworker) and I came upstairs to find Tracy much worse than she has previously been. I am now 100% certain that Tracy is indeed suffering from hysteria as Pat (Manageress) has been saying all along. She was completely unaware of her surroundings and familiar faces. We took her downstairs and tried to comfort her. Two members of staff, Sonia and Rita, were still around and Sonia felt that Tracy had chosen to regress and needed to do this with Judy. We agreed that to enable her to do this Sonia should tell Tracy that it was a secret between her (Sonia) and Tracy and that it was okay to do this. Tracy had indeed regressed and I had discussed this earlier with her Dad. He said she did do some thumb-sucking at times and had once asked for a feeding bottle. I had already told him that we would probably need to let her regress before we could get much further. Judy and I feel that Tracy has gone back to about eight years. She is in a bad state of fright. The staff lay two mattresses on the floor for Judy and Tracy with my bed pulled to the door of the end sleeping-in room, though I don't think we will be sleeping tonight. It is now 2.20am and if we can't get Tracy into a natural sleep soon, I will call the GP in to give her a sedative as she is very distressed and frightened.

Phoned GP at 2.45am and Tracy was given 5mg

Valium. Judy and I went back to bed for 4.30am.

***

The night is so very dark, the blackness all around me seems so solid that I can feel it pressing against me, pulling at me and slowing me down. I can't possibly see where I am going. If I had time to look I know I wouldn't be able to see my hands if I held them up in front of my face, but I am running, faster than I have ever run before. My legs are burning as every muscle is being pounded harder and harder as I push them to carry me forward.

I'm desperately trying to get away; fear giving me the extra push to keep on going. My heart is exploding in my chest, no longer pounding but ricocheting from my ribs, shaking every fibre of my body. Each breath I take sears through me, burning my throat and chest as I try to force enough air in and out of my lungs to keep up with the pounding of my body. I try to push myself harder and faster…I must get away. He is closing in on me and I can sense his hot, fetid breath on the back of my neck. I can smell the pungent aroma of cheap aftershave and sweat as I hear his rasping breath gaining on me.

I pound my legs harder, harder. The scream inside my head is deafening, but the only noise I am making is the wheezing of my lungs and the crashing of my body through the undergrowth. I just need to escape, to get away once and for all. I glance over my shoulder and I can see the glint of moonlight reflecting off the steel blade. I know without a doubt that he will kill me if he catches up with me, the hatred he feels for me is etched on his weathered face, it is there every time I catch him looking at me. He hates me and maybe with good reason, but I don't want to die like this. He is reaching out for me with his gnarly hands and long, manicured nails. I can feel his fingers slip from the silky fabric of my shirt giving me an extra burst of energy, a brief moment of hope. It is short lived, I have tried so very hard to get away, but I can't run any further.

My legs are as heavy as lead, my breath is coming in short gasps now, not enough to supply me with the oxygen I need. I feel myself slipping, falling, slipping...

Laying quite still, damp with my exertions, my heart still pounding in my chest and my breaths still coming in short rasps. I can feel the dream ebbing away but can't seem to pull myself out of it. I can see people looking at me. Three faces, one framed with a mass of yellow, wavy hair that flows down past her shoulders. Her face is familiar, quite round, with blue eyes and a very fair complexion; she is looking serious, almost angry. One other familiar face is framed with rich, auburn hair, cut into a bob and finished off with a full fringe. Her features are more angular, although there is a softness that seems to come from within. Her face is tanned and laughter lines spread from the corners of her eyes, yet there is no laughter there tonight, as she is also looking sombre and concerned. The last face is not known to me; her wizened, weathered face is surrounded by long grey hair crudely tied back away from her face. She looks like she is a hundred years old and has a witch-like appearance that makes me scream louder inside. The remnants of my dream seem to be confusing reality and I can't shake the fear that swells inside me. Surely, they can't be letting her near me; maybe he has sent her to finish the job he started.

One of the staff is holding me and I can feel the warmth of her body against mine, which brings me a little comfort. I can't quite catch what they are saying, as everything and everybody seem so far away. Almost dreamlike but I know I am no longer dreaming. I seem to be drifting in and out – here but not here – and all I can do is watch and lay still. My body feels heavy as if each limb were encased in lead and I can see they are troubled. I try to speak, but no sound comes out. I begin to feel strangely calm as if in this place between sleeping and waking, I cannot be hurt, safe from him, wanting to stay like this forever.

I see the gnarled face coming in close, her beady eyes watching me intently like a snake coiled ready for attack. I can see her mouth move as if she is trying to speak but in my current state of drifting I can only catch the odd word – 'catatonic' – *what on earth does that mean?*, 'trauma', I just don't understand what they are trying to say. They are pulling at my jumper and then holding my arm. I can't struggle or pull away as my body doesn't seem to be part of me anymore. I try to tell them it was just a dream, that they don't need to hurt me, but they don't hear me; it is as if I am not really there at all. As I feel a scratch on my arm, all I hear is the word 'doctor'.

***

The sunlight streaming in through the gaps in the heavy dark brown curtains wakes me up, and from the brightness I guess it must be mid-morning. I lay still for a moment trying to get my bearings as I am feeling groggy and a little confused. As I lay there slowly becoming more awake, I try to take in my surroundings.

There are two very large, soft, beige sofas, designed for comfort with thinning patches of corduroy on the arms and saggy seats showing that they had often been used. Several black and brown, large bean bags are strewn around indicating that this is not a place for airs and graces, but a room meant for relaxation and chilling out. In the corner, there is a television that is staring blankly back into the room. The television looks lost in this large room, with its high Victorian ceilings and cold, pale, wood chip walls. Everything about this room seems bleak to me; all of the attempts to make it feel warm and homely are lost on me. With beige furnishings and magnolia walls, it is too much like home, a stark reminder of the loneliness and desperation I have grown up in. I think it would be fair to say that it is probably the room I like least in the whole house.

I am at 'Medvale', a council run, therapeutic, children's home, which has been my home for the past few weeks. The staff have made me a bed on the floor; the duvet underneath me offers some comfort from the floor and I have my own duvet snuggled over me. Part of me doesn't want to wake up properly as it would be good to be able to stay in this semi-conscious state forever, then I would never have to deal with the real world again. I could just stay safe and warm always.

I don't remember being moved from my bed but, as they have put me in the TV room, I know I must have had a bad night. I am scared that the staff are going to be so angry with me for keeping everyone awake and for making them call out the doctor. I really couldn't help it and I didn't mean to keep everyone awake.

The door slowly opens and a lady pokes her tanned face around the door and peers into the room. I can see the concern in her eyes, which are puffy and showing signs of a poor night's sleep. When she sees me awake her face lights up with her usual beaming smile; her laughter lines furrowing and Helen, my key worker, my social worker and my guardian angel, replaces the worried woman from my dream.

Helen is one of the longest serving members of staff currently working at my children's home. She is amazingly insightful, seems to notice my moods and responds accordingly. Sometimes her behaviour is fun and childlike in an attempt to give me back my childhood that was so cruelly cut short. Other times she is gentle and caring, wrapping me up in an invisible duvet and protecting me from the pain that bombards me like a living entity.

Helen has a calming, soothing presence, which is reinforced by her soft Irish brogue. However, for all of her nurturing ways she is also a confident and powerful woman, who fights her corner and has often been called upon to fight mine for me. She has a fiery temper when she is crossed and incredible physical strength for a woman so slight.

Helen truly is the most wonderful woman in the world. It may be her job to care for me and guide me, but I know she really does care about me. She scoops me up and holds me tight, and promises me that everything is going to be okay. Right now, as I lay in her arms, I can believe her. I snuggle into her red jumper that is so soft against my face; I feel so safe and I know she will look after me. She carries me out to the dining room and puts me on a comfy chair while she prepares some tea and toast. She asks how I am and seems happy when I say okay. For now, there are no questions. I know the questions will come, but for now, I just want to forget.

We have breakfast together and then she lets me go up and have a bath; she has said I can stay home today and I am so relieved. I couldn't face school. I sit for a while in the room that I share with Mia. At fifteen years old, Mia is older than me and she is very kind. She is so much taller than I am and has blonde, short hair. She calls herself a tomboy and lives in her jeans and sweatshirts. She is great fun and she looks out for me the way a big sister should even though we are not related, and in return, I try to help her. She tells me about the things that used to happen to her at home and I try to be the best friend I can be; after all, we are all in the same boat now. We have partitioned our separate areas with our wardrobes and drawers to give ourselves some privacy for times like now when we need to be alone.

My mirror has photos of my Mum and my little sisters stuck to it, and I have even managed to get a photo of Tiggy, my short-haired, ginger tomcat, who I had to leave behind. I miss him terribly. Every night I used to leave my bedroom window open at my father's house so that Tiggy could come in and sleep on my bed. It was against the rules – the cats weren't allowed upstairs at night, but he was my best friend and I couldn't imagine sleeping without him. I told Tiggy everything, and he never judged me. He just went on loving me and wanting me to hold him. We got him when I was only one year old and often as a little girl I used to dress him up in doll's clothes and take him out in my doll's pram. He would lay there quite happily, purring away, relishing the attention, loving me hugging and squeezing him. I feel so bad about leaving him behind; I know he won't be happy without me, and I don't know if I can ever be happy without him to cuddle. When nobody else cared, when there was nobody else to hold me or fulfil my need for warmth and affection, Tiggy was there, warm, soft and happy to be cuddled for hours on end. I think he was what got me through the terrible, cold, lonely days of my childhood.

I go down the grand, sweeping staircase of the children's home and find Helen sitting in the office. "Can I have my cat here?" I asked her.

"I'm sorry, Honey, you're not allowed pets here," Helen replied.

I tried telling her how important it was, but she wouldn't listen. She tried to assure me that he would be better off where he is; what does she know? With no one to cuddle him and give him love, I know I've left him to a miserable existence.

Now come the questions: are my dreams memories of something bad that happened? Who is chasing me? Well, that one is easy – my father, always my father. I know they want to help but how can I tell them, they don't understand how scared I am. My dreams are not memories but visions of what is to come. He will want his revenge and who can blame him. The nightmares have been coming every night for a long time; sometimes I wake up and I'm not in my bed at all, I find myself curled up underneath where I guess I feel safe. They seem to be getting worse, more vivid, and increasingly real. I dread going to bed knowing that he will come for me again and fearing that one day I will not escape.

Helen seems sure there is more to it; she thinks he has done something to me but how can I even begin to explain it. For as long as I can remember I have always been scared of him. She's asked if I'll see a doctor – a psychiatrist – but assures me she doesn't think I'm mad. She can't possibly think what I did were the actions of a

7

sane person. I agree and she offers me a cigarette. I inhale deeply and try to relax; however, I feel wound so tight I could explode.

I go up the stairs to my room and turn on my stereo; flopping down on my bed, I press my face into my pillow feeling the anger and pain bubbling in me like lava waiting to erupt. As the hot tears run down my cheeks, Phil Collins sings the words I want my Mum to hear so badly: "Take a look at me now, there's just an empty space. There's nothing left here to remind me, just a memory of your face." I play the song over and over until eventually sleep quiets the tears.

I just want my Mummy; I want to go home.

Mia wakes me to tell me it is dinner time and I go through the motions of having dinner. I feel exhausted; when everyone has finished and we are allowed to leave the table, I go back to my room to lose myself in songs that say how I am feeling so much better than I could ever do. I hope the staff can hear them and can understand that I am trying to tell them how much I am hurting right now.

***

Extract from Staff Communications Book
Date: 6/4/84
Staff: Pat R.

I, Pat, phoned Dave Oubridge (line manager) to tell him about last night and ask for authorisation for a night nurse if necessary. I also phoned Dr Anthea Blofeld (child psychiatrist) to ask if she could come and talk to us at the staff meeting about Tracy's behaviour, and how to handle it. Anthea says we are handling Tracy exactly right. She asked if we want her in a hospital or on medication. I said no to the hospital because she needs as normal surroundings as possible or her behaviour will become more bizarre, and no to medication because it won't help and she'll resist it. I said that we might well need a night

*nurse for a while though, because we can't work all day
and all night too. Anthea and the Department of Family
and Child Psychiatry (DFCP) will support and will
contact us again on Monday.*

*I brought her downstairs to meet her needs and to
prevent her disturbing the other children.*

*I put her on the sofa in the TV room and provided her
with a quilt, with 'silky' and 'little fluff'. Then I arranged
the beanbags beside the sofa and lay on them within reach
of Tracy, just touching her to soothe her occasionally, and
I listened. Tracy is telling us a lot in what she is now
saying.*

*I spoke to her very little – just saying a couple of times
that we all loved her and that she is safe at Medvale – she
cannot hurt anyone. Sonia and I decided to split the 'Night
Watch' between us; I stayed until 4.30am and then Sonia
took over.*

*It is important to let Tracy do this when she needs to
but within our limits and without secondary gain.
Therefore, I would suggest the TV room as we arranged it
tonight – no audience and no prior arrangement. It is
important to remember that it is her subconscious mind
talking and it is her subconscious mind that hears every
word said in her presence. So only say in front of her what
you want her to hear. No drama, fear, shock, surprise or
even tension – just calm, matter-of-fact caring, as though
this happens every day of the week (God forbid). This is
like a scab on a wound; it will cease to exist when she no
longer needs it. Poor kid.*

***

Tonight the nightmares come again but this time my father
is trying to kill the staff at Medvale and then the staff turn
on me. It is not my fault, but they come at me with murder
in their eyes. I start to run. I see two members of staff, my
keyworker Judy and another called Sonia, and run towards
them. And in the way only dreams can, they become one,

9

and that one is my Mum. I know she will keep me safe I run as hard as I can, my arms outstretched. She is reaching for me but when she grabs me it isn't with the love and tenderness I expect. Her nails dig into my skin and she's holding me too tight, I can't pull away. She's holding me for him so that he can finish what he started.

I start to scream and desperately try to pull away. The harder I struggle the tighter she holds me, my voice is faltering, and I have no strength left to scream. Then I realise it's not my Mum, Sonia is holding me. I am safe at Medvale, I begin to relax and drift into a more fitful sleep. This time, I wake on a mattress on the floor of Stuart's room. Stuart is a child here, but he is only around during the holidays, leaving his room empty for a lot of the time. I pull the quilt up around my shoulders and just lay there listening to the bustle of the house. I feel lousy and terribly guilty. I don't mean to keep everyone awake, I really don't want to dream anymore.

I seem to have spent most of the day in bed and feel totally washed out. I know the staff are angry with me and think I am doing this deliberately, but I just want this to end. There is no end to this misery, though, as another bad night and these dreams seem to become increasingly real and more intense. I am sure my Dad will win in the end and I will be dead, no longer a burden to all of those around me. I wake this time and feel disorientated before I realise I am in the television room. I lay on the sofa, under my duvet, listening to everyone getting ready for breakfast, hoping that no one comes in, as I just want to curl up and die. Mia pops her head around the door wanting to make sure I am okay. I hate seeing her so worried and can't apologise enough.

I spend most of my time with Mia; we are so close and I can share so much with her and her with me. Sonia has asked Mia if she can be my special helper and I am hers, that way we can always be there to help each other. We are allowed to go out for a walk and then after dinner Mia comes with me to meet Carl. Carl used to be my boyfriend and I have promised to meet him to try and stop him from coming here. He only wants sex and I know that it will be over quickly and he will give me some space for a while. Mia wanders off while I let Carl do what he needs to and then we meet back up and wander through Rochester High Street talking about the crap that our lives have thrown at us. I don't tell her what Carl and his friends did to me. Instead, I focus on the problems I have with my father.

There really isn't anything to do and I can't shake the black mood from my dream. I keep playing it over and over in my head; why can't my father just leave me alone? Mia is a great friend, we have known each other for such a short space of time and she is already like a sister to me. I talk things over with her as we stare out over the River Medway. Standing on the bridge, with the moonlight reflecting off the ripples in the water, I feel so melancholy. There is a chill in the air and I pull my jacket tighter around me. I long to be with my Mum and I guess deep down I know that isn't going to happen. I feel so alone. Before I know what I am doing I have climbed over the railing, Mia's voice sounds so distant almost as if she isn't calling me at all. The water looks so inviting and I let myself fall forward.

I'm jerked backwards as Mia is pulling with all her strength. I fall, sobbing on the pavement where Mia holds me tight and lets me cry. We make our way home but we are so late and we know we are going to be in trouble. I'm still crying and Mia explains everything to Rita, who is on duty tonight. She is an older lady with a shock of white hair. I am always quite wary around her as sometimes she can be kind and gentle, but she has a mean side that is strict and unforgiving.

She tries to comfort me but what can she say; I don't want to live without my Mum. I know I shouldn't have put Mia through that, but I couldn't seem to stop myself, it was as if she wasn't there at all. I just want my Mum. We are both grounded again for being late.

Tonight Mia has decided to read me a story she wrote

at school. The story seemed to work because as she reads I drift off to sleep and, instead of being chased, I dream of the dog in the story.

This seems to set a precedent because now a member of staff reads to each of us every night, they lay next to us on the bed, or sit on the edge and read until we sleep. Just feeling so warm and safe and knowing they are there, help to keep the nightmares at bay. They still happen, but they are not so bad, not so real, or quite as vivid. I am beginning to wonder if maybe the staff here can keep me safe from my Dad after all.

I wake up feeling really low; part of me really wants to believe they care, but then they keep making me see my Dad. *Doesn't anybody understand I tried to kill him for a reason?* They have started talking about having family sessions now; surely if they really loved me, they wouldn't make me see him again. I know they are going to try making me go home, then my Dad will know he can do whatever he wants to me.

***

Extract from Staff Communications Book
Date: 9/4/84
Staff: Pat R.

Rita found a letter from Tracy under her pillow at 9am. It was a suicide note addressed to Judy, Mia (Medvale child) and Sonia. Rita contacted the school and they are going to keep a close check on her all day. We must collect her from the office later.

At 10.30am Peter (staff) followed Tracy from Top school to Bottom school; she went in. Note: envelope DID NOT carry Helen's name, carried Sonia's, therefore, could be working Helen against Sonia: 'Everything's happening like New Road?' Tracy is very scared of her ability to kill – this DOES NEED expressing emotionally.

11.05am, rang the school to ask if they could manage

at lunchtime. The whole staff group are aware and are keeping a close but unobtrusive watch. I let them know that Peter (staff) had been about when she changed schools. They are doing everything they can to support us.

12.10pm, Chris Cahill (previous social worker), rang about Tracy visiting Anthea Blofeld (psychiatrist). Filled him in on what had been happening since Thursday. Chris is saying that Anthea is reluctant to become involved in Chris's case. Chris said that he needs time to think but has always in the past felt that Tracy is very attention seeking and he has played down her behaviour. Said that of course, New Road are very direct and we didn't get any of this when she was there.

Explained that we are aware of Tracy's attention seeking behaviour and we had played everything down, but that in my opinion there was no way that Tracy was acting on Thursday night. He told me what he knew about Tracy and said that Dr Blofeld could see her tomorrow at 11am. I filled Chris in on all the details and agreed to take Tracy to see Dr Blofeld. Told him that we needed to know exactly what she was about – need for psychiatric report – in order to know how to deal with it. He seemed quite understanding.

Extract from Staff Communications Book
Date: 9/4/84
Staff: Judy R.

I collected her from school. She was quiet and withdrawn. I told her that we had to talk. I absolutely blasted her for suicide note but referred to last few days behaviour (without saying bedtime behaviour – I told her exactly what I thought of her – selfish, uncaring, cowards way out, deceitful, etc., etc. A lot sunk in. I went through the letter bit by bit – she's only just started talking so not to give up yet. Medvale/New Road – we won't make her go back to Dad, loving us – she doesn't or she wouldn't want to kill herself, etc., etc., I told her the effect of killing herself

13

would have on all of us and me – it was unfair to do that.

I piled her up with guilt about wanting to kill herself. Told her to deal with things directly i.e. use her strength in the right way and I'm expecting/demanding that she does so and now. I told her about being angry – we can cope – and also about wanting to kill people; we can cope and she must bring those things to us now and directly, and not in a round-about way. Brought her out from that and then asked her what she remembers about Thursday and Saturday night. She says she was asleep then half woke up having a bad dream (same as she told me before). She set the house on fire; Dad ran out after her with a knife to kill her. Also, Mum had a knife and Debbie (sister), and all were trying to kill her.

Was aware of people around her, not knowing whom. Knew people were talking to her, yet couldn't speak or move in response. Can't remember me being there. Sonia was telling her something about me (that was the chat about it being okay to be a little girl with me and maybe why she has been calling Sonia 'Mummy'), but couldn't remember what. Remembered seeing her Dad's face through Helen's, then Helen's face becoming her Dad's face (maybe seeing me as Mum, Helen as Dad).

I feel these are real memories, as to my knowledge no one has spoken to her about what she was saying and what happened. I told Tracy that there was nothing to worry about; perfectly normal, not mad, lots of kids do it, but we need to try to stop it because she's not getting enough sleep, nor are we. For those reasons, I'm taking her to see Dr Blofeld, who works with Chris, to see if she has any ideas. Tracy seemed quite happy about this and I stressed not because there is anything wrong with her, but so we could all get some sleep.

***

Great! Now Judy and Helen are furious with me because Rita was nosing around my bedroom and found the note I had written. They weren't supposed to find it until I was dead and gone. *Why doesn't anybody realise that I would be better off dead?* I can't live like this anymore. I withdraw into myself, the place inside my head where they can't hurt me. I hear her words, telling me how selfish, uncaring and deceitful I am; doesn't she realise how bad I feel anyway? I know I am all of those things and more; I am an evil, twisted, sick murderer. She thinks she can protect me, stop me from killing someone or killing myself; how on Earth does she think talking about it will help? I can't even begin to explain why this is happening to me. Helen moves on to talking about my nightmares. I tell her again that Dad is going to kill me and that I don't mean to keep people awake, and that I just want to sleep like everyone else, but I can tell she thinks I am just playing games.

Helen wants me to see the psychiatrist tomorrow; she insists that I am not mad and wants me to go to prove it to me. I agree to go. Hopefully it won't matter soon anyway as I will be gone.

***

Extract from Staff Communications Book
Date: 10/4/84
Staff: Judy R.

Took Tracy to see Dr Blofeld. She was fine. I had a quick chat with Dr Blofeld to put her in the picture. Then Tracy saw her for an hour and I saw Anthea on my own after. Basically, she said that Tracy had told her she was no longer suicidal because she didn't want to hurt us and her confusions/loves/hates/ concerning family. Anthea felt that what we are doing regarding night-time behaviour was absolutely right, but we need to give her half an hour quiet time to relax her brain at bedtime. Possibly a story or a quiet chat.

If she goes into it again not to talk to her as that will

only stimulate her mind, but just to watch her and if we feel it appropriate, to hold her hand or cuddle her.

She will write to the local GP as if it continues for periods longer that a couple of hours she would recommend that we sedate her as physically, Tracy will be doing herself damage. Anthea said that her biggest fear was that she would get pregnant.

***

My meeting with the psychiatrist is not a great success. Judy drives me there and one of the boys who live in Medvale, Stuart, comes along for the ride. I sit quietly, all the way, I'm not sure what to expect. We approach an imposing building, not unlike Medvale, the home that I am living in. I get ushered into a room, alone with an old woman, who looks very prim and proper. Her name is Anthea. I sit down and she starts to talk to me about my childhood. She wants to know about my family, whom I lived with before, like any of this is going to help. I know she thinks I'm hostile, but I can't see how any of this is going to make things better. She can't change what happened to me; she can't make the bad stuff go away.

Anthea asks why I'm in care, so I tell her it's because I chored some dough off my old man. She asks me again, not seeming to understand me, so I explain I stole some money from my father. In the end, she gives up and sends me back out to Judy. They talk for a while and then Judy takes me home. The conclusion, apparently, is that I am not mad. How this woman can say that when I hardly spoke to her at all, I'm not sure. She can't know what I did or why I did it.

Back in my room I find the shard of glass I found on my way to school. I knew it would come in handy so I hid it in my chest of drawers. Holding it now I dig deep into my left arm, the tears flow down my face, but it does not hurt. The pain I feel inside fills me but as I watch the small droplets of blood, grow and spread, I feel a strange release.

I know this won't kill me as much as I want it to. I'm not brave enough to go that deep and make the blood really flow. Part of me wants to, as I don't want to carry on living like this. I cut again, and again, each a little deeper.

I cut my wrist today,
And now I realise what you say.
Life is short,
But Pain is long.
My mind is warped,
By what went on.
The only way to help me now,
Is to make me realise life's worthwhile.
Tracy Pain Aged 14

***

Extract from Staff Communications Book
Date: 13/4/84
Staff: Helen M.

The doctor had received a letter from Dr Blofeld about Tracy. He has prescribed the medication recommended by Dr Blofeld, but he felt that it would be far more beneficial for Tracy to have it in a very mild form on a daily basis for a while rather than in large doses when necessary. I explained that Medvale is not the usual children's home and that we work towards bringing feelings, hurt, pain, etc., to the fore to help our kids work through them – suppression is not what we are about. I told him some of Tracy's problems, starting to regress, etc., and no way would we want any of this interrupted because of drugs suppressing her emotions. Dr Bally (GP) felt sure that this would not happen. He said that if necessary he would see Tracy as often as needed.

I cannot agree to Tracy being medicated on a regular basis. I want to discuss this with Judy and then the whole team on Wednesday. In the meantime, the prescription is

*in the medicine box. It can be filled but only with the view
to giving it to Tracy if and when she is experiencing the
same sort of distressing, disturbing nights as she has had
recently.*

***

Judy gave me a beaker of juice tonight to drink with my
story; it is so comforting, to be able to be little again and
makes me feel so safe and loved. I felt safe enough tonight
to ask Judy if she could hear the baby crying too. She said
it was probably a cat, so I guess that I am right and nobody
else hears her crying. I won't ask anyone else as I don't
trust them not to think I am completely crazy; I know she
is there, I just wish there was a way to stop her crying. My
dreams don't seem to be disturbing everyone at the
moment, thankfully, although I still have such vivid
dreams every night, often waking, shaking and damp with
exertion.

***

Extract from Staff Communications Book
Date: 6/5/84
Staff: Helen M.

*Tracy was under her quilt when I came on duty. She had
not eaten dinner and was very worried about the visit with
her Dad. She came down to the office and we discussed the
visit. She was angry and upset at first. Went through all
sorts of things with her; how she thought he had kicked
Mum out while having his baby, and how she thought she
was in love with Peter Pascal (manager at previous
children's home). Dad said that she had witnessed a nasty
row between him and Mum the night she left (they did not
know that Tracy was there). He had slapped Mum's face
and told her that he could kill her for what she was doing
to him and the kids. He had known about her affair for a*

year and they had both been attending Marriage guidance to try to save the marriage. He had just found out that she was still seeing the other man and was pregnant by him.

Cheered up quite quickly but chose not to watch the film with the rest of the group. She was warm and close with me all evening, then later she gave me this letter. She was fine at bedtime, had a story sweets, etc. When I went up to say goodnight to Mia, Tracy was rambling away. Sonia was sitting on Mia's bed but holding Tracy's hand. I knew that Tracy wasn't really in a turn so I said to Sonia, Tracy is going to sleep properly now. We went downstairs. Ten minutes later I went back up. Tracy was wide awake, sitting up, couldn't sleep, nightmares about Mum leaving home. Mia says she is talking in her sleep. I told Tracy to lay down. Both were asleep at 1.15am. At 1.45am, there was a noise from the bedroom. Both girls were sitting up having a chat still awake at 2.15am.

Extract from Staff Communications Book
Date: 23/5/84
Staff: Judy R.

A long heavy session with Dad, Helen and I. Tracy gave him her notes to read about him trying to kill her. Lots of new bits to work on. The outcome was that Dad denied trying to kill her. Tracy maintains that he did, but all other things he said she agreed were open and honest. Agreed that bit of it not resolved so we would have weekly sessions with Dad and Tracy also to include Debbie (sister) and eventually a final one with Mum.

Tracy was upset after but not properly able to cry. Snivelled when I took her to bed – also some glimpses of anger. I told her that I had got her a (baby) bottle and did she want it? Yes. Helen and I gave her a story and snuggled her down. She didn't drink the bottle but cuddled it and regressed. A slightly glazed look on her face – possibly some nightmare behaviour bits coming up. Told her to go to sleep properly and left her. Needs careful

19

watching tomorrow. Please phone the school and let them know that she may be wobbly.

Staff: Helen M.

My God, Peter Pain needs some work.

***

I can't bear the thought of going to school today; my whole body feels ready to explode and I need to be alone. I get ready for school and make out that things are okay. The staff here can be so suspicious; they don't seem to trust me at all. I put on a couple of extra layers of clothes, as I know it gets cold at night and although I don't need them now I may do later. The staff seem fine when I leave and I walk down the road as if I am going to school but before I reach the church, I am crying so I go in the churchyard and sit on the bench. The anger is bubbling in me: *why am I such a nasty person?* It's no wonder no one can love me. I find some shards of glass and start cutting my wrist again.

What bothers me the most is not knowing I can kill someone; it's not even knowing I want to kill someone. It's knowing that I don't care. How can one little girl hold so much hate, so much emptiness, be so lonely that nothing matters anymore? That life doesn't matter anymore. Why do I hurt so much that I need to hurt others? Why now do I punish myself so? The hope that someone, somewhere, notices and cares enough to stop me is only a mere glimmer. The stark truth is that I am on my own and always have been.

I begin to feel a little calmer and decide to go to school after all; they shout at me for being late and no one notices my arm as my baggy school jumper keeps it covered. The one good thing about being at school is that no one seems to care; I can drift off and be in my own little world. The girls around me chat and mess about and I enjoy the distraction. Mrs Green leaves the room while waiting for our static electricity test to develop. We have all been asked to rub balloons on our hair and stick them high up on the walls to see how long they take to lose their charge and drop to the floor. I use this opportunity to climb on my stool and glue a balloon to the ceiling. As the lesson progresses, Mrs Green becomes increasingly distracted by the balloon that is still stuck to the ceiling. I am not sure how I contain my laughter; this is certainly working to lift my mood.

I walk home at the end of the day and when Mia asks about going roller skating tonight, I know what I must do. I leave them all at the skating rink and head towards the Pentagon; I can't go home, not now. They really don't understand what I have done; if they really knew what I had done, what I had planned and what evil thoughts fill my head, they wouldn't love me. They would have me locked away, which is what I deserve. They keep saying I should tell them, *but how can I?*

Chapter 2

1980 – Aged 10

Murderous Thoughts

At ten years old, I was small for my age. I had blonde hair that just hung in no particular style and I was very thin. I didn't enjoy eating and had always battled with my parents at dinner time, although I had an incredibly sweet tooth and would quite happily eat sweets and cakes morning, noon and night. I wasn't very good at maths but excelled in English and had a reading age of someone much older.

Reading gave me a way of escaping from my life; I could lose myself in other worlds, in families that were loving and caring. Where children had the power to make a difference. *The Famous Five* and *Secret Seven* were by far my favourite books to begin with; the children in these stories got to escape and had amazing adventures, which left them admired and loved by the adults around them.

Unfortunately or, fortunately, depending on how you looked at it, this led to me reading what my father would say were books that were totally unsuitable. He confiscated a book called Head Hunters from me, which was about an African tribe that practised cannibalism. A little late for some of the other horror titles that I had already read, like *Suffer the Children* by John Saul. This book had hit a chord in me that was difficult to describe, I felt as if I was reading about myself. As if I was the little girl in the book that was shutting out the world and hiding a big secret. That if I could do something really bad I would be taken away and kept safe. It was from this book that I got the idea for my plan.

I had thought long and hard about the plan and, although I could not answer why I felt the need to follow that path, I knew it was the right thing for me to do. Just imagining the shock everyone would feel when they found out how evil I really was, gave me ripples of pleasure; they would all pay for hating me so much. I was sure that this was just the beginning and that people would remember me and pay – most of all pay – for the hurt they had caused.

I planned to lure my friends Evelyn, Maisie and Katrina to the Conny Banks, as it was somewhere that we often played. Like me, they were also ten years old and although we played together I don't think they really liked me, I had always been different and a bit of an outsider. They were nice enough, but I often caught them giving me strange looks and whispering about me when they thought I couldn't hear.

The Conny Banks was a place where we often played; a rolling field surrounded by woodland, with plenty of places to hide, and not many people around so I knew I was unlikely to be disturbed. I was sure they would meet me there quite willingly as it was a good place to play or pick berries. Then I planned to take them into the woods and during an innocent game of hide and seek I would pick them out one by one and trap them in the kind of trap they used for animals.

I would have to make sure the hole was already dug out, deep enough so that they couldn't climb out, however hard they might try. I could dig it out a couple of days before. I played there often and no one was really bothered about what I did during the day, as long as I was home in time to cook dinner for the family. I had seen these animal traps on television and read about how to cover the hole with sticks, leaves and bracken. I couldn't see any reason why this wouldn't work. Many little paths ran through the woods where I could do this without being spotted. The good thing about being a little girl was that I could go about completely unnoticed; after all, who would suspect a small child of harbouring such evil plans.

The others wouldn't realise what had happened until it

was too late. I imagined them skipping along without a worry in the world, then seeing them falling, clawing at the walls as they desperately tried to save themselves. I pictured the look of horror on their faces as the realisation of what was happening registered with their unsuspecting minds. I knew they would shout and scream for help, but I was sure that they wouldn't be heard. It was quite remote there and they were only small. I hoped that their fear would wear them out quickly and then eventually when they were weak from hunger and fear, I could strangle them until their bodies were limp and unresponsive.

I felt quite detached while I thought about my plan, confident that they would die and then people might care. I didn't see them as my friends anymore, just children that needed to be taken care of. Trying to get them to come with me proved harder than I anticipated; we had played there plenty of times before, but I couldn't seem to persuade them to come with me. Although I was convinced that they couldn't possibly have known what I was planning, they didn't seem to want to be my friends anymore.

I found myself thinking it over and over in my head, picturing their faces, mud and tear stained, begging for me to release them. Feeling, for once that I was important, that I was in charge and I wanted them to suffer.

At around the same time I woke to find a young girl had been brutally murdered. The headlines said they had found the body of a young girl and underneath was her photo. When I saw her, I felt goosebumps erupt over my body, the hairs on the back of my neck prickled and I was sure that not only had I seen her before, but that I was the reason for her demise. She was but ten years old, a pretty girl with long blonde hair. Logic would say that I could not have killed her. I didn't even know of the town that she died in and I was only ten years old myself. Nevertheless, in my mind I felt that I was to blame; after all, hadn't I just planned to murder my friends in an equally horrific manner. I stared at her photo for a long time with a heavy feeling inside of me.

I knew I was mad; no sane child would think the things I did, would plan to do such horrific things to her friends. I could not stop those thoughts coming into my head. I was so unhappy, so lonely and so deeply angry.

Chapter 3

1984 – Aged 14

Medvale: The Beginning

The police bring me home in the middle of the night and I know I will have to speak to Helen and Judy in the morning. I am not sure what I will be able to tell them, as I don't know where to start or how to explain what is going on in my head at the moment. All I know is that I am so full of emotion I just want to explode, but I can't even cry.

Helen and Judy want me to start writing my life story; they think it will help me understand how I have got to where I am today and in doing so will act as a cathartic release for the painful and angry feelings I harbour. Well, I wasn't expecting that, I really thought they would be so angry with me.

I enjoy writing about my life although it is not always easy, I want people to know why I am here, in this children's home. To know the journey I have taken, the journey I am still taking and at fourteen years old, the end that I envisage for myself for I sense that it will be sooner rather than later.

I find it difficult to talk, having spent many years being criticised and put down for how I thought and felt, I learnt how to keep my mouth shut. Writing is a way of telling everyone how I really feel without getting tongue-tied and feeling that I can't explain myself. I often write letters to the staff here, as it is so much easier than trying to tell them how I feel. I have kept a diary for a while now. I write as if I am talking to someone and find it is a good way of sharing my deepest thoughts without the risk of getting myself into trouble. Writing became my preferred method of communication – then and now – and has been my constant companion throughout my life. Allowing me to explore, reflect and examine all aspects of my life and convey these to the people in my life that I would not otherwise have the courage to do.

It makes sense to start my life storybook from the beginning when I was born and so this is where I begin…

Chapter 4

1970 – 1978: Birth to Aged 8

The Early Years with Mum and Dad

I was born on 24th January 1970, the second child of Margaret and Peter Pain. My mother was kind and nurturing and stayed at home to care for me and my older sister, Debbie. I spent my early years totally cocooned in her warmth and love, following her around, sucking my thumb and twiddling her petticoats that were smooth and silky and gave me so much comfort. I was her baby and I never left her side. Many an evening she would settle on the floor so that I could sit behind her on the sofa and brush her smooth brown hair. I adored her totally and even now can feel her swaying with me on her feet listening to songs by Showaddywaddy, her gentle voice, knowing all of the words, playing over and over again until I knew the words too and could sing along with her.

Debbie was two years and four days my senior and would never let me forget it. We looked alike and were often mistaken as twins, although our personalities were so very different.

Mum made soft toys, to bring in extra money and always made things to sell at the school fair. She was the hub of the house and if a room needed decorating or a cake needed baking she would be the one to do it. She made Debbie and me a slide one year, out of wood that she cut, put together and varnished. It was fantastic and lasted years, a huge hit at our birthday parties and a testament to her workmanship.

It seemed to me to be an idyllic life. We really only saw my father on holidays, and even then he would bring with him his over-stuffed black, briefcase and a box full of bundles of paperwork to be done. We had many good times; we would always stay with my Nan (his Mum) in Somerset and go on day trips to the beach, or to climb Glastonbury Tor.

Granddad was around only until I was about five years old, and I remember his grey hair atop a round, smiling face. Nan's neighbour, Bert, had a lovely dog called Peg and he let us come to his house to play with her and to feed her. His house was full of amazing things, glass cases with stuffed birds inside, antique tools and dusty, unused rooms. He loved letting us explore and was always there to explain what things were; he was there to talk to and most importantly to listen.

Life was much better then; we all seemed happy and although Debbie was mean to me sometimes, that's just what big sisters did and I could give as much as I took. Often we would walk home from swimming on opposite sides of the street because we had fallen out, that's just the way things were.

Christmas's were the best holidays; my father would drive us down to Somerset a few days before Christmas. A couple of times my other Nan would join us, which was even better. I could never sleep Christmas Eve; Debbie and I used to put out a drink and a pie for Father Christmas and I always made sure there was a carrot for the reindeer, which made it so exciting. We would lay out our stockings that had been embroidered, lovingly by our Mum, so that they were special to each of us.

I would be so excited about Father Christmas coming that I would stay awake for hours just wishing I could sleep so that Christmas could come even quicker. If I were lucky, I would hear the sleigh bells as he approached and one year he left big sooty footprints all through my Nan's house, from the fireplace and up the stairs. She was fuming when she woke up Christmas morning and had to clean up. Father Christmas always filled our stockings to overflowing; I would wake up and feel the weight of my stocking resting against my feet. With butterflies making me shiver in anticipation, I would tentatively poke, squeeze and shake my gifts, trying desperately to guess what delight each one held. I was never disappointed although the horse I wrote on the top of my list for several years only ever turned out to be a plastic toy horse that my Sindy doll enjoyed far more than I ever would.

I sometimes wonder if the detachment I feel now to the world has always been there in different forms. I was never aware of any problems at home; in fact, I only ever heard my parents argue twice and that was in the middle of the night. I remember sitting at the top of the stairs crying as I listened to my father shouting at my Mummy. The second time, he was telling her to stop seeing David – I could not believe how mean he could be. David worked at Sainsbury's where my Mummy did the shopping, she couldn't help but see him. But that was my father all over, always expecting the impossible. I was very much a Mummy's girl and was a very young eight-year old. I still sucked my thumb and twiddled my 'nyla' and was totally cocooned in my Mummy's love.

My 'nyla' started life as a petticoat; when I was tiny, I used to lay on my Mummy's lap and twiddle her petticoat when I was tired. Eventually, Mummy gave me one of my own, which I took everywhere. I overheard her telling a friend that I liked the feel of the nylon and that's where I got the name 'nyla'. Mummy had an awful job trying to clean it and I had even been known to swing from the washing line clutching it while it dried.

I wore knee-length socks and pretty dresses that Mummy had made for me. I took my dolls out in their pram, made mud pies, raced my pet snails and did all the other things that little girls do. I was just a little girl and life was so simple. I lived in my own little world where only good things happened.

The day that all ended, the day that my entire life shattered into a thousand pieces, the day that my illusion of happiness crumbled into dust was just a stone's throw away.

Chapter 5

1978 – Aged 8

The Day My Life Ended

I woke up in the room that I shared with my sister Debbie and ran straight into Mummy's room. She wasn't there, but I didn't worry because sometimes after she had been out late with Aunty Frieda she would sleep on the sofa so that she didn't disturb anyone. I skipped downstairs and flung open the living room door – no Mummy. I started calling her; she couldn't be far.

I started racing from room to room, *where was she?* My father caught up with me in the kitchen, and I could see Debbie standing just behind him. He held me by my upper arms and told me that my Mummy had gone to stay with Sid and Sue and she wasn't coming back. He said that she had been seeing David and she didn't want to live with us anymore. He said that they had agreed that it would be better to keep Debbie and me together; he said that Debbie wanted to live with him and he asked me where I would rather live, with him or my Mummy. My head whirled, my thoughts spun and I didn't even hear myself mutter 'you'.

In my head I was screaming, *I don't want to live with Debbie! I want my Mummy! I just want my Mummy!*

I didn't cry, my mind and body went numb. He was a liar! I remembered their argument when he told her to stop seeing David; he threatened to kill her and had made it clear that if she left, she couldn't take Debbie or me with her. In my eyes, she didn't have a choice.

Either later that day or the next day, Mummy came to collect her things. There were no dramatics. I just stood on the doorstep and cried as she carried her things out to Uncle Sid's car. I didn't say goodbye, I couldn't bring myself to speak at all. I stood watching her, the tears hot on my cheeks, my nose running. I remember very little of the next year. At eight years old I had lost the will to live.

***

Over time with the help of friends and relations, I managed to fill in some of the gaps of that year and regained a few memories. We – Debbie and I – apparently spent some time with my Nan in Somerset. Mummy even wrote to me while we were there. We saw Mummy every couple of weeks to start with and then every Saturday. Mummy told me that she was pregnant and I was sure that would mean she would get back together with my father. I knew they said it was David's baby, but as she shared a bed with my father, I was convinced it could be his too. We ate pork chops and streaky slices a lot because that was all that my father could cook.

Mummy eventually got a house with David; a two-bedroomed terraced house in Gillingham, which was close to the station and the town centre. It needed a lot of work doing to it and David and his brother Sid worked long hours making it a comfortable home. Their first daughter, Elizabeth, was born on 16th March 1979.

I really had only gone through the motions this year; my emotions had totally shut down, I never cried, a rift grew between Debbie and I. I think she knew I never wanted to be there. I don't think she even wanted me there. She seemed to understand and even sympathise with my father – I blamed him, totally. He had told Mummy to stop seeing David even though he knew she couldn't do that because he worked in Sainsbury's. He also wouldn't admit that the baby could have been his. I hated him for making my Mummy leave us and I would never forgive him, and I hated Debbie for taking his side.

It was almost like being under a spell; that's how blank that year was for me, but I suddenly woke up, a year later, when I bumped into a lady that had recently moved in up the road. She was quite tall, around five-foot six, slim build with dark hair that flowed past her shoulders and had a full fringe that framed her face. She wore jeans and a yellow T-shirt and appeared happy and relaxed. She was taking her Mum's Dachshunds for a walk and stopped to let me stroke them. They were adorable; one black and tan, the other just plain tan. Both were very friendly and wanting to be fussed over. My father got talking to her and she started to spend a lot of time with us.

Her name was Tracey (with an E) and she was nineteen years old; she was always spoiling us, buying us sweets and clothes and spending lots of time playing with us. The day my father broke the news that Tracey would be moving in with us, she gave Debbie and I a cat money box each that was filled with pennies. My cat was blue and striped like a tiger; Debbie's was pink. I was so pleased, she brought warmth and happiness back into the house and she seemed to really love us.

Things changed once she had moved in – she changed. We were no longer allowed to call her Tracey; we had to call her Mum, and we had to call my Mummy by her name, Margaret.

I really struggled with this, not only because she was not old enough to be my Mum, but mainly because I had a Mum. I didn't need or indeed want another one.

On one occasion, while I was ironing, I slipped up and called her Tracey. She screamed at me that I should call her Mum. I shouted back: 'But you're not my Mum!' and she grabbed the iron from me and slapped me across the face. I honestly believed she was going to hit me with the iron. Hot tears welled up and threatened to spill down my cheeks and I struggled to hide them; I didn't want her to think she had won. I didn't argue anymore, but my anger burned more furiously than ever.

She soon gave us chores to do. We had to take turns in vacuuming downstairs after school, polishing every day, vacuuming upstairs once a week, cleaning the bathroom every week, cleaning the cooker every Sunday after cooking the roast dinner, cooking dinner for them every night, when all I was allowed was a sandwich or half a tin of soup. Washing or drying up every night. Doing the washing every Saturday, including stripping the beds and then ironing it all on a Sunday. Because she was a nurse and worked shifts, she couldn't possibly be expected to clean the house as well.

She became more and more fastidious, insisting that there was not a speck of dust or dirt to be found. If I had accidentally missed something, she would make me do the entire job again and she would even pull out the furniture to make sure I hadn't vacuumed around it.

Although she didn't often hit me, she shouted every day and I was scared that she might snap at any moment. Every night I longed to catch a glimpse of the children's programmes that I knew would be on when we returned from school, but heaven forbid we should be caught with the TV on before our chores were completed.

My father let Tracey buy a Dachshund puppy that was supposed to be what is classed as a toy, but she was actually a miniature. The dog was so small that when we first got her, she could fit in the palm of my hand, she was tiny. Tracey called her Dappy. It was a silly name and although I loved her dearly, I longed to get a proper dog. Dappy would offer people her paw when they came to the house but no one noticed because she was so small, it was such a shame.

Tracey spent time in the hospital with a slipped disc and for a while, she was kind again; however, before I knew it, she was back out and ordering me around again. It was like living with two different people. One minute she would be kind and loving, the next she would be screeching at me. I never knew where I stood.

She went into hospital suddenly one day with no explanation; I was very excited and thought she was going to have a baby as my Mummy had done. I shared this with my friends at school; it was very exciting and I couldn't believe it when I got home to find her and my father standing in the front room. They were so angry; my father said I should never say such things, like having a baby was something so bad.

Apparently, she had a nervous breakdown; she hadn't been able to cope with looking after us, and my behaviour had just made things worse. She also had anorexia; she believed that she was fat when, in fact, she was pitifully thin. Her bones jutted out and gave her very sharp features. She went into hospital a couple of times, which gave me some respite from the daily onslaught. And each time when she came home things would be calm for a while, before reverting to the hell I had begun to think of as home.

Chapter 6

1984 – Aged 14

Medvale: The Overdose

Extract from Staff Communications Book
Date: 24/5/84
Staff: Sonia C.

Having taken tablets, I (Sonia) have taken Tracy to Medway Hospital. We first phoned to see whether an ambulance was needed or not. Was told by the hospital that it would be quicker by car and that she would be seen straight away. Tracy wouldn't tell me how many tablets she had taken. She couldn't be easily woken up but managed to stand and walk. I would imagine that if many or any taken it was this morning. (When I checked on her at 1.15am she was fine and fast asleep.) Tablet bottle found beside her in her bed.

The school was informed that Tracy is sick.

I asked Mia and Lacey (other Medvale children) if they had any idea at all as to Tracy's taking of these tablets. None. Lacey said that Tracy was talking the other day about 'killing herself' and that she had told her it was stupid. Mia said she didn't know what the time was, but she can recollect that someone, 'a figure', was around in the bedroom and heard a voice saying, 'Shit, where are they?' Mia now informs me that the voice she heard was just after everyone had gone out of the room after the stories etc., 11.00pm. Didn't get out of bed after – as Mia was lying all over her. She noticed that Tracy was laying staring at the window.

Staff: Rita W.

Sonia has just phoned from the hospital – 8.30am. Doesn't know whether or not Tracy will be admitted as they do not know what tablets she has taken. Tracy is stating that she took these tablets at 1.00am. Her blood pressure, breathing and temperature are all normal.

I tried to phone Peter Pain, but he had just left for work. Mother is not on the phone. Apparently, the tablets were stolen from a girl's school bag.

Helen rang to say that she and Tracy were now at All Saints Hospital, Christopher Ward. As far as the hospital are concerned, Tracy hasn't taken anything!!!! Awaiting psychiatrist.

Staff: Helen M.

Visited Tracy with Darla and Mia (other Medvale children). Took all her night gear etc., and Duncan (Judy's toy elephant) at Judy's suggestion (he had an overdose too). Tracy was lying like the dying swan with both girls sitting on each side of her holding her hand. I felt a great deal of anger towards her tonight as it was pitiful to watch the girls' very real emotional reactions to what she had done. Both were crying, Darla so loudly that the staff came out onto the ward to see what the hell was going on.

Tracy gave me this letter and said the doctor had come to see her but not a shrink. I spoke to the doctor earlier. He did not feel that Tracy had taken anything but will keep her under observation for tonight. Discharge tomorrow morning. Dr Blofeld is not worried about seeing Tracy (this from Chris Cahill); she knows Medvale and feels that we can do a better job with her than she can. Silky, furry owl and (baby) bottle were taken in at Tracy's request. Told the staff about her regression; they seemed amazed.

***

I'm so full of emotion, anger, hatred, hurt, pain and longing. I sometimes feel that I am going to explode. Every now and then a little seeps out before I can get it under control, but I'm beginning to think that suicide won't hurt them as much as I once thought. For that to happen, they would have to care and I really don't think that they do. But they should care, they should understand how hurt I am. I think it's time to stop hurting myself and to use the pain inside of me to make them listen. I have a special place that I go to when I'm in trouble or when the pain gets so bad I can't contain it any longer. To get there, I have to step outside of reality and sink inside of myself. Lately, I seem to be going there more and more; I wonder if one day I'll go and I won't be able to come back, destined to live my life in my own secluded, safe world. It does sound appealing.

Nobody took me seriously when I tried to kill my family, not just once but four times! They really don't get it, but I'll show them. I know I can kill and maybe then they would sit up and listen to me. I think the first member of staff I shall kill should be Sonia, as she is so sarcastic and full of herself. She really doesn't like me, I think maybe she's jealous that Mia loves me and talks to me a lot more than she does to Sonia, even though Sonia is her key worker. Either way I think she should go first. I could strangle her next time she is sleeping in; I'm sure if I took her by surprise that she would die quite easily.

This seemed like a good plan but at school a girl called Shona has brought in a bottle of fifteen period-pain tablets; I don't want to steal from her, she is my friend, but I know the time will come when I might need to take them. Helen and Judy keep making me talk to my father, trying to get to the bottom of my fear of him. They really don't understand and I guess neither do I. He sits there so smug, denying that he has ever hurt me, with no idea why I am so scared of him. The fact that I can't remember the year after Mum left makes me think that there is something I don't want to remember, something that scared me so much that

I have blocked it out completely. They arrange for him to come back next Wednesday; *why can't they see what this is doing to me?* Maybe there is a good reason why I shouldn't try to remember.

***

I lay awake and listen to Mia's breathing fall into a steady rhythm. I really can't go on like this. I unscrew the top of my baby bottle and wash down all fifteen tablets with my orange juice. I reach across and hold Mia's hand while she sleeps; I can't seem to stop crying. Life is so unfair. Eventually, I cry myself to sleep hoping that tonight will be my last.

***

I felt myself wake up as the sun streamed in through the window. WHY? *Why can't I even die?* I scream this in my head and the tears of despair start to flow. Sonia wants to know what is going on. When I tell her she tells me to get dressed and she takes me to Medway Hospital to have my stomach pumped. Helen comes and waits with me and they keep showing me charts of pills so they can work out what I took. I wish now that I hadn't taken the label off the bottle; I just didn't want Shona to know I had stolen her tablets. Apparently, they can't find any trace of the tablets in my body and they don't believe I took anything. They move me to All Saints Hospital for overnight observation, but even Helen doesn't believe I took them. This day is becoming more and more surreal. I should have died they would have believed me then. I can't stop crying and having two of the other children from Medvale – Mia and Darla – visit, just makes me feel even worse. *Why would I lie?* I had my stomach pumped when I was eleven years old; I wouldn't do it again for fun, would I?

***

I must admit that I was much closer to success last time, back when I was eleven, the tablets I took then nearly did the job. I had raided the medicine cabinet at my father's house and Tracey had all manner of tablets, in all shapes, sizes and colours. I just took a selection, as I had no idea what any of them did and I figured taking a lot would kill me, whatever they were. I took them to school and took them all at break time; my best friends Valerie and Molly were with me, and I think they thought it was one big laugh.

I really don't remember the lessons between break and dinner; I remember queuing up for dinner but that is all. Apparently, after dinner I went to class and asked to be excused because I said I felt unwell. My friends said I looked green and I had stuff dribbling out of my mouth. The teacher excused me and in a wave of guilt, Valerie and Molly confessed all to the teacher. They hurried into the toilets and frantically tried to keep me awake while they called Tracey and my father. Mrs Furley, the deputy headmistress, drove me to the hospital in her little black sports car, while Tracey kept rubbing my temples, trying to keep me awake.

At the hospital, they pumped my stomach and after a long sleep, I had to explain my actions to a psychiatrist. I had to pretend I didn't mean it because he was a friend of Tracey's; they worked together in the hospital and if I told the truth, I knew my father would kill me. If only my friends hadn't grassed on me, it would all have been over. No more pain.

When I got home my Dad told me that having stolen from Tracey, she would be the one to punish me. I felt relieved because I knew her punishment would be less severe. I was right, she hit the backs of my hands ten times with a ruler, which hardly hurt at all, and that was that. No one spoke about it again.

***

Extract from Staff Communications Book
Date: 29/5/84
Staff: Judy R.

Helen and I had a long session with Tracy regarding suicide. We told her exactly how we felt – angry because:

> *The effect on the other kids.*
> *She didn't even take the tablets.*
> *She knew the right way of sorting things out but chose not to.*
> *She broke yet another promise to us.*

We have gone backwards quite a lot – Tracy unable to say much at all and now in an absolutely EVIL mood. When we asked her how Dad would feel about her saying he'd tried to kill her, she smiled with obvious pleasure and really turned from there on in – said she wanted to kill Dad again and was obviously sat there plotting and scheming. We pointed out the fact that she has a review in one month's time and had better get her act together by then.

She really is in a bad way at the moment. I think a lot to do with being sussed, i.e. by trying to kill herself we'd stop family sessions – no way! Left the session in an angry way and is scheming something – Helen felt that she will run tonight. We'd left it that she do some thinking and bring something in writing to me later.

All staff, please watch her very closely now, as she really is in a dangerous mood.

Fine all shift – earlier nasty mood has gone 'underground' again but we still need to watch her. Cuddled up to me watching television. Seemed much more at ease with me.

Extract from Staff Communications Book
Date: 30/5/84
Staff: Judy R.

Tracy was confronted in the community meeting tonight over her 'overdose'. We recounted exactly what we originally thought had happened and its effect on staff and kids, and then told the kids the rear of the details so they knew that Tracy hadn't taken any pills. Wanted to get out of her family sessions and knew exactly what effect she would have on the others. She got the full brunt of the staffs' anger and from some children.

Tracy sat throughout (for about a half-hour) totally unmoved and looking smug and calculating though at times angry. She said little and what she did say was dismissive – '...you lot don't care, why should I bother, not worth it, no one is honest with me...' in a very bitter, callous way. At one point, Darla started crying and said, 'She's not going to do it again, is she? She can't because I love her,' and one by one all the children cried and said to her how upset they were and how much they cared for her. Tracy did not respond in any way and remained totally unmoved and even rejected the other children.

Eventually, Lacey said she knew exactly how Tracy felt, that she was trying to block everyone out because she did care and it was easier to hate than to love. Lacey was crying and Pat asked if she could move over to help Tracy, which she did. Tracy finally broke with Lacey talking to her and they cried together.

Helen then took Tracy out of the room and, having returned a short time after, Tracy went over to Mia, started crying and was then able to say she was sorry to the group. Helen and I felt that Tracy had opened by a little chink and we felt therefore that we would hold tonight's family session as planned as:

a) We may bring her out even more now; and,
b) If we didn't then she had achieved her aim.

The family session went very well indeed. We started by going back over Tracy's letters to Dad and Peter Pain responded to a lot of what Tracy had written. He clarified for her a lot of the detail about Mum leaving home and why Tracy couldn't live with her, i.e. Mum's boyfriend had made it clear that he wouldn't have the children.

Tracy seemed a lot more relaxed and for a long period was able to keep her thumb out of her mouth and look at Dad. We established that the knife incidents never took place and Tracy at that time was not afraid of Dad. We talked about Dad's marriage to Tracey – how things had been fine at first and all had been happy but when she came out of the hospital after her breakdown, she changed completely, was very Victorian and quite cruel towards the children.

At this point Tracy's fear of her father began; she was afraid of her step-mum and the way her Dad always 'sided' with her even when Tracy was innocent. She was afraid of the effect and control that step-mum has on Dad and what step-mum could make Dad do to Tracy. This fear intensified during the month before New Road, when Dad took a very disciplinarian line with her and actually hit her if school work was not up to the standards he set.

Peter Pain was able to say to Tracy that he regrets a lot of the mistakes he made, but explained why it was important that 'parents stick together' and how he was trying to save his second marriage. Tracy seemed to understand all this and was much more responsive being able to talk to him, agree with him and ask him questions with help from Helen. We established that Peter had never been able to say these things to Tracy nor indeed ever really speak to her about anything, other than in his role of controlling father, before Tracy admitted she had never been able to tell Dad how unhappy she was or take any problems to him.

We, therefore, suggested that before we could rebuild father/daughter relationship, we had to help them respond/talk to one another as human beings first. Peter

43

admitted he would find that difficult but would try and Tracy responded positively to the suggestion.

The session ended with Dad and Tracy having a happy, friendly chat about her cat and Tracy left the room in a very positive frame of mind. Before Peter left, Mia brought him a note from Tracy saying how much better she feels towards him and how she wanted to go over and kiss him at the meeting, but couldn't, but maybe she could next week.

Helen and I felt it was a very positive session and that we were beginning to make some progress. Tracy was very happy and relaxed when we went to say goodnight. Her restrictions have also been lifted today.

***

I can feel reality slipping away; I'm in a place where consequences don't matter. Nobody can hurt me anymore and if I hurt people then so be it. I have nothing left to lose. Wednesday is meeting day, the staff have meetings all day, then us children have a meeting on our own to discuss what we want to bring to the staff's attention and then finally the community meeting, where the staff and children all sit in a circle and air their grievances. Many a time these have gone on all evening while we wait for someone to own up to stealing something, or why we try to work out as a group how best to help one another.

I know tonight's meeting is going to be hard. I have hurt and angered everyone. My defences are up and I detach myself from my emotions as I sit here in the community meeting listening to everybody tell me what I already know. I am a nasty, horrible, evil person that should have died and saved everybody from the pain of knowing me.

Nobody believes I took an overdose and now they think I pretended just to scare everyone. They really hate me and think I just want attention. They don't realise that I just want it all to be over. My ability to block them out is a skill I have honed well over the years, sinking into myself so that their words become meaningless and their presence blurry. It really doesn't matter what I say as they don't believe me, and there is nothing I can do to make them understand how desperate I am to die and escape from my father forever.

Lacey came to sit with me and she knows how to reach inside of me and bring me back to the moment. We share a close bond that has been forged in the misery of what life has thrown at us and it is this link that makes me feel bad for what I have done to the other children. We are, after all, all in the same boat and they don't deserve any more upset, especially not from someone like me.

Once I start crying it feels impossible to stop. Helen takes me out of the group for a while and eventually I am able to apologise to them; luckily no one questions whether I did it or not anymore, the assumption being that I didn't. They take my apology as some kind of admission that I was pretending and, if that makes them happy, then fine. I know what I did, I know why I did it and I know that one day I will do it again, but next time it will work.

***

Extract from Staff Communications Book
Date: 17/6/84
Staff: Helen M.

I had Tracy in the office for a chat. She is still very non-committal and said that she really did not know why she ran etc., etc. I told her that she was not being asked that. I told her that I knew that something was amiss with her most of last week and that she might as well start talking about it. She didn't want to. She asked what time Dad was picking her up on Thursday. I told her that she seemed to want very much to give us the impression that she wanted things to be right with Dad when he was here and then did not offer a lot when he was here. 'Why?' She was evasive, as usual and then said, 'I suppose I'd better tell you, you probably know already.'

She went off and came back two minutes later with a folder of her plans regarding her Dad. Her eyes were all funny and she started crying, as we have never seen Tracy cry before. She came onto my lap, regressed (genuine), and cried for a long time. She went back out to the group but stuck close to me. She was still not right at bedtime and was crying again when I read to Mia

I spoke gently, but firmly to her, tucked her in all over again and told her to go to sleep. I checked on her at 11.45pm and she was crawling all over the bed – usual hysterical behaviour but no speech, just dry, racking sobs. Paul (staff) and I brought her downstairs. She was shaking severely, sobbing and had staring eyes, then a complete catatonic state and then sobs again. She was searching for my hand etc. Went into a natural sleep at 1.45am.

Judy and I have decided that we now need to involve psychiatric help for Tracy but not D.C.F.P. as we feel that she would see this as a retrograde step. I am contacting a psychiatrist tomorrow for his advice, as we want Tracy seen as soon as possible.

***

They keep making me see my father, every couple of weeks we have started having 'family meetings'. I await these times with dread, my stomach churns. My heart is heavy and I cannot see any purpose to these meetings. There will never be reconciliation and I cannot fathom how everyone seems to be ignoring the main thing. *I tried to kill him!* I didn't do that for fun or just to gain attention, I did it because I hate him, I hate everything about him.

They have tried telling him that all I want is love and affection but he can't even do that. He did try to cuddle me after one meeting, but it was so false it made my flesh crawl. There seemed to be a perverse sexual feel to it that was very, very wrong. I try to find the part of me that would feel sorry for a man that grew up in a loveless family, not receiving hugs and cuddles from his Mum. Without the warmth that humans need to grow, but to have lived through that and not be able to better yourself for your children's sake, to make your children suffer as you have suffered, eliminates any compassion I feel I should have.

I have begun to think that the only way they will take me seriously is if I show them how serious I am. I have worked out a plan and written copious notes on the most effective way to execute this. If this works, they will realise then that I am serious when I say I hate him and want him to die. I read a book and the girl in it used rat poison to kill her family. When mixed in his sugary coffee the bitterness of the coffee masks the taste somewhat. I know I could buy this and I am sure they will jump at the idea of me having a home visit; after all, they seem to think building our relationship is so important.

I feel so torn between telling Judy and keeping it to myself. I hate lying to her and Helen but I can't take the risk that they will make me go back with him one day. I know that is what they are hoping will happen; supposedly, children are better off with their families and this should be encouraged whenever possible.

My mind wanders and my imagination walks me through every step of their murder, from sprinkling the poison in their drinks – my heart thundering in my chest and my hands using up all my concentration to minimise the trembling – then watching the horror on their faces when they realise that they are dying. I have read that it is a painful death but no more than they deserve, I sit for a long time just watching and waiting. Making sure that the last rasping breaths I hear are really their last ever. I know by then I will have completely shut down and as they lead me away, I will know it is all over.

Back to reality, I have to see him regularly now and it is killing me. I try so hard to be the daughter he wants me to be, but every time I see him, the fear wells up inside me and I just want to put an end to it once and for all. Helen is angry that I am not making an effort when I am with him; why can't she just let it go? Why doesn't anyone believe I am serious when I say I hate him?

***

Extract from Staff Communications Book
Date: 21/6/84
Staff: Helen M.

I had a very good session with Tracy following a letter she gave me when I came on duty. Tracy was in a very sensible mood and wanted to start putting things right for herself. She was really honest and open about how confused she gets when she tries to rationalise things. I feel that it was the most verbal and constructive session we have had with her so far.

We talked about how she wants to talk in family sessions but dries up completely as soon as she is in Dad's company. The reason is fear; fear of him being violent towards her (even though she accepts that Judy and I would not allow this to happen). Fear, too, of hurting Dad by things she might say or do if she got angry and fear that 'as always, I will only make things worse'!

I explained to Tracy that Judy and I could try to convince her forever more that her fears were unfounded, but she will only be really convinced when she starts talking in our family sessions about them, and by doing so will be able to disperse of them once and for all. Tracy was genuinely worried about taking them to our sessions but was willing to try with Judy's and my help, e.g. if Tracy can only say one sentence, Judy or I will continue for her. Next time, two sentences and so on.

We talked about Tracy's anger, how she holds on to it for fear of hurting people and then ends up by hurting them more; e.g. Tracy was furiously angry with Mum for leaving but has never expressed this for fear of upsetting

48

her. Tracy was able to accept that Judy and I will set up the first session with her Mum on her own, followed on by Mum joining some family sessions if she wants to. Tracy was also able to accept that Mum will very likely be most upset by much of what Tracy has to say to her, but that it will be her own unresolved guilt, which will be upsetting her and not Tracy. I explained to Tracy that in a way, she would be helping Mum too. Tracy was willing to try.

We talked about Tracy's sexual experiences and when she first had sexual intercourse (aged eight) with a fifteen-year-old boy. To date, at the age of fourteen, Tracy has been with approximately twenty males.

We went through how she has tried to replace her Mum's affections and the only way she could do this was by giving sex to anyone who wanted it, just so that she could get close to another human being. Dad was totally undemonstrative. We talked about what the sex act should be like and that at fourteen years old and younger, no girl is emotionally ready for it. Tracy said that she has never once enjoyed any of it but that it was what was expected of her from boys, and it seemed to please them. I told Tracy that Judy and I would start sessions on this with her as soon as possible. There is loads of work to be done here.

It was a really good session. A letter is to go to Anthea Blofeld when I come in on Tuesday laying out the recent events and requesting a referral for Tracy to the Maudsley Hospital in London to have EEG tests etc. done.

***

The community meeting didn't end until 10.00pm tonight as no one will own up about who scratched Mia's record? Lots of people think it is me but I swear it isn't. After the meeting I have a meeting with Helen and Judy and they said they were glad I wrote down about the fire as it straightened a lot out for them. They thought I had worked everything out about when Mum left but now they've realised that I've worked it out in my mind, but not in my heart. The meeting with Dad ended at 11.00pm and was pretty upsetting, but nothing I can't cope with. Helen has a really high temperature now, worse luck!

I have a meeting with Helen after school and she wants me to write all my feelings down for her, which I will do over the weekend. She asks about sex and I tell her about how often I have done it. She thinks I am just trying to find a father figure as my Dad hasn't been able to show me any love or affection. She thinks I will give sex to anyone just to be loved. I know she thinks I am too young and she wants to talk to me some more about it, but she doesn't understand that it doesn't matter to me. Men can do and have done whatever they like to me. I just switch off and let them get on with it, that way they are happy and no one has to get hurt.

Helen is collecting me on Monday after school and we are going out for a meal, which will be great!

Chapter 7

1978 – Aged 8

Loves First Kiss

My session with Helen reminded me of my first boyfriend. I was only eight when Gordon and his friend Ivor started hanging around our group. They were a lot older than most of us, Gordon with his shock of black hair and rugged look and Ivor, blonde, tall and forever in Gordon's shadow. Both of them were so kind to me, paying me attention when the other big kids just teased me for being a baby.

I think I fell in love with Gordon when he lifted me onto the handrail in the alleyway, kissed me and told me he loved me. I felt special that the big boys were interested in me, that Gordon loved me even though I was the youngest in our group; he called me baby face, but in a nice way, not mean and spiteful like some of the others.

He showed me the difference between English and French kisses and then told me that grown-ups kiss the French way. I didn't really like it but I wanted them to think I was a big girl so I let him kiss me and stick his tongue in my mouth. Gordon and Ivor both let me sit on their motorbikes and they made me feel so grown-up, so when Gordon offered to take me for a ride on his bike I jumped at the chance. Gordon sat at the front and I sat behind, with Ivor behind me so that I didn't fall off.

I felt really safe, sandwiched between the two leather clad boys and held on tight to Gordon. They took me to the cemetery at the top of my Dad's hill, where we drove in and pulled up under the trees. Nobody was about and it was getting late. Gordon lifted me off the bike and we sat on the grass; he had told me in the alley about the special things grown-ups do to show they love each other. He said he wanted to show me because he loved me so much and I wanted him to because I loved him too. He said it was a secret and that I mustn't tell and he would love me forever.

I remember him putting his hand up my dress and into my knickers; he touched me gently and pushed his finger deep inside me. He pulled down my knickers and told me to lay on the grass. He was heavy on top of me, and he pushed himself into me. Ivor was there, keeping watch at first, but they both loved me and when Gordon had finished Ian laid on top of me. I don't remember getting home, just standing in the front room trying to explain why I was late.

I was in so much trouble; Dad was furious. When I said Gordon and Ivor had taken me to the cemetery on the bike – he went crazy and stormed out to find them. I was scared about what he would do. When he came back, he was still angry and forbade me to see them ever again. I tried telling him that I loved them, but I remember him shouting at me, saying they were far too old for me and that they couldn't possibly love me.

But what did he know? I knew they loved me, and they had shown me they loved me, it was our secret.

I had never seen my Dad so angry, I didn't dare tell him that I had been doing grown up things, I think he would have killed me.

I think this added to the growing hate I had for my father; he drove my Mum away, drove Ivor and Gordon away, too. In my eyes, he took away everyone that ever loved me. I could have understood why if he had loved me but he certainly didn't. He never once cuddled me or showed me any affection of any sort. Gordon and Ivor did, which is why I believed them when they told me they loved me. *Did I know it was wrong?* At eight years old I didn't have the words to explain what had happened, all I knew was that my Dad would be angry when all I wanted was to be loved.

It's strange that no one asked about what happened back then. Everyone just took it for granted that as I gave myself so willingly to boys and men, I must have asked for it and I suppose I did, as I never complained. *Why would I?* At least someone loved me.

Chapter 8

1984 – Aged 14

Medvale: Crazy, Angry Times

Extract from Staff Communications Book
Date: 22/8/84
Staff: Pat S.

Absolutely no emotion was shown about Mia leaving.

Walking around the dining room, saying that it was like a morgue, and trying to change the atmosphere by putting on lively music. Later on, she went very quiet, watched the film for a while and then went to bed. I went up to see if she was okay. She was in bed reading. I asked if she wanted to talk and was it her time to feel sad (Mia leaving), but Tracy did not want to talk.

***

Mia is leaving; they have found her foster parents that she likes and she is going to leave next week. She is sad but happy too, I know she doesn't want to leave us but at the same time you can see she is excited about her new life. I hope she will be happy. I hope I don't have to leave as I can't imagine living a normal life right now. I have spiralled down and seem to be getting lower and lower. There's not a family out there that would want to live with me and I am certainly never going to live with my father again. I know he says he wants me home but I know that's just so he can have his revenge. They believe he is such a good person; however, one day I'll make them see what he has done to me.

***

I was determined to have a chat with Tracy because she was annoying me at various times with her moods. I approached her in the bedroom but there was too much noise so we used Pat's office. I went to get her from the bedroom and she was in tears (although nothing had been wrong!). In Pat's office, none of it was my business, she had already talked to lots of social workers and what was wrong was between her and her Mum. Okay, but I was only concerned. She then burst into tears. I cuddled her.

We went around many houses – Mum, Tracy wants to live there, strong in last two weeks but birth of another baby means even less likelihood, therefore, mixed feelings over birth. Dad, significantly, not mentioned, when I brought him up, death was the only answer again. No apparent desire for Mum, Dad, Debbie, Tracy reunion. Tracy not close to any child anymore. 'Yes, Stuart (Medvale child) may feel I am close to him', 'no nothing happening between us', no overt feelings or concern about the loss of Mia; Tracy saying she doesn't want any help and can figure out everything for herself although it hasn't ever worked out before.

After the bit about Mum and Dad not getting together, talked about families. Tracy talked about Helen and Judy being important, had spent a lot of the holiday with Helen, Helen important, Tracy saying that Judy is not now as important (I think different, not unimportant – see later). Families – yes, Tracy has seen Helen's family and would like to be fostered by Helen! (I think fantasies are about!) I think transference is happening where Helen is now the good Mum Tracy wants and Judy is the bad Dad, although obviously not a man. I think that Tracy may be putting a barrier between her and Judy as with Tracy/Dad. Twice Tracy was very sorrowful and cried but little other emotion. I think she is depressed and in a bit of a hole.

Staff: Sandra B.

Very close this evening. Followed me around the kitchen when I made tea, waited around until I returned to the television room. Cuddled up, stating she's feeling 'weird', but couldn't describe in what way. Playing with a penknife, rubbing her hands up and down my arm. Very quiet but warm. Then floods of tears. I asked her if she wanted to talk. 'Yes.' We went up to her bedroom where we laid and chatted for a while. Said the same as she had to Peter – Mum being pregnant, not sure whether she's happy about it or not, missing Mia – didn't respond to Mia going last night. Feeling unsafe. Missing Helen etc. Not Judy – basically, what she said to Peter, but something is definitely erupting.

Staff: Peter J.

Crying again later, brought down, cuddled with me and then went to bed at 12.15am.

***

This morning Peter had a talk with me and I can't seem to stop crying. I just can't cope anymore. Sandra spent most of the night with me but I could've killed her; I don't want to get close to people and she is becoming far too close to me. I don't trust myself around her at all and yet I feel compelled to be with her, it is very confusing but very powerful.

I feel unsafe here right now; I am scared of what I am going to do.

***

Extract from Staff Communications Book
Date: 24/8/84
Staff: Sandra B.

Tracy asked to speak to me. I went up and she was lying on her bed. She cuddled up to me and then said, 'You'd better take these from me.' She had a packet of tablets which she got (stolen) from the family. I praised her for not taking any and asked why she hadn't. Something told her not to; she's had them for a while – life was pointless – didn't trust anyone; will be glad to see Helen tomorrow when she goes over to clean out Ben (mouse). He's all she's got now. I pointed out that we were here for her and that we all loved her. She talked about Mia going; missing her, but couldn't show it on Wednesday. She cried a little. She still wants to kill Dad and doesn't care about Mum! I asked her if she still is doing her life storybook. She said she was and that she had got up to the fires with her Dad. I asked if she is going to carry on. 'Yes.' She came down much better and is now working in the dining room on her life story. Has a large swelling on her right arm.

I am finding Tracy a little weird. She is following me everywhere but I am feeling very warm towards her.

She again sought me out and we had the same sort of chat – life's not worth working at. I disagreed and said that she is to give all these feelings to Helen and Judy. I told her that she must have thought life was worth going on as she wouldn't have given me the tablets this morning. She smiled and agreed. Better. Mentioned that she was wandering around the bedroom looking for something she had in her drawer. Not there. Is now looking again and if she finds 'it' she will give it to me.

Staff: Pat R.

Tracy has asked to talk to me after the barbeque and has come to me several times just briefly, to rest her head on my shoulder. She is obviously hurting. Tracy is trying to

57

cope.

Tracy told me she is full of feelings and never seems to get to the end of sorting them out. 'Knows things' through her life storybook but still has feelings that stop her 'accepting' it (her words). I delved further. It transpired that at first, when she and Mia were friends, Mia was like her sister. Then when Lacey came, Mia became like her mother and Lacey like her sister (exact parallel of home). Mia has now gone like Mum, Tracy is angry.

I used the 'empty chair' technique to see if Tracy could voice feelings for Mia. She became very upset – frightened white, nervously chewing lip and tears were close – but couldn't speak. So, I doubled for Tracy, speaking to Mia about how Tracy loved and needed her and now she was gone. Then, after a little interval for Tracy to recover a bit, I spoke of anger, hatred and guilt. Then I worked with Tracy to distinguish quite clearly that Mia is her friend, not her Mum, and highlighted all the differences.

Then, having cleared the ground, I was able to approach Tracy's anger at her Mum as a totally separate entity. I asked if Tracy could speak to her mother in the 'empty chair': 'No!' Could she cope with me doing so? 'No' Very frightened sitting on my lap, holding on tight. So I shared an experience with her of feelings I had for my mother, hoping that this would make Tracy's seem less nightmarish. This appeared to work, and she curled up on my lap in a much more relaxed way.

I asked her if her fear was that if she got angry she would kill her mother – she nodded. I asked if it was possible then, that she had put the anger that belonged to Mum, towards Dad, because he was there, and she needed a dream Mum to hang on to – she nodded. I then explained that if that were so, it could explain how intense she had had to make her anger to Dad. Somewhere she had been aware that it wasn't wholly true – that it was therefore very unlikely that she would hurt her Mum in any way.

I asked if Tracy had found this as frightening as she had thought, and she gave me a rather surprised smile and *said, 'No.' I cuddled her for a while and gradually reduced the tension while we decided the next step. Since Tracy recognised she has to face all this now and can't stop (and that she can't hide in games anymore, having grown out of them).*

Tracy decided she would think, perhaps write, and then talk to Sandra as Helen is away. (Interesting – is Tracy trying to take on Mia's relationship with Sandra.) Tracy needs to express her rage with her mother in full emotion and then cry out her grief. She hasn't a close enough relationship with me to do that so couldn't quite reach it tonight, even though she's very accessible, and it's all bubbling just below the surface. I hope someone else can get to her as soon as possible.

***

I carried on my talk with Sandra this morning and gave her the pills I have. As much as I want to die right now, she makes me feel so guilty; I hope she can see how torn I am between doing the right thing and just ending it all. I have other tablets that I stole from Shona, but I can't find them; if I do, I will give them to her too. I don't need any temptations right now. Pat talked to me after the NAYPIC (National Association of Young People in Care) barbeque about Mia leaving, and I agreed to talk to Sandra tomorrow as well, I am really not okay.

I am so scared!

***

Extract from Staff Communications Book
Date: 25/8/84
Staff: Pat R.

Very quiet. Returned to bed sucking her bottle. Very shaky and insecure.

Staff: Sandra B.

I took Tracy upstairs to talk, as there was too much row downstairs. First, I sat on the bed with her but she was not too relaxed so we laid down, and she cuddled up to me. Went over brief things she had said to Pat; angry with Mum, doesn't want to hurt Mum 'cos she loves her too much – wants to kill Dad as he's the next nearest person to her. Spoke about her feelings towards Mia leaving – angry with her, if she were here now would hurt Mia. When Mia left, it was like her Mum leaving again. I also said that Mia was Tracy's friend, and a friend is different from her Mum. She has definitely realised the fact that Mia was close to me and is seeing that closeness as putting from her to me (transference).

She spoke of the other night (Thursday) when I went and said goodnight to her; of when we sat in the television room she sat and cuddled up to me, wanting a cuddle but didn't want to get too close to me. All the time she was playing with her penknife. When I said goodnight to her, I laid and cuddled her for a while. She was looking odd; eyes fixed – evil expression. She told me she wanted to talk but was confused at where to start and what to say.

When she told me today of her feelings, I wasn't surprised. She didn't want to get close to anyone, became angry at getting close to me as she had previously decided she was going to make it on her own. Didn't need anyone, didn't need to get close, etc., so her anger made her want to hurt me. The knife she has was under her pillow – blade open, so she stated (she first thought of this in the television room). I asked her why she didn't show her anger. She was afraid of Peter. Why? Because if I'd hurt you he would have acted like Dad, hit me, shout at me, etc. (boy am I glad of that!).

Her anger must have been broken when Peter came into the bedroom and we brought her downstairs. Peter held her but that same look was in her eyes, fixed on me. It did frighten me a little, I must admit. Today again, I asked

60

her why she was wandering around the bedroom at 5.30am on Thursday morning. She said, 'Okay, I'll tell you it all. I had a bottle of pills hidden in the drawer. I pinched them from school. I felt guilty for wanting to hurt you and to make it up decided to hand over all the tablets I had.' She was concerned because she couldn't find them (little did she know that Judy had already found them).

I asked her how she felt now: 'Frightened, you won't tell my Dad will you?' She was sweating and shaking and then cried openly. I let her cry for about ten minutes and then suggested that she would have to talk with Judy and Helen at some stage. It was very okay to bring her anger out here, we can handle it and that I couldn't promise her that her Dad wouldn't find out.

I brought her down for a cigarette and lunch. Seemed okay. One other thing I forgot to record this evening on her way upstairs, someone asked her (I can't remember who): 'Has your mum had her baby yet?'

'No, but I hope she dies having it!' No further comment.

Staff: Judy R.

Went out with Mia to Chatham for an hour. I quickly searched her bed and drawers when she was out – no weapons or anything else. Also, read her diary – no entry for 4–5 days, but most recent ones scribbled in bad writing. Entries on holiday in Somerset all talking about missing Medvale, getting close to the family (and worried about getting hurt) but being able to block out feelings about Medvale; not sure it will work, the test being when Mia leaves and 'I may have to take the pills then'. Only other bits of interest are two different boys wanting to 'fuck' her – one she conned twenty fags out of; the other, she said she would if he paid her!

While I don't wish to be a 'scare-monger', Tracy does need watching like a hawk, I think, especially at night. We should never forget what she has attempted before (fires, *poison, etc.) and should always be alert and please don't give her any money other than bus fares, etc.*

***

Sandra is one of the sweetest women I have ever been lucky enough to meet. She is tall, slim built and has shoulder length, blonde hair that frames her face with delicate flicks. Her face is full of understanding and warmth; I can almost see my pain reflected in her eyes. When I'm near her I just want to pour my heart out to her, but I know I can't. After much consideration, I decide that I must kill Sandra. She evokes such powerful emotions in me; when I am near her, my heart aches for the love I wish she could give me that I know isn't mine to have. I don't want to feel like this, to hurt so much and to risk exposing so much of myself.

I am not sure how I get through school the next day, I feel sick to the bottom of my stomach just thinking about what I need to do. Killing someone is the only way I can see to stop the pain I am feeling, and then they will have to lock me away so justice can be done.

I am having sessions with Helen and/or Judy virtually every day at the moment and my mood seems to swing from feeling really positive and close to them both, to really negative and wanting to end it all.

I have been spoken to about involving one of the other children, Matilda, in trying to kill me; well, that's her version of events. Personally, I remember a dream, at least I thought it was a dream where Matilda was singing my name and trying to strangle me, and then suffocate me with a pillow. I didn't fight back, I would be quite happy to die right now but when I woke half an hour later she claimed I had tried to kill myself. Now, she is telling the staff I am trying to get her to kill me.

I can see they are angry with me and Helen keeps talking about psychiatric care. I wish they would lock me away; I couldn't hurt anyone then and couldn't hurt myself. I deserve to be punished for what I done and I will carry on punishing myself if no one else will do it for me.

***

Extract from Staff Communications Book
Date: 29/8/84
Staff: Pat R.

Community Meeting: Very angry but absolutely freaked by the group tonight – afraid because she knew her anger was about to be brought out at Medvale (though not tonight) and freaked by her own admission that she knew this was so and wanted us to reach her.

Staff: Sandra B.

From the moment I walked into this building today and saw Tracy (who had been out), I felt uneasy at her presence. I put my arms around her and all she did was to pull away and stated she hated me. Never have I felt as uneasy as I did in the community meeting. She said that her anger was over something I'd said the other night about her Mum. Before this – at the dinner table – she was fine with Judy, chatting about her mum and the baby. The moment I sat down she changed. Evil looks, wouldn't speak to me, etc. Paul was winding her up really well, asking if he could make her angry – 'No.' I asked if I could – 'Yes.'

Getting back to the community meeting – if looks could kill, well I wouldn't be writing this. I was more than happy when Judy asked if I wanted her to see Tracy with me (as Tracy had said that she would see me later about what I had said). So, at about 11.30pm, we both had a session with Tracy. She was quite okay with that. She produced two notes the first of which she wrote after our chat on Saturday and the second a few hours later.

I asked her to relate back what it was I said about her

Mum. Reply: 'You told me I was angry with my Mum for leaving.'

Judy then said, 'Well, you are aren't you?'

Tracy said, 'I have no reason to be – my Mum doesn't deserve me to be angry with her.' Judy reminded her of past sessions with Helen and herself, her anger over Mum and Dad and asked why she now denied it. I then reminded her of the comment she had made on the stairs about someone asking about Mum's baby and how she had said that she hoped Mum would die giving birth. She flatly denied it and then I got that evil look again. She made me feel really terrified.

Judy put it to her that it is fine to get angry with the right people and in the right way – not a way that could be damaging. I pointed out that Helen and Judy were working very closely with her and that they were her key workers, and that they were the people to bring all this to and not me. Told her that it was fine for her to talk to me or any member of staff who was around (as I happened to be on Saturday and Sunday), but to hold on to all the parts that they have been working towards for six months.

Tracy said that she had transferred all her hate from her father to me. Not so – I was getting too close and she didn't want that, so yet again Tracy is playing and setting up roles. She admitted that she can talk to me and finds it difficult to handle. Judy asked her if she still hated me – 'Yes, just a little.' The decision was, possibly, if she still feels the same when Helen gets back then Helen, Judy, Tracy and I will discuss it, but hopes it will pass (so do I). Off to bed angry at 12.30am.

Extract from Staff Communications Book
Date: 30/8/84
Staff: Sandra B.

When I went up to bed at 2.35am, I heard crying from Lacey and Tracy's room. I found Tracy sitting huddled in a ball on the bed – actually crying real tears. I sat with her for a while and told her it was time she was asleep. She said that she couldn't sleep and she was afraid. (Paul and I were around.) She clung to my hands and began the mumbling. She was saying, 'I'm sorry, I want my Mum,' all the usual babbling. Then she said, 'I hate my Mum.' I told her that I was aware that she was awake and stressed that she must sleep.

Paul then came into the room and touched her face. She flinched away towards me, hanging on tightly saying, 'Don't leave me.' I repeated that we had all have a long, hard day and that she should talk all this over with Helen and Judy. She started to sleep mumbling again, '...the only answer is to kill him. Death is the only answer.' I asked whose. Her own. 'When you're dead everything's okay,' etc., etc. I again said that I was aware that she was not asleep and that I could hear every word she was saying.

Paul sat outside the bedroom. I felt okay, not spaced out with her as I had felt on Wednesday. She said that she could talk to me and I asked, 'Why me?' She said that she couldn't talk or tell 'them' (Helen and Judy). I asked her why. 'They will tell my Dad.' I told her that everything she told me would go back to Helen and Judy anyway. She was okay with that also. At 3.30am, I told her to settle and if she wanted to talk to any member of staff to hang on to it and talk when she needed to. She said she would talk again to me. Also when Helen returns she wants to talk to Helen and Judy with me present if that was okay. She said, 'I love you,' and then seemed to settle.

***

It was a long community meeting just about anger, as everyone was extremely angry. I feel like a kettle boiling but I can't be switched off; I am really scared of letting my anger out as the only way I know how to is by killing and I can't do that here.

The meeting with my Dad was fine; I am far too distracted in my head even to contemplate what we talked about. I am finding it easier and easier to switch to the person that people want to see when he is around; fear paralyses any part of me that wants to be really honest with him in the room, the smile and carry on girl takes over for me.

I had a meeting with Sandra and Judy as I felt like killing Sandra because I was scared of being close to her. But they are fucking liars! Saying I said evil things about my Mum; *why would I be angry with her?* I can't blame her for leaving my Dad, I couldn't live with him either. I didn't get to sleep until 4.00am as I was crying so much. I don't know why they are doing this to me.

I had a couple of talks with Sandra as I keep feeling okay one minute and then angry the next. In the night, I tore some skin off my arm as I was so angry and this morning I tried to slash my wrists with some glass that I found outside. Luckily, no one cares enough to notice, so I don't have to explain myself. After all, what would I say? If I don't hurt myself, then I will hurt someone else, so it's a no-brainer really.

Chapter 9

1979–1983 – Aged 9–13

Living in Hell: The First Fire

The time we lived with my step-mum Tracey, was probably the hardest, and maybe her unbalanced mind played a part in destabilising my mind. I can't speak for my sister, but she endured the same hell as me and was not left unscathed. It was clear to me that my father loved my sister, and in his eyes she could do no wrong, driving a wedge between us that would never truly heal.

Still carrying the resentment I felt about him forcing my Mum out, I took my anguish to school and, as a result, my work and my friendships suffered. I tried hard to keep my friends and took to stealing money from my father's dressing table every morning so that I could buy sweets to give to the children at school. At first it seemed to work but they wanted more and more from me so that in the end I was buying around five pounds worth of sweets a day and still felt that nobody really liked me. Nobody wanted to play with me, and I didn't know how to ask.

In a way getting caught was a relief; my father was furious, and for once I didn't even try to deny what I had done. He was shocked that it had been going on for so long and worked out that I must have stolen about £1000 over the six months I had been stealing from him. He had apparently accused Tracey time and time again of overspending her housekeeping, not thinking for one minute that I could be the culprit.

He called the police, and two burly police officers came to the house. They sat on the settee with me in between them. I must have looked tiny to them; ten years old and weighing no more than five stone. They spoke to me about how worried my father was about me and how stealing was a bad thing and could end up with me in prison. I sat there listening, wishing and wishing that they would just take me away. Even prison sounded better than living like this.

I could feel the anger seeping from my father; I knew he hated me. Why couldn't those policemen see what was happening? I was scared when it was time for them to go; I knew I was still in trouble, and wondered what punishment was in store for me.

My father ordered me upstairs and made me bend over the bed, where he hit me several times across the back of the legs with his slipper, sending burning hot pain shooting through my body. He left me there, crying into the duvet, my legs and bottom throbbing and burning. I hated him so much.

I lay in bed that night planning how I could run away, maybe my Aunt Frieda would let me stay with her. I didn't have anyone else I could turn to, and I knew she had helped my Mum escape. In the morning, I packed a bag with underwear, pyjamas, Nyla and some food and decided to go after school.

I walked up to the bus stop from school and waited for what seemed like an eternity. The long wait gave me time to think, and I knew deep down that Aunty Frieda would just phone my father and send me home. I couldn't escape. I walked home crying; nobody noticed that I was late, and I quietly got on with my daily chores. One day I would get out of here, I promised myself.

A man from the NSPCC came out to see me. I felt relieved that maybe somebody might listen to me now and see how bad I felt. My hopes were dashed within moments of him meeting my father. They got on famously, talking about cricket and drinking tea and I became very much an afterthought. If only I could have a few moments alone, maybe I could have told him, but I could see how he had been sucked in to believing what a great guy my father was and he would never believe me.

My father – in his efforts to humiliate me further – made me tell the man that I wanted to be a stripper when I grew up (sneering the whole time). I switched off when the lecture started about the dirty old men that go to places like that. The one thing I learnt to hate at a very young age was hypocrisy and there was my father, with his bedroom full of porn magazines, sneering at my desire to be a stripper. I used to just vacuum around them under his bed until curiosity got the better of me and then I found I liked what I saw! Nine years old was probably a little young to be vacuuming the house and it was certainly too young to be introduced to the world of pornography. I wasn't sure what made me look in the box on top of his wardrobe, but it was full up with magazines of naked women.

All the things that I couldn't tell that man from the NSPCC, who scorned my desire to be like the girls my father so obviously liked. The man asked if everything was alright and I quietly muttered, 'I'm fine.' He went away happy and my father looked at me with a smug, contemptuous look, knowing that he had won again.

I knew I was beaten and for a time lost myself in a world of books and fantasies of murder. For one so young, I was in a very bad place with no obvious means of escape, but then I found books. Escaping into books opened up a whole new world to me, a world where people had the power to fulfil their destiny. Where the weak could rise and slay their enemies, where people were loved and cared for.

The day in, day out, constant criticism wore me down. I knew nobody loved me because I didn't deserve to be loved; I was an evil, disobedient child that needed to learn how to be a loving, dutiful daughter, like my big sister Debbie. 'Why can't you be like your sister?' I lost count of how many times I heard that and how many different people asked the same question. I never answered because I knew the answer would only infuriate them more, but I didn't want to be like Debbie. I didn't want to smile and play, at being happy families, pretending everything was fine when our life was far from fine. I couldn't obey without questioning the never-ending demands of a stepmother who treated us like slaves when we should have been enjoying our childhood.

At times, I admired Debbie for quietly being able to put up with the abuse, but I could see she was unhappy. I often wondered why our life drove us so far apart when we were both suffering and could have supported each other through the bad times. Ultimately, Debbie blamed me for most of the discord within the family; she never understood why I acted the way I did, strongly believing that if I behaved then everything would be harmonious once again. In her eyes, if I didn't want my father to be angry with me, if I was as scared of my father as I claimed to be, then why did I go out of my way to oppose him?

Debbie was always telling me how my father had got people spying on me to make sure I behaved on my way to and from school. I believed her and even saw a black Ford panel van several times following me to and from school, stopping and starting as I made my way along my usual school route. I knew it was the same van and made a note of the registration – LBA 475T. There was no depth to which he wouldn't stoop to control my every move; I had no life of my own and believed I never would.

I let my mind wander to thoughts of release, a way out of the hell where he could use me to do his bidding, and then squash me under his shoe like a cockroach. I just wanted an end to it all, and thought that maybe if I were dead they would be sorry, they would be sad that they didn't love me while they had the chance.

I pictured myself stepping off the kerb and imagined the impact as the car tossed me into the air, my body thudding against the windshield and my broken body bouncing, and landing disjointed on the cold tarmac. I felt the life ebb away from me with a pool of blood spreading around me. As I rose out of my body, I looked down and saw them all standing over my grave. They looked sad and I hoped they were sorry that they didn't care about me while they could.

Maybe if my Mum had loved me, she wouldn't have left me with him. She must have known that my father hated me and how dangerous and controlling he was. I envisaged my demise in so many different ways but was too much of a coward to go through with it. Even when I tried walking out in front of cars they just swerved to avoid me. When I did get hit and knocked to the ground once, the driver just leaned out of her window and told me to 'bloody watch where I was going'! Not stopping to see if I was okay. It was almost like I had a sign on me making it okay for people to hurt me.

Running away seemed the only answer. I couldn't keep on with the masquerade of happy families that we were expected to play. After school, I went to a friend's house to give myself time to make plans. This was only a delaying tactic, as I couldn't bear the thought of being out all alone but the thought of going home terrified me more, I felt so trapped.

When I had exhausted the goodwill of her parents and before it got late enough for them to ask questions, I made out it was time to go home. I gathered my things as slowly as I could get away with. I knew I was not going back home, I knew that I wanted everyone to suffer as I had. The early part of the evening I was more on edge; every car and every person could be someone sent to look for me, and I didn't want to get caught. I walked fast so that I looked like I had a place to go in the hope that no one would stop to question me.

As the night wore on, and the people became fewer I could afford to slow down and wallow in my thoughts while I was walking. I had nowhere to go; no one to turn to for help. They all thought it was just me attention seeking, trying to find ways to hurt my father. Poor innocent 'Daddy' who didn't deserve such an ungrateful, unloving daughter, why couldn't they see? See him for what he truly was.

I sat on the wall and imagined myself living with my

Mum, feeling warm and safe. Although I couldn't remember all the words to the songs I liked, I sang the choruses in my head over and over again. Songs like *Cry Boy Cry* by Blue Zoo, which meant something to me and my father had bought me the record as payment for cleaning his offices.

Every week I vacuumed the two storeys of his office building and in exchange he would buy me whatever single I liked. To me, it seemed like a good deal and I got records which I could never have afforded without this.

I kept walking, searching for doorways or secluded corners of car parks, somewhere, anywhere that I could hide and be safe. The cold crept in slowly and I wrapped my coat tighter and tighter around my body trying to keep it out. I found that looking at the lights in people's windows warmed me a little and made me think about the lives that other people lived, full of warmth and laughter and happiness. However, slowly these lights go out. One by one and then the only lights left were the street lights that gave everything a surreal yellow tinge or the shop lights that were harsh and cold and offered no comfort to me.

A van pulled up, and a man inside called to me; however, before they had a chance to stop and get out I was running as fast as I could away from there. I ran into the woods and hid in the bushes convinced that they would catch me. I could see torches moving along the paths and could hear people calling my name. My father and a few others passed close by, and I held my breath terrified that he would find me but he went by, continuing to call my name. I overheard them talk about the police looking for me and could see several other torchlights combing the higher ground opposite me. Eventually, they got further away and finally disappeared totally.

I sat in the bushes for a long time, too scared to move in case they were trying to trick me, but eventually I crept out carrying my bag close to me. I found a more comfortable spot where I felt safe enough to doze through the night, although I seemed to be keeping one ear open, alert to the possibility of approaching footsteps. As daylight dawned, I headed towards the shops, freezing cold and damp waiting for some signs of life so that I did not feel so alone.

When I thought it was a reasonable time I knocked on my friend's door, totally unprepared for the news that greeted me. She had told her parents everything, and they had spoken to my father and the police. They seemed very caring but wanted me to return home, yet they didn't understand that I couldn't go back, my father would kill me. I insisted on walking to school, and Valerie walked with me; I guessed her parents wanted to be sure that I would get there.

As I approached the school, there were four police cars waiting by the road and my father waiting by the school gate. I froze, a rabbit frozen in the headlights, the hunted caught in a trap, wanting to run but knowing there was nowhere else I could go. I made a token attempt at running back the way I had just come but was stopped quickly by the police who wanted to know where I had been. When I told them that I slept in the woods they gave me a lecture on how a rapist was loose in the woods last night, and I could have been raped or even murdered.

Little did they know that to have been murdered would have been a better option than going back with my father. They insisted that I returned home, and I felt crushed, there was no more fight left in me, and all I could do was bow my head and take the punishment that I knew was coming my way. My father was furious, I had embarrassed him in front of the police and our neighbours as, apparently, our neighbours had joined in the search and the lady next door had ruined her shoes in the woods, which I now needed to repay. I hadn't asked them to come looking for me, I hadn't wanted to be found. I was sent next door to apologise, given the slipper and then sent to my room.

My hatred for that family burned a little stronger with every failed attempt to escape, but I supposed the anger I had for my incompetence should have been directed at me.

The local police got to know me and instead of taking me back to the police station they took me straight home when they found me walking the streets at night. Despite desperately trying to make them understand how scared I was; my pleas to be taken away fell on deaf ears. My father came to the door in his dressing gown, thanked them, slammed the door in their faces and dragged me along the hallway into the dining room. I could see their silhouettes through the glass, so I knew they were still standing on the doorstep, yet they did nothing to intervene. My father was furious and kept pushing and hitting me so that I stayed cowered on the floor. Luckily he was barefooted so that he only left a small bruise on my face when he kicked me. All the while unleashing a verbal attack that in many ways was worse than the physical pain he inflicted. Apparently my social worker, Chris, had told him to be stricter with me and to him this meant corporal punishment, which he seemed to relish. If the regimented way I had to lay out the contents of my bag each night wasn't bad enough, he would hit me for any book that was missing or any grade that was lower than an A.

It was not long before the need to run away came again, living there was driving me totally crazy. They hated me; I hated them, I was convinced that there must have been a better way to live. My friends from school went with me to the hairdressers in Rochester and watched as I convinced the hairdresser that I was allowed to have a Mohican. She shaved it completely bald on either side of my head, leaving the centre strip quite long. When it was spiked up it looked fantastic, and it portrayed the confident person that I longed to be.

I caught a train to Charing Cross and spent the evening wandering around. Without any plan or place to go I must have looked quite bizarre, but I was careful not to linger in any one place for too long. I knew better than to draw attention to myself because if I was caught they would send me straight back to my father.

A short, dark-haired man in his forties approached me and using the promise of food, convinced me to have sex with him. He got what he wanted but I didn't and remained hungry for the rest of the night, although at least he pointed me back in the direction of the train station.

As the night wore on, and cold began to creep into my bones, I looked for shop doorways that would offer some comfort for the night. A passer-by told me that the newspaper printers were nearby, and as they worked late into the night, their doorways offered a little warmth as well as shelter. I huddled up and tried to keep as warm as I could. I must have drifted off because while my guard was down, I was approached by the police. The police could see in an instant that I was far too young to be alone on the streets. They took me back to the police station, and I spent several hours giving the officers false names and details, my favourite being Anna Alucard. It took them a while to realise that Alucard was Dracula backwards, and they were not impressed.

Eventually, they wore me down, and I told them everything. They insisted on calling my father although I begged them not to and told them he was sure to kill me, especially once he had seen what I had done to my hair! My pleas fell on deaf ears, and I guessed he thought he would help by telling my father to go easy on me, as I was scared he would hurt me.

Therefore, with even more ammunition than he had or needed my father collected me and although I was sent directly to bed on our return home, I knew I would have to face his wrath in the morning. I managed to block out a lot of the rage that flew from his mouth. I had heard it all before, how stupid and worthless I was, and now I looked like a tramp. He insisted that I brushed my hair down when I went to school, leaving me looking like I had a basin cut. Anything to try and humiliate me that little bit more.

One night the answer came to me; if I could kill my

family then I would be free. Free from oppression, free from criticism and free to find someone who might truly care about me.

Once I had realised what I had to do it wasn't difficult. I was the only member of my family who didn't eat gravy. If I could poison the gravy, then nobody would be suspicious of me not eating it. The only thing I could think of in the house that could be used as a poison was the Babybio plant food. I knew weed killer was a good poison, but we didn't have any so I figured plant food must have been worth a try.

As usual, I cooked the dinner for the family, which gave me plenty of time to contaminate the gravy. I shook about half of the bottle into the gravy and stirred it in. I was worried that if I used too much, they would taste it and I would be found out, but also worried that if I did not use enough then they wouldn't die and I would never be free.

I shook all the way through dinner and struggled to eat, but there was nothing strange in that, eating was never a strong point of mine. I was waiting for them to notice, convinced that when they did my life would be in danger because of what I had done.

It didn't work; they didn't even notice that I had done anything to the gravy, and if they had, they certainly didn't say anything.

In an effort to be popular at school, I told everyone I would be having a party at my house at the weekend and to invite anyone they wanted as my parents wouldn't be there. I figured that once I had killed them I could throw their bodies over the wall in the cellar so that nobody would find them. The cellar had always been dark, damp and eerie. I believed that it was haunted; even the cats and dog were too terrified to descend the stone steps into the darkness. Old jars, demijohns and other neglected paraphernalia cluttered the floor and shelves. There was a wall built across it that totally blocked off half of the room, but that had a two-foot gap at the top. I had summoned up the courage to look over it one day and the other side was just a huge pile of rubble. It wouldn't have surprised me if somebody was already buried there, it would make the perfect place.

Before going to school the next day, I poured out half a pint of milk and filled the bottle with paint stripper. I put it back in the fridge, and I figured that would kill them. Walking to school I suddenly realised that Tracey would probably give it to Tiggy, and my lovely cat would die too.

I spent the day crying on and off; I couldn't tell my friends what was wrong but I didn't want Tiggy to die, he didn't deserve that.

When the end of school bell sounded, I bolted from class and ran all the way home. The milk had gone; I was convinced I had been caught when I saw Tracey looking at me. My heart was beating so hard, and it was all I could do to stop myself from shaking, but she told me that she thought the milk had gone off, so she had thrown it away. How could they not have seen what I had done?

The next day inspiration came from an unexpected source. The girls at school were talking about an older girl who had been sent to a children's home for setting light to her house. It was the beginnings of a plan. I told the girls the party was still on. I guess I hadn't thought it through; after all, my aim was to kill them, not to burn the house down.

I planned on waking up at my usual 3.00am but overslept and woke at 6.30am instead. I thought everyone was still asleep so with my heart hammering in my chest, I crept into my father's room. They were both asleep, and I managed to steal ten pounds from the dressing table, which wasn't as easy as it used to be because he had become a lot more careful with his money since I had been caught the first time.

I soaked some tissues in turpentine and laid them outside my father's bedroom door. Along the landing was a row of boxes that I figured would help fuel the fire. I was so scared that they would wake when they heard the sound of the match lighting; I lit it in my bedroom and walked slowly to his bedroom door.

The tissue caught quickly, and I hurried downstairs, scooped up Dappy, grabbed my coat and bag and then left the house.

I hurried down the alleyways, adrenaline pumping through me. I couldn't believe I had done it. I took a very long walk to school, stopping to talk to lots of people on the way, as everyone wanted to stroke the dog. I stopped for a while and just cuddled Dappy, I knew I had saved her from burning to death. I just hoped Tiggy and Skippy had escaped as well.

News that I had brought my dog to school travelled like wildfire. As I walked down the main corridor, Mrs Trollope, my Headmistress, was striding the other way demanding to know why I had brought my dog into school. Before I had a chance to answer, my father intercepted me. He lifted my hands to his nose, sniffed and said, 'It was you wasn't it? Why, why would you do that?'

'I wanted to kill you,' was all I could answer. Mrs Trollope, sensing the seriousness of the situation, ushered us both into her office where my father told her what had happened. He said he had woken to a fire at his bedroom door and had tried unsuccessfully to put it out by smothering it with a shirt. But when that had just burst into flames he had managed to put it out using his quilt. Tracey had accused me straight away; he said he didn't want to believe it and then went on to say that as Debbie had been in the bath she could have boiled like a potato.

I tried hard not to laugh at that point, but I couldn't hold it in, it just sounded funny, someone boiling like a potato.

The horror was evident on their faces, which stopped my laughter in its tracks. I withdrew into myself and didn't listen as they talked about what they would do with me. Mrs Trollope decided to call my social worker, and they agreed that I needed to be taken into care. My relief was short lived when they said I would have to go home with

Tracey, pack a suitcase and wait for my social worker to pick me up.

My fear welled up inside. *How could she have sent me home with them?* Surely she must have realised how angry they were with me and how much danger I was in. I couldn't say anything. I pleaded with my eyes for some understanding but there was none.

I sat in the car and tried to make myself as small as possible, to shield myself away from his wrath. I knew I was a worthless piece of shit; I didn't need him to keep telling me. Luckily, he left me at the house with Tracey and, as she seemed to think it was punishment enough for me to be going, she left me to pack on my own. Although I couldn't totally relax until Chris my social worker came to take me away, I figured I had made it out alive.

Chapter 10

1984 – Aged 14

Medvale: The Therapy Continues

Extract from Staff Communications Book
Date: 1/9/84
Staff: Sandra B.

Crying on her bed and looking at a photo of herself with her Mum, I checked with Pat about comforting her and also that she was aware of where I was. I lay and cuddled her for about an hour, she was sobbing. She was playing sad, slow records, which helped her to cry. I remarked again on the marks on her arm. She obviously wanted me to notice her wrist as she was scratching it. Again, she has run glass across her left wrist (today, so she tells me). My answer to that was, 'Far be it for me to put you right, but anyone who's going to cut their wrists must do it much further up,' and I showed her where. She smiled and threw her arms around me and had another cry. Then she handed me a torn photo of Mum. She came downstairs much better. It certainly was a genuine cry.

Bed at 11.15pm, she asked for a story and then produced a razor, saying, 'It's sharp enough.' I asked for what and carried on with the story. She was asleep before the end. Very clingy. I took the razor from her.

Extract from Staff Communications Book
Date: 2/9/84
Staff: Judy R.

I had a word with Tracy and told her that what she was doing last week was wrong, that I had told her it was and

*as far as I was concerned she had now put things right.
There was no need to punish herself and I didn't want to
see any more cuts or scratches and that she was hurting
enough inside without hurting outside too. She smiled and
agreed. I asked her to bring me any razor blades etc. that
she had. She said that she didn't have any. Then she told
me about the bottle of pills and I then told her when and
why I had taken them. She seemed relieved though I
suspect that she may later be angry that I searched her
things. She also told me that Mum had phoned and how
angry she now felt towards her Mum.*

*To follow on from Sandra's entry on Wednesday night,
I told Tracy that I didn't believe her about transferring
(switched was her word) anger from Dad to Sandra and I
put it to her that the anger and hate stemmed from a)
feeling close to Sandra and worried because being close =
getting hurt. Therefore, it is easier to be angry and hate,
than risk being hurt and b) the main reason was that she
had found herself opening up and talking to Sandra about
things that she had successfully kept from Helen and me
for six months and probably wouldn't have told us had we
been around that night. She was scared and then angry
because she had put herself in that 'vulnerable' position
and was hating Sandra for 'getting that out of her'.*

Extract from Staff Communications Book
Date: 3/9/84
Staff: Pat R.

*The change in Tracy since she knew that Helen was on the
premises has to be seen to be believed – much more secure
and happy.*

Staff: Helen M.

*Close and clingy. Made herself a (baby) bottle and took it
to her room. When I went up, I said that I thought she had
stopped having a bottle and she said that she just felt like*

one tonight. She did not want a story but showed me her photos instead. We did not talk about anything heavy this shift but I told her that our sessions would be starting again very soon.

Extract from Staff Communications Book
Date: 9/9/84
Staff: Helen M.

Judy and I had a session with Tracy this morning and went through her rejection of Judy, Judy's feelings towards her and the way in which Tracy is trying to use Sandra. Also, her expectations of me as her foster Mum, her hate for her Mum, her inability to let go of anger, sorrow, hate, and how she will never really feel safe here until she does. I fronted her with the hate and anger she was feeling towards Darla at the last community meeting. She agreed and accepts that she has to lift the lid in order to move forward. I felt Tracy's pain and sorrow at the end and spent time holding her. Last night she was telling me about a nightmare she had the previous night, exactly the same as the one she had told me about before (Tracy had never told me). She was in the dining room, frightened; I was looking for her because she had murdered my children, Darren and Karen.

Staff: Judy R.

Tracy was able to say that her rejection of me stemmed from May/June when I was away a lot – I was like Mum to her, and then I went away so she blocked me out and has never moved from that. I spoke to Tracy about me not needing cuddles and affection from her and as long as she was getting that from Helen, it was okay but that she needed to talk/work with me or I was wasting my time. I pointed out to her that it was interesting that Helen has been away for two weeks but no rejection. Little response from Tracy today – angry/hurt, clammed up and sullen.

Staff: Helen M.

We had a good family session spent going over all the events leading up to the first fire. Debbie has now joined in with us and contributed an awful lot today, which was very painful for her. She was able to cry and express real feelings for the first time. Peter was suffering too and this rendered him far less vocal than he usually is. Each session will now be focussed on one incident, which only Judy and I will know about before we start. Tracy coped well and was very honest about how she had planned to kill the family, but was now pleased she had not succeeded. The family stayed together afterwards and played pool.

Extract from Staff Communications Book
Date: 10/9/84
Staff: Helen M.

I saw Tracy again regarding sexual feelings towards female staff. She denied having any but I know that she is lying. She is very, very angry with me and has been since this morning, but she would not give reasons, still it will come out eventually.

I had a phone call from Peter (staff) to say that Tracy was telling people here that she had been forbidden to talk to any member of staff about her problems, except her two lousy keyworkers. I was furious and came back in to tackle her. She tried hard to say that that was what Judy and I had said this morning. I told her that she was lying and sent her out for fifteen minutes to think about it.

She was still very angry and sullen when she returned. I was sitting very close in front of her inviting her to let her anger out. At one stage, she stared me out for nearly half an hour with the most evil look I have ever seen in my life. She flinched when I touched her and I had just started needing to hold her when Peter came in. It was a good job that he did because I could never have restrained her on my own. We had to hold her for twenty minutes and she gave us a lot, but there is still more to come. What she did give was very real. Afterwards, she sat on my lap, cuddling like a baby and crying very real tears. After half an hour, I put her to bed and lay with her until she was sleeping.

***

One of the staff called Paul is taking Matilda and me to Carnaby Street today so we can spend our clothing allowance that we have been saving. I think we both have nearly one hundred pounds each, so we should be able to get loads. We are going on the train. I am so excited, and I feel so safe with Paul and Matilda. Paul just seems to accept us as we are, without telling us we should look and behave in a certain way.

Paul seems to be a bit of a hippy himself, with shoulder length brown hair that is very thin on top, always wearing jeans and T-shirts. He must be in his twenties and is one of the few men that ignores my advances, and is just happy to spend time with me. I feel I can say anything to him, and to get to go out for the day, is such a treat. We spend a long time looking in the shops and even manage to persuade a couple of punks to let us take their photos with us. We go into Harrods and buy a few bits; it is so posh, Matilda and I get some strange looks. We have so much fun, and Paul is great, just letting us be ourselves without feeling the need to rein us in or keep us on a short lead.

Other days are not so great; frequent sessions with Helen and Judy often bring up very negative feelings for me, the release of which is meant to be cathartic. Although, this is not always the case and when it isn't, it just seems to fuel my already huge pit of self-destruction.

I have a session with Helen and Judy today, and they tell me to stop latching onto Sandra, so now I am not going to talk to anyone anymore about my problems. Oh...and Helen wants me to let my anger out, stupid fucker. *How can I?* Does she really have a death wish?

The meeting with Dad and Debbie is okay; we talk about the first fire, and how it made everyone feel. It is difficult to be honest though when Debbie is sitting in front of me, crying about how much I have hurt her. This isn't about her; it never has been, it is him I want to kill.

Helen comes in about 9.00pm as I want to see her. I am so angry with her; I try so hard to block out her angry outburst as yet again it is all my fault. Sinking into my world where the words just blend into a single drone doesn't work and now Peter joins in. I try so hard to keep control of myself but can't, and all I want to do is hurt them as much as I am hurting. I end up laying across the chairs with Peter holding me down. He is lying with all his weight across my chest. I can't breathe but they don't believe me, they think I am just pretending! I wonder if I am going to die, right here, right now, as I can't fight anymore. I start crying and eventually they let me sit up. Helen holds me, and I get the feeling that this is not the last time they will restrain me. I am still so angry. It's not fair. I should have killed them both. I WANT MY MUM! I only wish life could be how it used to be.

Chapter 11

1983 – Aged 13

New Road Children's Home

Chris, my social worker, came to take me from my father's house to the New Road Children's Home. The relief I felt, washed away any nerves I may have had about going somewhere new. I had made it out alive, which meant I could begin to be myself.

As his car slowed down, I took my first look at the children's home where I would be living. The house itself was old and imposing, set by the main road, we swung into the sweeping gravel drive and parked outside a huge wooden door. It reminded me of a horror film and I fully expected a towering giant to slowly open the door; instead, a short, stocky, lady with a round beaming face framed with short brown hair, opened the door and welcomed me in. She introduced herself as Linda and took us across the huge open foyer to the office. A tall man with curly blonde hair smiled and finished his call. He introduced himself as Peter and explained that he was the manager of New Road, which was the name of the children's home that I had been sent to. He seemed so kind, and I could see something in his eyes that seemed to echo a pain that was mirrored by my own. I believed from that moment that he cared for me and could feel my pain. We sat down and they talked to me about what I had done and told me that my father had signed a section 20, which meant I was there voluntarily. That meant he could take me home whenever he wanted. I froze and I felt the colour draining from my face. I was not even safe from him there. I thought that I wouldn't have to see him ever again.

They seemed to realise the panic this had put me in and

quickly tried to reassure me that it wouldn't happen. That if my father wanted me home then it would be discussed and planned, so I didn't need to worry. I was not convinced, but I suppose I knew even then that I would never be safe from him, and I would spend the rest of my life looking over my shoulder.

Linda took me around the house and explained the rules as we went. The back stairs were only for the boys as it led from their bedrooms to their bathroom and girls and boys were not allowed to spend time alone together. She explained that as we lived as a family it was wrong to have girlfriend/boyfriend relationships with each other, and it would just cause lots of problems. Initially, I had my room to myself and was grateful for the privacy, although there were two other beds in my room, so when others moved in, I had to share. I was allowed to put up posters and photos, and I asked Mum to send me in a photo of my little sisters, Elizabeth, Rebecca and Miranda so that I could put it on my dressing table. I missed my Mum so much. I just wished I could have lived with her; I knew I would be happy then.

As the days went by, I met the other members of staff and I was told that Brian and Judy were my key workers. I was pleased with this as Judy was an older lady, who was kind and gentle and reminded me a little of my mum. Brian was also older, with a shock of white hair. He was very tall and towered above me, yet he was also gentle and kind and I felt safe with him.

I was upset that Peter hadn't been my key worker because as time went by I fell more and more in love with him. I began to hate Linda because she had a special relationship with Peter, and they were always laughing and joking together. I convinced myself that she was sharing his bed instead of me, and I resented her for this.

A girl came over one day from another home called Patrixbourne, and we got on very well together and started seeing each other every day, meeting up down the town and just hanging around together. She talked me into having my ears pierced as she said she knew how to do it and had done it before. I went with her to Patrixbourne and sitting in the kitchen, she held some ice on my ear for a few minutes before getting a bodkin and shoving it through my ear. The pain was intense, but I didn't want her to think I was a baby, so I let her do the other one too. It felt like my ears were on fire. She put some studs in and I must admit, although very red, it did look good. I was pleased that at last, I had my ears pierced too. Debbie had had her ears pierced for what seemed like ages and I just wanted to be like her.

The following day, Fiona, a younger member of staff who had wavy black hair and quite sharp features, came up to my room to tell me that Tracey had come to visit me. I was very shocked and unsure about how to react. Fiona guided me downstairs babbling on about how nice it was that she had bothered to come and see me, not once asking herself why she had come here.

We went into the games room, and Tracey immediately started shouting at me for getting my ears pierced. Before I knew what was happening her hand whipped out, and she slapped me across the face. Fiona stood staring, mouth open, completely shocked by what had transpired. I ran upstairs trying so hard not to cry so that she wouldn't know she had beaten me; I was so angry I was shaking, and in the end gave into my tears. Fiona came up and had apparently sent Tracey on her way; she repeatedly apologised as she hadn't expected that to happen and said if she had known she wouldn't have let her come in. What had Fiona expected? I had tried to kill Tracey after all; she wasn't likely to be happy about it was she? Fiona wasn't happy about my ears as she hadn't realised I had got my friend to pierce them, and she thought they would probably become infected. As if I gave a shit about what happened to my ears, they were the least of my problems. I stayed in my room and curled up on my bed, the only place in the whole world that I felt safe.

Despite all their reassurances, I knew then that I would

have to deal with my family on my own that there would never be any real escape until they were all dead.

A boy came to visit who used to live there, he was gorgeous: sixteen years old, tall, slender, and with short, spiky, blonde hair. We got on straight away and before I knew what was happening, we were kissing and fondling each other. As he pressed against me, I knew he wanted me, and I wanted him too, so we went out into the garden where we could have a little privacy.

Linda caught us having sex in the garden; she was furious and sent me to my room. Two police officers came – one woman and one man – and they asked me to tell them everything that had happened. I think because I was so adamant that I wanted it to happen they decided to put it down as heavy petting so that the boy didn't get into trouble. I was glad because it wasn't his fault. The next I heard was that he had told some of the girls from my school that I was a bucket crutch, so the taunting and reputation for being a slag began.

A few weeks after Tracey's first visit she came back to say goodbye. She had moved out of my father's and wanted to say goodbye properly because she didn't plan on ever seeing me again. She was so nice, so calm; I didn't want it to be goodbye forever, but she made it very clear that she wanted nothing more to do with me. It took me a long time to realise that my father probably blamed her for the way I had behaved, because with her gone, neither him nor the staff could see why I couldn't go home and this became the new game plan.

Despite my fears and trepidation the little girl in me wanted to go home, wanted to see Tiggy and for things to be okay again.

Once the decision had been made, it seemed that I went home almost straight away and I was told I could keep in touch with Judy for some support once I was home. I didn't feel ready, and I was scared but also hopeful that without Tracey living there things would get better.

Within two days I knew nothing had changed. I was

still unhappy, Debbie still hated me and my Dad didn't want anything to do with me. I was so alone there; nobody cared whether I was dead or alive. I tried telling Judy, but she said I needed to give it time and said it would be better if I stayed away for a while to give myself a chance to make it work at home. She didn't care either; I was sure Linda was still seeing Peter and I often walked to his house and saw what I thought was her car outside. I felt that I was going mad and wrote him poems and letters about how much I loved him; he never answered, he didn't really care after all. All I wanted was for him to love me as much as I loved him, but he didn't even know I existed. I lied to the girls at school and told them that he loved me back, that we had had sex and that I was probably pregnant with his child. I wanted that to happen so much that I almost convinced myself that it was true. He knew he could have had sex with me whenever he wanted, so why didn't he want me? Was I that difficult to love?

As things became worse, I began to hurt myself. Slamming my arm in doors until it needed to be heavily bandaged, cutting myself with pieces of broken glass and hitting my knee with a hammer until I needed crutches to help me walk. Frequently, I would sit on the bannister upstairs wanting to jump, trying hard not to be a coward. Imagining myself tumbling down each step, my body twisting and buckling, knowing that if I could break my bones I could go to the hospital and be with people who would care about me.

Chapter 12

1984 – Aged 14

The Second Fire

It was Wednesday 29th February, 1984. I got up early knowing that that would be the day, the day that I set myself free from the nightmare that was called home. The morning was grey, the sun had barely risen above the tree line but the sky was so cloudy and grey, there was little hope of any warmth from the sun. I hadn't been able to get any turpentine, and I was worried that the smell would give me away, but I knew alcohol burns and there was plenty in my father's drinks cabinet in the dining room.

I took a bottle of gin, as I guessed that would burn. I soaked some tissues and lined them up outside my father's and Debbie's bedrooms. There was money on his dressing table, so I helped myself to forty pounds. My hands and my whole body was shaking; I was so scared that he would wake up and find me. When I checked, their breathing was heavy and regular but I was so worried that it wouldn't last and then I would never escape.

Like last time, I lit a match in my room so that the sound of it lighting wouldn't wake them. The tissues caught straight away, and as the yellow flicker took hold, I scooped up my bags and ran down the hill. I would not allow myself the pleasure of watching it burn and losing myself in the flames. I followed the alleyways and back roads to the train station and knew I had to be confident while asking for a ticket to London, so that I didn't raise their suspicions. I couldn't afford for the police to catch me.

The train to London felt warm and safe but at every station I had to be on my guard in case the police were already looking for me. At Victoria station, I bought random tickets and three trains later I found myself getting off in a town called Oxford. It seemed like quite a lively town and far enough away to be safe for a while, and as I wandered around I spotted a café across the car park and figured it was time I got myself a cup of tea.

A tall lad with short blonde hair was smiling behind the counter, and we flirted a little while he brought me my drink. He said that he was twenty-two and before I knew it I had agreed to join him outside on his break and had convinced him I was sixteen. He talked me into giving him a blowjob around the back of the café and then I let him have sex with me; it seemed a good way of keeping him on my side.

We went back into the café so I could have another cup of tea, and his mates were there, although he had to work he was happy for me to go with his mates down the pub. They stayed for a couple of drinks and then they left me in the pub to go back to work at the café. I am not sure how long I stayed there, but I think I must have blacked out. Eventually, I woke up in the car park opposite the café. I had no memory of how I got there or how long I had been there, but it had become dark and was turning cold. I was still completely wasted, so I went to find my new friend. When I arrived at the café and fell through the door, my friend and his mate carried me to a table and made every attempt to get me to drink black coffee to sober me up.

They kept asking me what train I needed to get and about my ticket, but I couldn't answer. Between them, they helped me to the train station but I was in no fit state to get a train and I had to confess that I didn't have a ticket. Eventually, I admitted that I was only fourteen years old and that I had run away from home.

They took me back to the café and eventually I sobered up enough to tell them about the fire and that I had no home to go back to. They kept talking to me and really seemed to care, so when I saw the police officers walk through the door, I was completely unprepared. I tried to run but was still far too wobbly to make a proper escape; the blonde guy held me and tried to reassure me that it was for the best. I couldn't believe he had betrayed me; I wished I could've made him see what he had done. They would lock me up for a long time – *murder!* I would be going down for murder.

I wasted a lot of time in the police station giving them false names and refusing to tell them where I lived. In the end, I let it slip that I had a social worker so they took me to a children's home/remand centre called Yarnton House with the plan of calling my social worker, Chris, the following morning. I didn't mention the fire and luckily they didn't know who I really was, so they couldn't put the two together. I didn't feel upset about my father at all; it was almost like it was a completely different world and that I was nothing to do with it.

I woke up with a pounding headache and at first I didn't know where I was. I lay still looking at the wall while the memories of the previous day came creeping back. I didn't know what would happen, although I expected they would arrest me and lock me up. At least I would be free.

The staff telephoned Chris while I was standing in the office. I wished they had let me sit down because I was totally unprepared for the news they gave me. Not only had my father survived the fire, Chris told the staff that my father would have to pick me up. I could not believe this was happening. I could feel the panic rising like a living thing inside of me; my breathing quickened, my body trembled, I felt hot, clammy, and just needed to get out of there. I couldn't believe it! My father would go crazy. *How could they even think of sending me home with the man I tried to kill?* Did they honestly not think that he would want revenge for what I had done to him and his family? I tried to argue and they let me speak to Chris on the phone. I was crying and sobbing down the phone as Chris explained that he could not come and get me, however, he had spoken to my father who had assured him that I would be fine and that he would find somewhere else for me to stay tomorrow. I couldn't end the call and just handed the receiver back to the lady behind the desk. I had to get out of there but the staff were watching me like a hawk. I got together with another girl who was also desperate to run away but they were so suspicious. I couldn't stop crying; I didn't want my father to come, I was terrified.

I tried to find excuses to go to my bedroom, because if I could get away from the staff for long enough, I thought I could have jumped out of the window. I wanted to put myself into the hospital so that I wouldn't have to go home. The staff wouldn't leave me alone though. I didn't understand how they could let him collect me if they knew I was so upset that I would try to do something so drastic.

My father and his girlfriend Carol picked me up. They didn't say anything; he was very angry, and the atmosphere was thick enough to cut with a knife. We drove home in a stony silence and the warmth of the car mixed with the comforting smell of cigarettes made me drowsy. I couldn't let myself fall asleep, I was so scared that the silence would be broken and I would get what was coming to me. It was a long drive from Oxford, and every mile was a mile of extra anger, extra reasons to hate me.

When we got home, I went straight to bed without being told and lay there fully clothed, listening and waiting in dread, for the familiar thud of his footsteps. Knowing at some point, I would get what I deserved. Eventually, they made their way to bed, and I allowed myself to drift off into an unsettled sleep.

His shouts wrenched me awake. I had to get up and get myself ready as we had a meeting with Chris. I scrambled out of bed and pulled on the clothes that were closest to me, not daring to spend time because he wouldn't be kept waiting.

Just before we left the house, he flew at me, the anger that had been brewing, finally unleashed. Pinning me against the wall, shouting, with his face so close to mine I

94

could feel his spit peppering my face. He waved a clear plastic bag at me with the evidence of the fire in it. The tissues were only singed, but enough evidence to put me away for a long time, as he so readily pointed out. He seemed to relish the power he had over me; I had given him everything he needed to control my life forever.

He obviously hated me so why wouldn't he just let me go? Even prison would have been better than living like that. The hallway fire pressed into my back and I desperately tried to block out his unleashed fury. I knew that he desperately wanted to hit me, it was written all over his face, and I believed that the only thing that was stopping him was our imminent meeting with Chris. After all, it was always about how he looked in front of other people, he had to be seen to be doing the right thing. If I turned up with bruises, it would have messed that up for him.

I couldn't wait to get out of there; I was sure Chris would have to find me somewhere to live. Chris said that I could stay at my Mum's until they could find me somewhere to go, and I was so relieved. I didn't ever want to go back there.

My Mum was upset, and I hated seeing her like that, I just wished I could have lived with her then none of this would have happened. Staying with her for those few days were probably some of the best days of my life. I just wanted to be with my Mummy, and although I missed Tiggy to bits, I wanted to stay at my Mum's house, forever.

Chris found me a new children's home to live in called Medvale, and I was due to visit the next day with a plan of moving in the following day. I was relieved that I wouldn't have to go home but sad that they still wouldn't let me live with my Mum. I didn't understand why not. I got on okay with her new husband, David. I had known him for a long time and he was not mean like my father. I could have even helped Mum with the little ones, as I was good with babies.

Chapter 13

1984 – Aged 14

Medvale: Spiralling Down

Extract from Staff Communications Book
Date: 13/9/84
Staff: Helen M.

Tracy had some problems at school when she handed in her French book for marking with NF on the cover. She was very abusive to the teacher when she tackled her about it and she now has to report to her form tutor. Her school bag was smothered in bright red, foul graffiti when she came home. I was supposed to take her shopping for a present for Mum's new baby. Pat S. took her, as there was only the two of us on. She got a dress; I have loaned her the money and she will repay me each week. She phoned Mum and arranged for us to visit this evening. She was in good form and said sorry about her bag and put it in the washing machine. She wrote a note of apology to her teacher and talked openly about her feelings towards Sandra, and wants to put things right in a proper way. She was full of chat on the way to Mum's and showed lots of care for Mum and all the kids; she held the baby for a long time and Mum was warm towards her. When we left, I could feel Tracy's sadness and sorrow like a heavy cloak. She followed me into the office and just climbed onto me and howled such sad real tears. We talked about how guilty she feels about recent hate feelings towards Mum when she really loves her very much; how hard it is for her to accept that she cannot be a part of that family. Very close and loving to me and fine with the rest of the child group later. Tracy also wants to put things right with Judy.

Extract from Staff Communications Book
Date: 15/9/84
Staff: Peter J.

Appeared okay. At 10.00 pm was in bed, seemingly asleep. I put her light out. At 10.05pm, she came downstairs claiming no knowledge of sleep or of me putting the light out.

Extract from Staff Communications Book
Date: 16/9/84
Staff: Judy R.

Had a good family session. All three went over the period that big Tracey (step-mum) lived with them. All were able to see that after big Tracey had come out of the hospital (being mentally ill), she got loads of attention, and how our Tracy's behaviour started as trying to attention seek and developed into learning patterns of behaviour from big Tracey (mentally ill). All three gave a lot.

Extract from Staff Communications Book
Date: 17/9/84
Staff: Helen M.

I had a meeting with Dr Balachander (GP) today regarding Tracy and having EEG tests done on her. He is happy to refer her to the Maudsley but is going to give her a very thorough medical first and on the strength of that, she will or will not be referred. Judy and I are very pleased about this. The doctor knows that we are anti-medicating or labelling kids here at Medvale and would only want the tests done to eliminate any neurological disorder.

Extract from Staff Communications Book
Date: 21/9/84
Staff: Pat R.

*Calm and friendly. She showed me her 'feelings' paper
and talked about it for a bit. She had a (baby) bottle and
settled fine. Did a lot of homework. Helen wants Tracy to
have a (baby) bottle every night again at Tracy's request.*

Extract from Staff Communications Book
Date: 23/9/84
Staff: Sandra B.

*Fairly close but I feel something is brewing again – not
against me but maybe because she had a meeting with Dad
and Debbie tonight.*

Extract from Staff Communications Book
Date: 25/9/84
Staff: Rita W.

*At 2.15 am, Sandra went to check on Tracy, who is sitting
up in her bed and there is a red line around her neck.
Sandra will write this up in the morning. Gave her tablets
for a headache.*

Staff: Sandra B.

*Checked on all the kids at 2.15am. Tracy was sitting bolt
upright again weird. She has obviously tried to hurt
herself (mark around the neck). I told her that she must get
some sleep and told her that I had noticed the mark
around her neck and that she must not hurt herself. We
would not let her hurt herself. She gave me a big kiss and
cuddle, and said that she probably couldn't sleep. I told
her to try. She said that she was frightened. I told her not
to be frightened and she said that she was frightened of
hurting herself. I said that Helen would be in today (it's*

now 2.50am) and she would have to do some talking.
   Morning.
   I went in the taxi with Tracy and Lacey. Tracy was dropped off outside of the school. On my way back in the taxi, I saw Tracy heading up the Tideway. The taxi followed her at a distance. I wasn't prepared to tackle Tracy in the street, especially the mood she was in.
   I phoned Tracy's school and Tracy isn't there. I phoned the police and informed missing persons.

Staff: Suzanne B.

12.55pm. Tracy has just walked in and went straight upstairs without a word. She looks angry. I informed police and staff.

Staff: Helen M.

Tracy was withdrawn and sullen when I arrived in. I treated her with tender loving care in the staff room. There were many reasons for last night and this morning. Her boyfriend finished with her, guilt regarding Darius (Medvale child), fears about how close she is getting to Dad and Debbie, fearful too because she is now feeling she wants to go home, and all the other fears, which are nearly always present in Tracy regarding trusting people, caring too much. She had been to the roof of the Pentagon and very much wanted to jump off. Tracy responded very well to our session. She is going to school tomorrow (I have phoned them) and she will be attending the NAYPIC (National Association of Young People in Care) conference, in Oxford, at the weekend.

***

After the meeting with my father tonight, which went okay, Helen spoke to him and Debbie separately. I will have to speak to her about that; *why does she always tell them what I am doing?* I know she shows them everything I write, even though if I wanted to write to them, I bloody well would. I know they are all talking about me and it is driving me crazy.

***

I'm tightening the noose, soon I won't breathe.
It begins to get loose and I let out a sneeze.
Maybe a knife would make it much quicker,
But the blood on my arm, just gets thicker and thicker.
Until it clots and ends the flow, let's try something else,
But what? I don't know.

Tracy Pain Aged 14

***

Tonight my attempts to gain Sandra's attention have been in vain, as I am not her key child, Natasha is, and she is in need of Sandra's attention at the moment. Helen has told me that I am to speak to her or Peter and not to bring my troubles to Sandra, Helen doesn't understand. I know Sandra is the only one who would understand. I lay in bed thinking of ways I can end this; maybe if she found me dead she would regret not being there for me. They would all be sorry. I tie my braces around my neck, stretching the elastic as far as it will stretch. I tie it in a knot; I can't breathe very well, and I can feel my face swelling up, the room keeps fading out. I lay there waiting to die, there are black shapes floating in front of my eyes and my head starts to throb, I feel that I am drifting. After what seemed like an eternity – although in reality was only an hour – I give up. I guess they are right when they say you can't strangle yourself. I scrabble at the knot, eventually working it loose. I can't even kill myself properly; the hot tears stream down my face, and I go to the bathroom to look at the damage. My throat has red welts around it, and it is very puffy. Hopefully, I can cover them up in the morning. Sandra must have heard me moving about and spends a while talking to me; I can't even begin to tell her how desperately I want to die. She tells me to go back to sleep; instead, I try to strangle myself again with my braces, even less successfully than last time, as I have overstretched the elastic. I hardly sleep at all.

***

Morning is here and it is raining, which suits my mood perfectly. Nobody notices the marks around my neck as I manage to disguise them with my clothes. I'm beginning to think that nobody here cares about me either. I don't think they would even notice if I were dead. I don't bother going to school today; instead, I walk to Chatham and sit in my favourite place at the top of the multi-storey car park. From here I can look down on the world. Several times I have debated whether or not to jump, trying to work out if it would kill me or just injure me. It's only five storeys so I probably wouldn't die, unless I could land in front of a passing bus. I still sit here. I feel at peace and there are plenty of pieces of broken glass about for times, like now, when I feel that I can't continue.

Chapter 14

1984 – Aged 14

Medvale: Further Down

Extract from Staff Communications Book
Date: 30/9/84
Staff: Helen M.

Peculiar on her return from Oxford. I asked her if she had anything over the weekend that she shouldn't have had. Drink, speed and hash. I explained to her my care and concern I felt for her then and said how disappointed I was. I read to her and she had a bottle and a Kit Kat. Tracy will not be going to anymore overnight NAYPIC meetings.

Lacey says that Tracy is trying to get five pounds by Wednesday to buy drugs. She says that she doesn't want Tracy to know she's said anything. Tracy did ask me how she could get money for cigarettes. I think we should avoid giving Tracy any cash for the foreseeable future.

Extract from Staff Communications Book
Date: 1/10/84
Staff: Pat S.

I found Tracy crying in the dining room. I brought her into the office and gave her a cuddle. She didn't want to talk and was very quiet on the way to school. I had a feeling that she wouldn't stay there.

On the way to one of Medvale's children's schools at 9.15am, I saw Tracy standing outside St Bartholomew's Hospital. On my return, I phoned Rochester Police and reported Tracy missing. I told them that she was very down and could contemplate suicide.

Tracy returned at 12.30pm. Went straight to her room and we informed the police.

Staff: Pat R.

In tears early on (but I didn't feel I have got everything yet) – full of sadness. 'I want to go and live with my Mum but I can't.' No anger. No pretence. The worry that I have is, what she may do in attempting to blot out the feeling of real pain she now has, having abandoned the anger, the defences and the fantasies. Still quiet, pale and very sad.

Quickly asleep but still looks awful. Earlier she asked if she could do some work to earn some money; however, I refused and said that I didn't think she had talked about what the money was wanted for. Her challenge of this was tokenistic; she just wanted to know how much I knew, and dropped the subject when I said that the information had to come from her, not from me.

***

I cannot believe the staff are letting me and Lacey go to the NAYPIC conference in Oxford – *on our own!* It's going to be fantastic, the whole weekend with no staff. A chance to catch up with my friends from the café and all the others I met when I ran away there before I came to Medvale.

We get a little lost on the trains to London as we have to change trains, but with a couple of calls to Medvale, we are soon arriving at Oxford where the other NAYPIC members meet us. I must admit it really isn't what I expected, as there are a couple of meetings that we have to go to and the rest of the weekend we just get to know everyone, and there are loads of people here.

We do a serious amount of drinking. Lacey goes to bed and leaves me in a room with a few other people who have been drinking with us. They soon pass around joints and then tabs after which I guess I pass out, as I don't make it back to my room until the morning, feeling really rough. We go down to the café where I had been before. The blonde guy nearly died a death when he saw me, as the last time I saw him things were not good. Once he found out my age, I think he freaked about how much trouble he could get in. People really frown on a twenty-two-year old shagging a fourteen-year old! I let him take me out the back and screw me again – for old times' sake and to convince him that age isn't an issue. I spend the whole weekend totally wrecked and feeling weird, and I manage to forget about the shit going on in my head for most of the weekend, a definite result.

I feel so much worse since the weekend, and I know a part of that is guilt for letting Helen and Judy down. I just feel so low and desperately want to get something to make me feel better. I think going to Oxford was a bad idea, as I seem to have gone back to the place I was at before I ran away there. I feel scared, angry and out of control. Last time I ended up trying to kill my family, feeling the same now leaves me wondering what I should do this time, I just want to put an end to this pain one way or another.

Seeing Sandra is just really messing with my head. I love her so much and really want to pour my heart out to her, but then I find myself contemplating whether or not to put bleach in her tea. I figure it won't kill her so I don't bother and take myself to my room so I can sniff glue in privacy. Although I have to be careful not to overdo it as I made myself sick on it the other day. While I am feeling less inhibited, I write another letter to Sandra telling her how much I love her and how sorry I am for the way I am treating her. I don't want to hurt her, but I can't risk her getting too close to me.

***

Extract from Staff Communications Book
Date: 6/10/84
Staff: Helen M.

Super, no problems. She is much more contented since we did her list of objectives and promises, which she insisted on doing to help her reach goals she is setting herself.

Extract from Staff Communications Book
Date: 10/10/84
Staff: Judy R.

Pleased to have me back. I am getting good vibes from her. Chatty and close and settled with a story etc. at bedtime.

I forgot to log yesterday that she told me in a light-hearted way of a funny experience on her way home from school – she heard someone calling her and looked around but saw no one. Helen and I spoke to her regarding Darius and said there was nowt going on or would be, but she knew what we were on about and no strong denial. I told her not to flirt or respond to his flirting and to nip it in the bud or we'd be down on her like a tonne of bricks (if Lacey didn't get to her first which she agreed with – she is afraid of Lacey and her reaction). I think she will be okay but obviously needs watching with Darius. I also made her aware of coming home at lunchtimes (to see Darius).

Extract from Staff Communications Book
Date: 11/10/84
Staff: Judy R.

I read her diary – all stuff we knew about except 2nd October's entry saying that she was going to put bleach in Sandra's coffee (but didn't).

Extract from Staff Communications Book
Date: 17/10/84
Staff: Sonia C.

Looking dreadful earlier. She had some exchange with Sandra earlier during which she refused to talk and threw various bits out of the window. Tracy wanted me to control her tonight. I felt that she was working herself into a self-destructive state and that we had to bring some of those feelings outside of herself. I made her sit on my lap and made her ask me if she could go upstairs where I followed her shortly. She was playing a fatalistic record and sinking deeper. She told me it was about Sandra but: 'No point in talking. I've talked to everyone, and no one understands how important it is.' I made reassuring noises about understanding that she felt bad and those feelings were important, and we understood that. Tracy didn't really talk to me at all and I talked to her a lot, aware that I had her attention about how people often felt, why they felt x, y, z, how certain things made them feel better, etc.

I focussed on sexual desires, boundaries, Mum's feelings, how things get confused, why they often got confused, that you could feel both, that anger and sex were closely linked, about how kids try to meet and cannot meet needs in their parents, angry when parents decide kid isn't enough, etc. No denial to any of this – did tell me when I got other bits wrong. She asked if she could talk to Sandra. She is definitely scheming in a big way but I felt that she was better later.

Extract from Staff Communications Book
Date: 18/10/84
Staff: Sandra B.

To follow on from Sonia's entry last night, a lot of what Tracy was saying was about her feelings towards me, that she couldn't and wouldn't tell Helen, as she wouldn't understand. I said that she must see and talk to Helen and

Judy, and that she had been told before about her problems going to others, i.e., me, and not them. I said that she had been working so well lately, so why was she suddenly in this mood again. She said how Helen had said to her before that she mustn't talk to anyone else. I said that I was sure it was okay for her to talk to me when Helen or Judy were not on duty, providing she could then take all of what she had said to them.

She has a book upstairs about her feelings for me, lots of 'I love you, Sandra', and how she feels when she looks at me, other people being with me and not her. Nothing sexual at all. I asked too, why she thought that Helen or Judy wouldn't understand the way she felt for me. She replied: 'Cos they wouldn't.' I asked her what made her think that I would and asked her to explain it to me. She said it's a little of 'my real Mum' and also a little of her step Mum (she has told me that before). I said that I felt that she was afraid to, maybe tell Helen because she may say what she said before about it being sexual. She agreed. She said, 'But it's not really that way.' And that I am just different.

She doesn't want to hurt me anymore and that if anyone said she mustn't talk to me or can't possibly care for me she'd kill them – i.e., Helen. I said that I am sure it's okay for her to come to me. I also cared for her but she must think about all that I had said and talk to Helen about it. (I was not deleting Judy but Tracy was stressing on Helen a lot.) She talked about the suicide attempt, having her stomach pumped, them finding nothing. She knew she did take those tablets and other times she had talked rubbish about things i.e. being on cocaine, smoking pot, etc. she had always owned up in the end and that it wasn't true. Why, this time, was she convinced she took them?

I said that she had admitted earlier in the book that she exaggerated situations and maybe this one she was also exaggerating – maybe she took one or two or even more, but not enough to hurt her or show up in a stomach pump.

She said that Helen would freak over all of this, but I still kept stressing that she must talk to Helen and Judy.

Later when I said goodnight to her, she was really looking weird, fixed eyes, silence, holding 'Psycho 2' book. I took it away from her saying that it was all rubbish, like everything else she read. I told her that those sort of books are no good and told her to read something decent. She said, 'I know who you remind me of – my great, great Aunt.' I asked if she was nice or not? Tracy said that she's dead now but she was nice. She had an awful sneering grin on her face.

I told her to go to sleep, take care and kissed her goodnight. She said, 'Don't worry about me. They will take care of me.' I asked who 'they' were. 'Just they.' I wasn't prepared to get into anymore and left her staring and looking totally spaced out again.

Staff: Judy R.

Tracy told me when she came in that she wanted to talk to me. I told her that I wanted to see her too. She told me a) that she skived maths today – she agreed to go to the teacher tomorrow and ask what work she had missed and do it, and b) that she wanted to change her 'contract'. She has crossed off all her promises and said, 'I'm not able to keep them yet.' I told her that was okay – it was her idea and not a proper contract anyway and I would tell Helen. I asked her if that was all and she said it was. I asked if she was sure. 'Yes.' She obviously had no intention of discussing last night with me so I launched into what was a long and angry session.

I told her how angry and disappointed I felt that she is still playing games – complete denial. I went through all the times relevantly including last night, she knows that she can talk to Sandra but not about anything that should come to Helen and I, and not to use her in a keyworker role or set up and manipulate to get Sandra's attention, as I feel she did last night. Again denial.

I also told her that I knew that her next game was to do with the occult e.g. wearing all white and cross yesterday, 'they'll look after me' to Sandra and hearing voices on the way home from school, reading Psycho, etc., etc. I told her there was nothing unusual or abnormal about her i.e., she is not mentally sick or possessed etc. and to stop saying and doing things to try and convince people that she's weird or psycho or possessed. People like the real or normal her but disliked strongly the weird or unreal/pretend her and that she knew the difference and was making a deliberate choice to be like that – complete denial. I put to her yet again the need to sort it out (her biggest problem).

Tracy felt that all she now has to do is work through her list of objectives and she'll be off to foster parents. I said, 'No, Tracy, because this, i.e. your biggest problem isn't on the list.' I told her that if it is not worked through or even started on soon then at her next review we'll be saying no return home, no to foster parents and only choice is long-term residential care. She states again that she wants foster parents but won't acknowledge that she plays many games ('only a few') I wouldn't (or Helen) understand and that there is no point talking to her. I told her that I was sorry but she wasn't swapping key workers from me to Sandra, for a list of reasons.

We ended up going round in circles so I ended by saying that: 1) she was to do thinking and talking or writing to Helen or me; 2) we would set up a meeting with her, me and Helen so that she could hear it from all three of us; 3) that she would hand me all her horror, occult type books. She was very angry with me for all of the meeting and stared at me with real hate. She went up and brought down the books. She seemed 'fine' just after but was obviously stewing/plotting to do something.

As per last night, it is possible that she may try harming herself (or someone), so watch her closely, however, please try not to visibly over react to her. We do need to discuss her in detail next staff meeting to try and break this pattern of her playing games and work out a consistent approach from the whole team. I also feel that we need to fix a date for another review (not in the next few weeks but I feel we must have a date for her to get hold of).

Tracy asked to speak to me and told me that we may as well plan for long-term care because she is not playing games and I don't believe her, and it's not worth her trying them as she won't change my mind. I told her that I knew that she could work, was being bloody minded and it's a cop out, but I wasn't prepared to have another long session.

***

I feel so angry and restless at the moment. I can't seem to shake the feeling that something is seriously wrong. Sonia has a talk with me, mainly about homosexuality. Just because they know how I feel about Sandra doesn't give them the right to keep going on about it. I can't change the way I feel; I wish I could because I don't want to hurt anyone anymore. Sandra tries getting me to tell her how I feel about her, I don't know where to begin, my feelings are so intense and all-consuming. It feels like I need her to hold me forever to try and make this pain go away.

I feel really weird tonight. I have been reading Psycho and feel entrenched in the story, which is messing with my head. I keep thinking of my Great Aunt Rose and confusing her with Sandra, but Great Aunt Rose is dead. The images in my head scare me and I am no longer sure what is real and what is imagined. I don't want Sandra to leave me tonight. I am in a very scary place in my mind, but part of me wants to stay here because nobody can hurt me here.

Judy really pisses me off; she thinks I am just playing games to get Sandra's attention! She hasn't got a clue about what is going on in my head. I've told her that she had just as well start looking for long-term care because I am not working with people that don't believe a word I say!

***

Extract from Staff Communications Book
Date: 19/10/84
Staff: Pat S.

Up to something and walking about the garden with Lacey before school. Very sullen when we left. I dropped Tracy first.

At 11.30am, Tracy's school rang to say that she had not been at school today. We have not reported her missing. If she does not arrive back at Medvale after school, then report her missing. If she does return after school, then she is to go to her room and do school work.

Tracy walked in at 2.20pm. I spoke to her. She said that she had been in the Pentagon all day. I asked her why she hadn't gone to school and she said that she hated it there. I told her that she should talk to Helen and Judy about school and that it is the law that she goes to school and that is that. I also reminded her that the last words I said to her this morning were, 'If I'm needed I am on duty all day.' I sent her to do some school work.

I went to see Tracy just before tea. Her eyes were full of tears. She started crying but didn't want to talk so I just held her for a while and then she settled down and read a book.

Staff: Sandra B.

Lacey told me that Tracy had a bottle of Tippex in her room, which she was sniffing. I went up and asked her for it and she handed it over. I asked if she had any more but she said that she didn't and it was all in the office. She said that she didn't think Tippex was dangerous!

Extract from Staff Communications Book
Date: 20/10/84
Staff: Helen M.

I had a session with Tracy this morning regarding her running. Tracy now knows that we are not going backwards with her just because she is scared of what is ahead. Judy and I will be having a talk with her as soon as possible and once again setting her on the right road. I want everything to do with Tracy regarding her behaviour, moods, etc., to be played very low key. If she does anything that warrants it, then she should go straight to her room and come out again at the staff's discretion when she says she can cope.

Extract from Staff Communications Book
Date: 22/10/84
Staff: Helen M.

Don't give Tracy any large amounts of money at the moment, as she may be planning to run.

Staff: Sandra B.

Tracy was reported missing by Rita at 5.45pm. I have notified Peter Pain, who gave me Tracy's Mum's number. They both want to be informed as soon as possible if she returns.

Staff: Ross F.

A Mrs Marigold phoned at 6.15pm, to say that her daughter arrived home with Tracy (which she thought nothing of at the time) and then at about 6.10pm her daughter and Tracy left to go to the Grammar School where, they said, a social worker was collecting Tracy. I told her that there was no such arrangement made. Mrs Marigold then suggested that her husband could go and pick both girls up as the school is only two minutes from their house. I said yes to this and Sandra has gone to the Marigold's house hopeful to collect Tracy.

Sandra rang at 6.40pm. The Marigold's daughter arrived home with another friend. Tracy had apparently headed off to the Delce to meet a boy. Sandra said that she will try to head her off as she is already out that way so she will ring as soon as she has any news.

Staff: Paul M.

Sandra saw Tracy near Chatham Station but Tracy gave her the slip. The police were phoned with the new information.

Staff: Sandra B.

Mrs Simmonds (Tracy's Mum) rang at 9.00pm to ask if she was back. I told her she wasn't. I explained that I had been out and seen Tracy on the New Road. I told her that we would inform her immediately when we knew anything. When I went round to see Mr and Mrs Marigold, they said that they thought it strange that Tracy wanted to stay there until 6.30pm. She had told her friend, Harriet, and her Mum and Dad that she was meeting her social worker at 6.30pm by her school. Harriet walked round with Tracy but she went down to the Delce Road, saying that she was meeting a guy by the name of Joe at the Pentagon and that she would be okay. Harriet's Mum and Dad got on to Harriet, saying that she could or should have stopped Tracy. I said that it would have been difficult for anyone to have stopped her and unless Harriet knew of anything else about Tracy then not to feel guilty. As I said earlier, they wish to be informed when she is back as they feel partly responsible for not phoning earlier. I told them that we were pleased that they phoned when they did and that we would keep them informed. I then drove along towards Chatham (I was so near the Delce that I thought it would

113

be okay to see if I could stop her and fetch her back). I got as far as the viaduct near Chatham fire station when I saw Tracy walking towards Chatham Railway station or the Pentagon. I pulled up, called her and said I'd give her a lift home. She gave me an awful glare and kept on walking. She was soaked to the skin. I carried on, turned around, walked up into Victoria Gardens but saw no sign of her. I then returned to Medvale.

Staff: Paul M.

At 4am, Chatham police phoned to say they have Tracy. Rita went to pick her up and Helen has been informed. Helen said that Tracy might have her mouse with her.

Staff: Rita W.

The police had picked Tracy up outside Central Hall, Chatham. Paul and I had a long chat with Tracy. She started by saying she had it all planned out, to prove a point to Judy, who had told her she is always playing games. Tracy thought that if her plan had worked she would have been away for two or three days and Judy would have to believe that was true. I pointed out that all she had proved was that she did play games. She pretended not to understand that. She moaned about Judy. Tracy was angry about what Judy had said about her playing games with Sandra and didn't believe she cared for her and was also angry about long-term care. She said, 'Helen doesn't agree with Judy,' etc. etc.

I told her that I agreed with Judy. I didn't think she really cared for Sandra because caring meant: 1) wanting to be close – she ran from Sandra; 2) she played games and hurt Sandra's feelings; 3) she only pretended to share herself with Sandra and didn't often give anything real – just a load of rubbish most of the time.

She said that Paul and I sounded just like Judy, that we made her sick that we didn't understand, that we

114

disagreed so there was no point in discussing it. We said that she should convince us – we were willing to listen. The upshot was that she didn't want to take that on but voiced the long-term care again. She eventually said that she intends to go and live with her Mum when she's eighteen and out of our clutches. We talked about the reality of that being a possibility (i.e. Mum's past decision, David's opposition, etc., and also that it might be an idea if she consulted Mum first). We stressed to Tracy that whatever or wherever she ended up going or doing she needed to move on and stop playing games. We took the conversation in a safe area and sent her to bed when very okay.

* * *

School is okay, and I manage to stay all day. Harriet says I can go back to her house after school so I go there for a while. We tell her Mum that I am meeting my social worker later by the school so that she doesn't get suspicious about my unplanned visit. When I leave Harriet at the school, I walk to Chatham. Sandra drives past me, so I leg it down the alley. I miss her, but I have to show Judy that I'm not playing games. I love Sandra so much. I vent some of my anger by keying the cars outside New Road children's home and then walk over to my father's house where I carve the letters C.U.N.T. into the bonnet of his car. I am so angry and so hurt; so full of longing and pain. I walk to Walderslade in the rain trying to find Sandra's house. We went there once but I can't find the right road this time, and after lots of walking round I give up. I am cold, wet and hungry. Tomorrow I must find somewhere proper to sleep. I can't go back to Medvale now, and I can't see anything working out now. Without Sandra my life isn't worth living; everything I have ever loved has been taken from me, and I can't do this anymore.

I use the shop doorways along the high street as shelter although I am so wet already it doesn't make much of a difference; nothing seems to take away the cold that is permeating my bones. I keep moving as I am so scared of being found, but eventually I feel so exhausted I end up curling up in the doorway of Woolworths. I try to stay as warm as I can just wanting to sleep to blot out how I feel right now. I must have drifted off because suddenly the Old Bill wake me up, the bastards. It's 4.00 am, and they take me back to the police station. They know who I am, where I am from and before I know it, Rita has arrived to take me home. It's not fair; why can't people just leave me alone?

I am so angry, mainly about the things Judy has said; she doesn't understand, how could she? Even I don't understand why I feel the way I do about Sandra. Nevertheless, I know I am right and she is the person who would understand me the most if I could just have the time to tell her my story. Paul and Rita are on duty and talk to me about how I am feeling, about my Mum, Judy, Sandra and everything. I don't think they believe me either; they think I am playing games, just like Judy.

I don't understand why anyone would think that I am choosing to be this way, this unhappy, this angry, and this lonely. They eventually let me go to bed at 7.00am. I feel a little calmer but am so tired that luckily sleep stops me from dwelling on what I have done today. I know I must apologise to the children and to Sandra; I don't mean to scare them or hurt them, it's not their fault. I won't apologise to the other staff though; they hate me and don't trust me. I owe them nothing.

Chapter 15

1984 – Aged 14

Medvale: Goodbye, Little Ben

Extract from Staff Communications Book
Date: 31/10/84
Staff: Judy R.

Tracy asked to speak to Helen. She had taken Ben (mouse) for a walk after school and he'd jumped out of her sleeve and died. She had buried him in a nearby field. Helen then called me in and we talked a lot to Tracy, but she couldn't cry and is racked with guilt. She is shocked and numb and it hasn't hit her yet. She desperately needs to cry and needs watching very closely as it may bring out all her self-destruct tendencies and she may even attempt suicide, so please don't leave her unattended for periods and check her during the night.

Please phone school in the morning and explain to them and if she is upset at school for them to phone us immediately and we will collect her and bring her home. After the meeting, she wanted to be with the other kids and sat drawing a picture of a mouse. The other kids have been told he's dead, but she didn't want them to know.

Extract from Staff Communications Book
Date: 1/11/84
Staff: Helen M.

I had bad vibes about the mouse. I saw her and told her what I was feeling and she told me that she had killed him. She went on to say that she had set him free in the bushes and he must be dead by now. I checked with the people who were looking after Ben for her and they said that Tracy collected all of the mouse's stuff after school yesterday saying that she had found another home for him. Tracy told Natasha that she had dropped Ben and that she was glad that he was dead because she was fed up moving him around and the people he was with were not looking after him properly. Tracy was sad for most of the evening. Tears at bedtime but did not cry properly.

Extract from Staff Communications Book
Date: 2/11/84
Staff: Judy R.

Tracy was talking about her mouse this morning and wanted to walk to school. I gave her a look of distrust and she said, 'Don't worry, I'm going.' I told that I knew she was! She was a little tearful but didn't produce them. She has a load of scratch marks on her left arm, which she obviously wanted me to see. She told me that Ben was dead and that was why she had tried to harm herself. She wants to be with him etc., however, I told her that wasn't possible and that she should just feel that possibly he's in a better place. As Helen said earlier, she hasn't just let him loose. She was starting to say about him, she wants to say what she's done but she knows that Helen is in later.

Before she left for school, she said that she might be back as she wants to throw up. I told her to forget it and go to school and she would be fine. She replied, 'Oh sure, so would you throw up if you had done what I did.' I didn't say any more to her but sent her to school. She said, 'You might see me back about 10.30am,' and I said, 'We'd better not.'

Tracy came in from school early, demanded paracetamol, admitted she had walked out and started crying in the office with Sonia. I took her into Pat's office and put her on my lap where she cried for quite a while, deep sobs and lots of tears. I talked very gently to her and asked her to tell me about her talk with Helen then Sandra,

118

which she did. Then she told me that she knew he was dead, as he had fallen down a bank. She assured me that she hadn't touched him or hurt him in any way and left him where he was dead. I had doubts about the accuracy of the story but didn't push her, as she was feeling very bad.

I spoke at length about what she had done was a favour, relieving him of his misery, like shooting a horse with a broken leg or Battersea Dogs' Home putting down animals that had no one to care for them, that it was not a bad thing. I spoke in that way so that if she had wrung its neck, what I was saying was still relevant. I told her not to harm herself, as she didn't need punishing and to shout for me or anyone if she wasn't strong enough to stop herself, also to let tears out when they came and that it would take time to heal. Whatever the story is, Tracy feels very bad and unhappy, so please all give her care and understanding. Very okay afterwards.

***

These feelings I have won't leave me, and it is all I can do to push them down and try to lock them deep inside myself. I try to keep my distance from Sandra, because the feelings I have for her are too overwhelming, and I don't think anyone will ever understand what this is doing to me. I focus my thoughts on just getting through every day and spend as much time as I can with my adorable little mouse called Ben.

Ben is a dark brown pet mouse who I bought from a pet shop in Gillingham. He is adorable; his fur is like smooth velvet and when I hold him his tail curls around my fingers. He is very tame and loves to sit in my pockets or curl up in my sleeves. I love him and love having a pet I can call my own. After having to leave Tiggy behind at my father's house, Ben goes a little way to fill the void, although I will never forget the special relationship I had with Tiggy. I talk to Ben about all the things I used to share with Tiggy and he always listens and never judges me.

I really hoped that I would be allowed to keep Ben here with me at Medvale, but we are not allowed pets. Although they let him stay for a short time, I have to move him. I let him stay for a while with some friends in Gillingham, but after I keep getting no answer on the phone, I find they have moved without even telling me and have just left him in his cage in the hallway of their house. He could easily have died, so Helen agrees to take him in for a while. I am so pleased and I know it is difficult for her, as she doesn't like mice at all.

Helen cares for him and lets me come to her house every week to clean him out. She lives a long way from Medvale though, so I don't get to see him even half as much as I would like. A girl from school says that her mum can take care of him and I jump at the chance as she only lives down the road. It still isn't very good, though, as so many times I knock, to be told I can't see him or take him out as it isn't a good time; or they are busy...or even worse, they don't answer at all as they are out. I don't have a chance to love him and spend time with him like I should.

I give up. I can't stand this anymore. I seem to be moving my little mouse Ben, from person to person, and nobody loves him the way I do. Everyone offers to take care of him, but they just treat him like shit, I know he isn't happy. I love him so much but I can't see him like this anymore. I pick him up from my friend's house; they don't seem bothered and believe my story of finding him a more permanent home, so they let me have all his things too. I don't have a plan; I just want to keep him but I know I can't.

I sit crying in the churchyard for what seems like hours, cuddling him and stroking him, my heart is breaking but then I know what I have to do. I put him down on the grass and watch as he runs away from me; he doesn't look back, he knows what a bad 'mouse mum' I am. At least now he is free, something I can't see ever happening to me.

My restrictions are lifted and I am allowed to go to the Regency tonight, which is an under 18s disco. It is good fun and a great place to hang out and meet people. Some of the other children come and despite all the promises I have made to Helen and Judy, I end up letting Darius take me out the back to fuck me. He is so gorgeous, but I can't get too involved because of Lacey's relationship with him.

The enormity of this act doesn't hit me right away, but when we get home, Lacey is really upset. I instantly think that she has found out, but lucky for me she has a family problem and my secret is safe. Over the next couple of weeks, the reality of what I have done eats away at me. I have betrayed everyone; Lacey will be furious if she finds out and Darius will probably tell the staff about me. I wish I knew why I was so stupid. Judy is so pleased with me right now, but as time goes by I can sense tension all around me. I haven't felt so scared in such a long time, yet I begin to wonder if I might be pregnant, as we never used anything – I never have. That would be a disaster; everybody would hate me for sure but the more I think about it, the more convinced I become that I am pregnant.

Helen keeps wanting to talk to me about Ben. I just wish she would leave me alone – there is nothing to say. I know she thinks I am lying and that I have done something really bad, and maybe I have but right now there is something much worse that is taking up every thought in my head. I hate it here so much, and I am even thinking of phoning my father so that he can come and take me away. Surely, anything is better than living here like this. Helen is furious with me again and not just about me wanting to go back to my father's, although she knows I don't really want to and she hates it when I lie to her.

I keep trying to talk to her about Sandra, but she just thinks I am playing games. I'm not; I love Sandra so much it hurts. I want to tell her everything from my heart, and although I have been writing it all down in my green book, I know when I show her she still won't believe me. Helen just doesn't understand how much I'm hurting right now.

***

Extract from Staff Communications Book
Date: 15/11/84
Staff: Judy R.

I read in her diary that on Monday 5th November, Tracy went to the Regency and so did Darius. Quote: 'I ended up letting him fuck me; it was great, he's gorgeous but I'm not getting involved because of the mess with Lacey.' She is also (according to her diary) late for a period and thinks she is pregnant. I am not sure now how to tackle this as its information that I shouldn't have and, therefore, I can't confront her outright but I am furious with her yet again. Apparently, she told Sandra that she wanted to chat to me tonight and I hope that is why but somehow I doubt it.

    I am very off with Tracy, and have been hinting that I know something that is to do with her and Darius. She asked me what was wrong and I told her that I was not happy with her today, but she had to tell me about it, not that I tell her. Then she asked to speak to me and told me that she had only had one school meal this week and spent the other money on ten cigarettes and crisps etc., and owed us the money. I thanked her for telling me and said that because she had been honest, she didn't have to pay us the money back. But that wasn't what I was upset with her about and that it was something much more serious and I was waiting for her to tell me in her own time.

Extract from Staff Communications Book
Date: 16/11/84
Staff: Helen M.

Tracy is not to be given any money whatsoever. Dinner money to be paid into school by staff. School to be told to watch her extra carefully. When Lacey eventually shows anger it will be directed at Tracy and she will know this so may try and hurt Lacey first. I will have a urine specimen checked tomorrow in case of pregnancy, as full intercourse took place. Family session is cancelled.

Extract from Staff Communications Book
Date: 17/11/84
Staff: Helen M.

We held the meeting to explain to the children that Darius was leaving and why. Lacey's anger surfaced and she went for Tracy. It took Rita, Sandra and me all our strength to hold her. Tracy was sent to her room and told to stay there, and needs close watching.

WPC Sandy called in again, mainly to say that they will not be pressing charges but they may need to take a statement from Tracy – if so they will contact us next week. I took her to see Tracy as she wanted to know time and place of sexual intercourse. It happened at approximately 10.15pm in the field at the back of the Regency.

I saw both Tracy and Lacey with Sandra and went through the whole bit – have to live in the same house, the effect they will have on the rest of the child group if they carry on like this. I told Lacey that I was not making excuses for Tracy and normally we do not discuss the kid's backgrounds with them; however, I did tell Lacey how blocked Tracy is emotionally and how she is unable to respond at the moment to any male in a non-sexual way. Lacey asked if she could do something, got up and went to Tracy and they cried in each other's arms.

Although Tracy is on total restrictions, she isn't confined to her room and now needs picking up in a caring way. She sobbed on my lap for a long time after the above.

Extract from Staff Communications Book
Date: 18/11/84
Staff: Helen M.

Established the order of events and that Tracy was a willing participant and ended by saying she wasn't prepared to have a medical examination (apparently not even a minor can be made to have one) not to be a party to pressing charges against Darius.

Extract from Staff Communications Book
Date: 19/11/84
Staff: Secretary

The school rang – Tracy was in school this morning and had lunch, but she hasn't turned up for the first lesson this afternoon. They have had a good look for her but as the school is so big they can't say for certain that she isn't there, however, it doesn't look as if she is. If Tracy turns up they will let us know, and if she turns up here we will let them know.

Staff: Helen M.

Tracy was reported missing to the social work unit. WPC Best is dealing with it. They have got Oxford details.

Ross (staff) answered a phone call asking for the charges to be reversed and then the phone was hung up. Ten minutes later, Tracy rang saying that she was at the Pentagon. I went to collect her with Natasha and I have never seen Tracy in such a state. She was like an animal, trapped and scared to death. It was obvious that she had been crying for a long time and she started crying again as soon as she saw me. Natasha comforted her on the drive back and I saw her in Pat's office when we got in. She climbed on my lap and held on for dear life.

When she was able to talk, she said that she had been sitting at the top of the Pentagon car park for three hours and had planned to kill herself. At some stage, she had gone to the loo and discovered that she had started her period (I still want a urine specimen from her in the morning). She said that she woke up this morning feeling bad about Lacey, Darius, etc. She feels that she is a very bad person and if she was now pregnant, there was no point in living. I went through all the bits with her regarding Darius and once again I told her that she is working towards foster parents and must keep that in sight. She was still very upset afterwards.

Staff – I know that I keep saying this but Tracy is very capable of committing suicide. Until we get her on an even keel again, she needs watching closely.

Extract from Staff Communications Book
Date: 20/11/84
Staff: Helen M.

Urine test negative.

Extract from Staff Communications Book
Date: 21/11/84
Staff: Judy R.

Towards the end of the community meeting, Tracy went rigid and shaking. I put her on my lap and she clung tightly to me. Also spoke to Helen and me after about feeling responsible for Matilda and Lacey running. I told her that it was good that she felt like that and she shouldn't feel any guiltier than the other kids. I explained to her that Lacey regarding Darius is an obsession, like Tracy had for Peter Pascal – no rhyme or reason to it.

I also told her that last weekend is over and done with; no anger left in me, just love and she needs to put the pieces together now and learn from the experience, think positively and continue moving forward. Also told her that she needs to be strong for the rest of the group – they need her now, so she can repay what they've given her over the last few days. Much more positive after the talk and very okay afterwards.

Extract from Staff Communications Book
Date: 2/12/84
Staff: Helen M.

Had a very good sexuality session. We have covered unlawful sexual intercourse, poor self-image, abortion, relationships with boys, love and sex, masturbation, VD and herpes. Tracy feels that in future, instead of having sex because that is what is expected of her, she wants to and will be able to say no. We have not set up any more sessions but have left it to Tracy to come to me if she feels that there is anything else she wants to go through, with me or if any problems arise. Tracy is in a very positive frame of mind at the moment.

***

They know. Judy has found out that I think I am pregnant; I am not sure how unless someone else has been talking, but I only confided in one person. Helen and Judy are furious; Lacey is too angry to come anywhere near me, and they are saying that Darius will have to leave. I'm not allowed to see my Mum tomorrow even though I haven't seen her for four weeks, it's so unfair! They have cancelled my family session tonight so at least I don't have to see my father – every cloud has a silver-lining. I'm so sorry for what I've done, but I know nobody will believe me, they all hate me now, and I just want to die. Helen is going to take me for a pregnancy test, and I am just praying that I am not as Helen will make me have an abortion. I hate life so much.

***

Last session with just the Pains. Next week Carole (cohabitee) will join us, then planning review after which we will have one more session to discuss the outcome of the review and Tracy's future. We went back over the work we have done in previous family sessions and how this has affected the relationships between them. They all felt that they have gained from the sessions, each understanding the other much better now and more important, understanding that the reason Tracy is as she is, and it is not her fault, but to do with the whole family.

The family was close after the session, Dad telling the girls jokes, etc., and they responded warmly to him. He has many fears about what Tracy will decide she wants i.e. foster parents or return home, but will go along with whatever decision she makes. Tracy was very okay afterwards but told me that the session had left her feeling that she could easily go home, but she doesn't really want to.

Staff: Rita W.

Looking washed out, tired and scruffy.

Returned from the NAYPIC meeting on time. Tracy was as white as a sheet and said that she had just been sick. I invited her to tell me the truth, as I knew that she had been on drugs of some sort. She said that she got glue from the art room today and has been sniffing all day. She took it to the meeting with her and gave some to Brittany too, obviously very little as Brittany has no side effects at all.

Tracy's eyes dilated, her skin was cold and clammy to deathly white. I phoned the doctor who advised me to take her to the hospital. Vomiting too.

The doctor at the hospital checked her over and said that she was okay. He gave her a little lecture on glue and drugs. Tracy was obviously still feeling sick and wanting badly to put things right. No go tonight, I'm afraid. Home from the hospital at 12.00pm. Straight to bed with a bottle.

Extract from Staff Communications Book
Date: 5/12/84
Staff: Judy R.

Had a session after school with Helen and me regarding the glue-sniffing incident. She was honest and open. She is afraid of hurting Dad by going to foster parents and Mum too. Positive discussion about real feelings but she knew how disappointed in her we were that she hadn't asked to discuss her worries. She assured us that she won't glue sniff again and I believe her. Ended up much more positively and has been fine for the rest of the night.

Peter Pain phoned regarding the weekend so I filled him in with what glue was all about. He sounded upset and disappointed again. He said that he could see Helen after all on Friday if she is still free.

Chapter 16

1984 – Aged 14

Medvale: Sexuality Meeting. Time to Kill

Extract from Staff Communications Book
Date: 10/12/84
Staff: Helen M.

Would staff watch her please; this will be a bad week for her as she will be telling Dad about her decision regarding fostering at Wednesday's meeting.

Staff: Pat R.

Tracy attended a sexuality group this evening, led by Sonia. It was agreed that rape and incest would not be discussed. Previous to the group assembling, Rita discussed with Sonia the fact that a new child was present and a low key topic was needed for discussion. Hence, loyalty between boys and girls was brought up. Discussion ensued about lesbianism and homosexuality. Regression was discussed as were sexual feelings towards and from parents.

Staff: Sonia C.

Sexuality Group
    The group wanted to talk about Tracy and Matilda, saying that their 'joke' about being married was not funny for them and made them feel awkward. What transpired was the fear the other kids – particularly Tracy and another girl – had about their own sexual feelings for people of the same sex. We talked to the group a lot about

sexual development that it is quite okay and quite normal for them to have sexual feelings for people of the same sex.

Tracy said that she does have sexual feeling for people of the same sex, including staff here. The group accepted that she hadn't dealt properly with those feelings yet and was therefore not wanting to say who, when asked. All the kids talked about feeling uncomfortable when Tracy and Matilda joke about and the group talked to them about them not wanting them to do that. Tracy took it all on board.

Staff: Paul M.

Generally fine before the sexuality group. Presenting a lot but from a very safe/comfortable base. Tracy was not particularly okay beforehand, but the rest of the group were. I was told that the group would be a safe, gentle one.

After the sexuality group, Tracy didn't want to talk to anyone. She was very unhappy after the meeting. Totally weird. She tried to physically hurt Ross and me, yet didn't actually blow. She wanted to talk to me later but I was busy with Matilda, so she is probably even angrier now. Helen will be in at 7.00am to session her before school.

Staff: Pat R.

Before the sexuality group, the children were fine. Tracy, with two other kids, needed support as she had special worries, but the group had a safe feeling and they were presenting what they needed to present calmly and confidently. The atmosphere was good. After the sexuality group, the atmosphere was dreadful. It wasn't mischievous, high, over-excited or delinquent: it was fear. The children were terrified. Tracy, with a look in her eyes that I have not seen since she was just admitted, began walking from one end of Medvale to the other like a caged animal.

I withdrew Tracy from the group. She was full of anger

but unable to talk to me. I allowed Tracy to re-join the group but she remained very strange (angry and hunted) all night.

If I hadn't witnessed it, I wouldn't have believed such a transformation in a group possible; the atmosphere after the sexuality group was one, the like of which I haven't experienced to date in Medvale. Hopefully, by the end of the evening, the child group were as stable as possible, given the situation. We were unable to give all of the children all they needed.

Staff: Ross F.

Tracy was not at all okay. She tried to hurt me and at one point I thought she was going to blow. Before the sexuality group, she had asked me to read to her. I did this. There was still much anger in her. She stared into space and gripped my arm and I don't think she heard a word I read.

Extract from Staff Communications Book
Date: 11/12/84
Staff: Helen M.

I came into Medvale at 7.15am to try to pick Tracy up. I demand to know what went on in the sexuality group last night that in a very short space of time has undone months of hard work, which Judy, Tracy and I have done. Were the staff who took the meeting unaware of the fact that I have been giving Tracy sexuality counselling and that her real fears regarding her homosexuality have been dealt with so that she was very okay about it? She is no longer okay and I am disgusted to say the least.

I saw Tracy in the staff room. She was totally blocked at first and then actually able to say that she was freaked by the meeting last night. Because of the sexual feelings towards Sandra, Sonia, Ross and Paul now and because of the discussion on homosexuality when Tracy was asked to name the people she felt sexual towards, she now feels, bad, mad, paranoid about how the rest of the group and staff will feel about her. And she was unable to give names when asked in the group last night to do so. I spent a long time with her trying to get her sexuality back into some form of perspective. I asked her several times if she was okay for school. She said that she felt a bit better and wanted to go to school, so she was taken in a taxi by Ross. Gave me a big kiss goodbye and said, 'See you tonight.'

Staff: Suzanne B.

At 9.15am, Peter Pain rang to say that he saw Tracy on Clover Street. I rang the school and she had not arrived. I got in touch with the police instantly and gave them details. I emphasised that they could check the top car park in the Pentagon and that it was urgent.

Staff: Helen M.

I went out looking for Tracy at 10.15am. Peter and I found her in the Pentagon. We had alerted the security and it was they who found her. She was in a bad way with lots of anger. She was walking with Milo's friend, Matt, who she had bumped into. Her intention was to doss around for a while and then go to the roof and kill herself. I saw her in the staff room when we got back. The first thing she did was to hand me a packet of Durex. I searched her bag and coat for drugs but found nothing. Then we talked about why she had said that she was okay for school when she was not. She said that she only decided that she couldn't go in when she got to the gates.

All of her anger etc. was she said to do with last night's sexuality group. Again she said that she felt mad, bad, a queer, etc., etc. I kept reassuring her that none of this was so. She then went into one of her Tracy states, staring at a pair of scissors that were on the table. I could read that she was going to make a dive for them to attack me, and then herself, so I went and sat beside her and took her in

132

my arms. She was very stiff and her hands went straight to my throat. I left them there even though she was exerting pressure, but eventually had to try to remove them as I could hardly breathe. I could only manage to remove one and I had to call out for Peter to remove the other one. Tracy is very, very strong. Peter and I then had to restrain her. Eventually, she was okay enough to sit and have a cigarette. However, she didn't cry and she needed to badly, and she still dislikes herself intensely. At one stage, she tried hard to strangle Peter too.

Rita's account of the sexuality group
Staff: Rita W.

The group started late as Paul was seeing Milo (child) about setting up dates with his friend and Tracy and another girl. In the group Tracy and Matilda (child) said that it was a joke about their being married game. It was suggested that maybe Tracy and Matilda made a joke like this to hide their real feelings. Matthew (child) started to change the subject but Sonia said that she wanted to go back to Tracy and Matilda because it seemed important if people were worried about it. Tracy and Matilda said again that it was a joke. Tracy said that she had sexual feelings for members of the staff and Sonia asked her if she could say who. Tracy said that she couldn't, as she was still working on this and everyone accepted this. Tracy and Matilda talked about their feelings of closeness to one another and that was why they joked about being man and wife.

I asked Tracy about her closeness to Mia as she hadn't played that game with her. Tracy said that it was the same closeness but the joke hadn't started then. She didn't know why. Sonia said that this obviously worried the group; Tracy was further on than Matilda and did Tracy understand the group's feelings. Tracy said that she did but that there wasn't anything sexual with Matilda, although she had sexual feeling for staff members. The

133

subject moved on to regression at one point and Tracy said that she had had a problem with a friend who had visited at Medvale and seen her (baby) bottle. She had explained about it and thought that she understood, but the friend had given her a hard time for about three weeks. I had to leave before the group had finished because of the meeting I had arranged, however, it was clear that the group needed more input.

Staff: Helen M.

Tracy asked to see me. She was in a worse state than I have ever seen her. She wants to kill herself and me too. I held her tight and told her that she is safe, won't kill anyone, etc., etc. I told her that I would be right beside her all evening, which I was. She was still very wrong at bedtime, shaking, pupils dilated, etc. I made her a bed in the television room and I will sleep in there with her on a spare settee. She had a bottle, story and goody but was not okay. I expect to be kept awake tonight.

I checked her at 1.20am when she went onto the settee in the dining room; somehow, she had a blade and had been hacking away at her wrist under the quilt. Not serious and cleaned with TCP by Pat S while I held Tracy on my lap, I brought her into the office for a cigarette. She is terrified. We need to discuss Tracy seeing a psychiatrist as soon as possible.

Staff: Pat S.

Helen went into the television room with Tracy and I said that I would sleep in the office, as I feel that I need to be close at hand.

***

The last few days have been a living hell; everybody hates me. All because of a stupid joke with Matilda and the staff putting words in my mouth. I can't even begin to explain my feelings for some of the staff here, but they put everything down to sex – I love them, therefore, I must want to have sex with them! They haven't got a clue. Sex isn't like that to me; sex is something I do to keep people happy, and sex has nothing to do with love. The feelings I have for the staff here are so powerful and consuming and most definitely about love.

***

Extract from Staff Communications Book
Date: 12/12/84
Staff: Pat S.

Helen saw Tracy and asked if she was planning anything today (running etc.) but the answer was no.

Staff: Ross F.

Not okay. Back in bed this morning and hasn't got up yet – 10.45am.

Staff: Helen M.

Had a good meeting. She told Dad that she wants to be fostered and he accepted this in a very caring way. He wants to take Tracy to the cinema on Tuesday but will ring tonight. The family stayed playing pool for a while. Tracy was okay afterwards. Had a bottle, story and goodie.

Extract from Staff Communications Book
Date: 14/12/84
Staff: Pat S.

Had me up in the night at 4.20am, I was aware of someone standing in the doorway of the bedroom. She didn't wake me and was just standing there. She said that she had

135

stomach pains. I put her back into bed and made her a hot water bottle and a hot drink. She had a hot head and cold hands.

***

Again, I feel like killing Sandra but I have to wait a couple of days until she is next on duty. Pat S is sleeping in with her, which means Sandra will be in the staff sleeping-in room at the end of the house, near the back stairs. The day goes by with a blur, Sandra and Pat seem to sense that something is wrong; they keep asking me if I'm okay. *What can I say?* I can't possibly tell them what I am planning…they will never believe me. I cry a lot today; part of me doesn't want to hurt Sandra, she is so kind and so good but I really don't know what else to do. At bedtime, she reads to me and as she lays next to me, all I can do is cry. She tries to find out what is wrong; it isn't her fault that this has to happen. Eventually, she leaves me to my tears.

I drift off to sleep, but my internal clock wakes me at 3.15am, the whole house is quiet and dark. I lay there steeling myself for what I am about to do. I ask my Mum to forgive me although I fear she never will. I creep out of bed careful not to wake anyone; I don't need any distractions tonight. I walk very slowly, very quietly along the hallway; moonlight filters through the stained glass window and sheds a watery light across the landing. The night is so peaceful. I turn the handle of the sleeping-in room very slowly, careful not to make a single sound. I can hear the steady breathing coming from the mound of the duvet on the bed. My heart is hammering in my chest and I am sure the sound can be heard outside of my body. The fear of being discovered makes my heart beat louder and my body trembles. I creep towards the bed and as I approach, I realise that something is very wrong.

Pat jolts awake. I nearly scream with the shock of being caught. She asks what is wrong and I tell her that I feel sick. This isn't actually a lie, I really do feel sick to my stomach and I can't stop shaking. Pat takes me back to bed and tucks me in. I don't go back to sleep. The trembling slowly subsides and my heart rate slows to a more normal level. I can't believe that Sandra wasn't in there; she always sleeps in that room! They must have known my plans, what am I going to do now? I know I am in serious trouble.

I toss and turn for the remainder of the night, trying to work out how it went so wrong and how I can carry on.

Pat seems quite shocked in the morning when I say I feel well enough to go to school. I don't look well enough as I have been up all night but I need to get out, to get away and have time to think clearly. I asked why Sandra wasn't in her usual room last night and apparently the other sleeping-in room is for the senior member of staff, and as Sandra is more senior than Pat, she slept in there.

I skip school and go to the top of the Pentagon car park; here I get some peace, time to myself and my thoughts. The day drifts away and before I know it the sky is getting darker, the blood on my arm has clotted and it has started to sting. It never ceases to amaze me that it doesn't hurt when I cut myself, however deep I seem to press the glass. But, afterwards it stings so much.

I wander home and Helen is waiting for me; she is furious because of the game she thinks I was playing last night. I'm confused; she doesn't know about my plan to kill Sandra for that I could understand her anger. Instead, she is angry because she doesn't believe I felt ill, she thinks I was trying to get Sandra's sympathy vote. I can't even begin to tell her what is going on, so I try to zone out her voice until it is just a blur in the background. I have mastered this art from living with the constant criticism I received at home, I stare intently at the person who is shouting and then I defocus my eyes and somehow draw into myself. It's a great way of shutting out the barrage of noise aimed at me. Eventually, she gives up and sends me to my room. I don't think there is any way out of this hell I find myself in. I put my music on and cry myself to sleep.

***

Extract from Staff Communications Book
Date: 14/12/84
Staff: Sandra B.

Tracy was the first down this morning. She came to me in the office and asked why I had changed bedrooms. I said that I hadn't changed rooms and what was she going on about? She said, 'Never mind.' And it was left at that. When I was in the kitchen, she came in and said to me that I was lucky that I wasn't in that bedroom last night as she was going to kill me and was shocked that Pat S was in there. She had invented the stomach ache.

I played it all very low key and said, 'Really, how did you intend to do that?'

'With my hands, dear,' was her reply. She went on to say that she had woken up at 3.30am, felt weird, clammy and afraid. She stood outside the bedroom and then went in, and was stunned to hear Pat S ask if someone wanted her. Pat stresses that she was very aware that someone was outside but waited until Tracy showed her full self, dressed in shorts and V-neck sweater. She said that Tracy was not right and looked odd and felt weird. Pat came into my room and let me know where things were at with Tracy.

At 9.10am, I phoned the school and they said that she was in school, happy and smiling.

At 9.25am, the school rang. Tracy hadn't turned up for her first lesson but as the school was so large they sent three people to look for her. I will ring the school again in twenty minutes to see if she shows up for her second lesson. If not I will report her missing. Tracy has asked the school if she could have a refund of dinner money for the days she hadn't been there but they wouldn't give it to her, for which I thanked them. Earlier I had told her to hang on to whatever she needed to talk about until Judy comes in. She said that she would be able to talk okay about all that she was feeling. She said that this has been building up slowly but Monday's sexuality group topped it. In spite of all that she was saying, I still felt that she was okay for school. I was wrong.

Staff: Secretary

Pat S phoned around 9.35am to say that she had just seen Tracy walking very briskly towards Chatham (this was at New Road near Chatham Station). Tracy is wearing a V-neck jumper, white bag with graffiti on it, lace-up pixie shoes, black stockings and a dark coat.

Reported missing at 9.35am. Asked them to contact security in the Pentagon.

Pat S. rang again at 9.40am. She thought it might be important to know that Tracy said to her this morning, 'Enjoy the funeral,' twice and she wiped Pat's kiss off. Also gave Sandra a big hug.

At 10.20am, the operator rang with a reverse charge call, which I said I would accept. The person on the other end hung up. I asked the operator if the call was from a young girl – Yes. I asked if she knew where the call came from – a 4 number, so probably the Pentagon. Sandra informed the police.

Staff: Sandra B.

I accepted the reverse charge at 10.50am. It was Tracy. I asked her in a very caring way where she was and she said the Pentagon. I told her to hand herself into one of the security guards or a policeman, if she saw one. She said that she would. I couldn't fetch her as I had no car and thought it best that she was found and brought back by the police. I was caring because I want her back in this building before any punishment is enforced. Helen phoned in (before the call) and wants Tracy isolated from the rest of the group – clothes removed and anything that she can damage herself with. Total restrictions. I haven't informed the school, Helen or Pat until Tracy is in this building. I have informed the police of the phone call and told them that I have asked her to hand herself in. They will ring back.

Tracy has just walked in at 11.30am. She didn't hand herself in but walked home. She looks awful. I sent her straight to her room. I have removed her shoes, coat, etc. and informed the police and Helen, School and Pat.

Staff: Pat R.

I saw her in her room and was cross and very matter-of-fact. I told her that she was playing games, being silly and using the situation. I was banning her to the building forthwith, removing all her possessions (until such time that she has stopped playing games) and leaving the rest for Judy to deal with when she comes in. I told her to find some schoolwork immediately and agree on it with me and then get on with it.

Tracy, who had been sitting on her bed, with silky, crouched up and looking weird, stopped looking weird. She looked childishly cross, then got out her books, showed me some geography worksheets and started working. I then removed all her clothing to the senior sleeping-in room. I checked the room and removed a bottle of Gloy. I alerted Mrs Mac to keep an unobtrusive eye on her and to get me immediately if Tracy even moved, but I don't think she will.

Had some dinner in her room. Working hard and looking normal.

Staff: Judy R.

I told Tracy that I am sick of her and reiterated Pat's bits. Total restrictions. I am cancelling her visit to Mum tomorrow and I will be speaking to her later.

I brought Tracy down and talked to her. She recounted details of last night and told me that she had woken up at 3.00am and then decided to try to kill Sandra but she doesn't know why. She apologised for missing school and said that it had nothing to do with Sandra being on duty. I told her that Helen and I have fought very hard to stop her being labelled as mad or mentally ill, but she is heading down that road and I couldn't stop her. I told her that I am no longer able to grab her by the scruff of the neck and pull her up, stop her slipping back and kick her forward, again and again. That she is on her own now at her most major crossroads and until she decides to go in the right direction I can't help her. If she follows the road she is on she will never go home, not go to foster parents, possibly not even a long-term unit will hold her and she will end up in a psychiatric unit.

I have also told her that as a result of manipulating and playing games around Sandra that I will tell Sandra to have no contact i.e. 'special time' other than is absolutely necessary. No bedtime story, not out with Sandra to shop to get videos, etc., not dropped at school by Sandra, etc. Only contact in building and low key. I told her clearly that Sandra is not afraid of her only disappointed, and I have no fears for her safety, but I have made the decision to eliminate possibilities of Tracy manipulating/playing games and because she has abused that relationship, she will not benefit from it anymore.

Tracy is on total restrictions, and is not allowed out of the building, even to the garden. She is not even allowed out with staff unless Helen or I agree it. She is also for the moment isolated from the group until I decide otherwise. Tracy is quite clear about this. When I started talking to her, there was no anger in Tracy. When I finished, there was a lot of genuine sadness and for much of the time she was very close to tears. I asked if she was going to do anything silly tonight and she said that she wasn't, which I 90% believe.

I sent her back to her room after a cigarette and told

141

her to think and that I would be happy for her to be awake all night worrying because she needs to face the consequences of what she is doing. Also, for her to come to me when she is ready to stop playing games and talk seriously and genuinely. I phoned Margaret and cancelled tomorrow's visit. Margaret's message for Tracy was for her to behave and sort herself out, as they want her there for Boxing Day.

Staff: Pat R.

Very sad earlier and thoughtful. She could take either road at this crossroads, has to give up fantasy for reality and she knows it.

Staff: Judy R.

After finishing her school work, she was busy writing something she wants to discuss with me – looks like she has written out various entries from her diary. She didn't ask to speak to me tonight, however.

Extract from Staff Communications Book
Date: 15/12/84
Staff: Pat R.

Apparently, Tracy told Matilda she was on total restrictions because she missed school and because she tried to kill Sandra during the night. Matilda told Tracy that she doesn't want to share a room with her in that case. Apparently, this was what they were observed to be talking about last night ,just before they settled for the night.

Staff: Helen M.

Because of Tracy's deterioration following the sexuality group of the 10th December, I contacted her GP and asked for a referral to be made for Tracy to be seen at the Maudsley Hospital for EEG tests to be carried out in order to eliminate any neurological disorder.

In response to this, Medvale was contacted by the DCFP requesting a meeting between Dr Blofeld (psychiatrist) and Mr C Cahill (Tracy's previous social worker), Pat Riley and Helen Mills, Medvale staff. Tracy had been a client of DCFP's for approximately eighteen months prior to her admission to Medvale.

It was established once again at the meeting that everyone was aware that Tracy is a very badly emotionally disturbed girl. It was the opinion of Dr Blofeld and Chris Cahill that Tracy did not need to be seen at the Maudsley Hospital. They both felt that a great deal of in-depth work has and is being done with Tracy here at Medvale, and they did not feel that an EEG testing would show anything other than we already know. However, I pointed out that my co-worker (Judy Reed) and I had for some time now, felt (as Tracy had never had any such tests done) that eliminating any neurological disorder would be beneficial to Tracy, particularly given recent deterioration in behaviour.

Dr Blofeld stated that there was no guarantee that Tracy would not become psychotic at some stage in the future i.e. late teens but that in her opinion, given Tracy's age there was no evidence of this at present.

It was agreed that Dr Blofeld would request Tracy's GP to make the referral for the Maudsley Hospital. Obviously, Judy or I will take Tracy when we receive an appointment.

Staff: Pat R.

Judy saw Tracy, who produced very disturbed writings about her wish to kill people she loves. Because of the serious nature of the contents, I phoned Dave Oubridge at 11.30am, to discuss the situation and necessary safeguards. It is possible that Tracy would have had to produce her kill agenda before being free to make a normal life anyway. But this situation has not been triggered in a planned way by us (it followed on from the mishandled group meeting on 10.12.84) and we have not, therefore, been able to build in planned safeguards. Helen is off this weekend and Peter is on leave.

Dave and I discussed previous psychiatric back-up for us with Tracy (from Dr Blofeld) and I told him that we had referred Tracy via Dr Balachander to the Maudsley Hospital. Dave asked at what point would we decide that she needed immediate admission to hospital should this be considered. I said if Tracy produced her kill agenda and remained inaccessible afterwards.

I feel that this is, as Judy said, Tracy's major crossroads, when she chooses normal life or life as a psychiatric patient. Dave asked about back-up over the weekend from hospital services if this occurs; we concluded that such back-up will probably be hard to find. In the absolute last resort, therefore, I told him I would have to have Tracy sedated by the GP.

I told Dave that I would discuss the situation with Judy, decide on what we are going to do and phone back. He suggested that I phone Peter even though he is on leave and I agreed to do this.

Staff: Judy R.

Tracy asked to speak to me and produced writings and her diary for me to read certain entries. I read them and asked why she felt that she needed to prove she could kill – she didn't know. I then asked if her decision was to go down that road: 'No, not really,' I said that her writings indicated to me that was the road she had chosen. I didn't believe the motives/reasons as they were not the ones she had previously discussed e.g. fear of being close to people and that if I ever believed her written account then I would be reading the writing of a very, very sick person and did she want me to believe that? No. I told her that I had

144

nothing further to say and sent her back to her room. She showed a touch of anger but went up to her room okay.

Staff, do not tackle Tracy on your own, either be with her in company or make sure other staff know where you are at all times. I feel that Tracy will produce something and am fairly certain that it will be during the night rather than daytime. For this reason, I have discussed with Pat the idea of a waking shift at night. I want to be called in to deal with Tracy if circumstances are extreme enough to require it.

Staff: Pat R.

Interesting mood switches. She looks awful. Is very sad when she sees me but yuk when she sees Judy. She is still restricted to her room. She ate a good dinner.

Staff: Judy R.

Tracy spoke to me just before I went off duty. She wants to go down the right road now. She still doesn't know why Thursday happened but thought she just wanted to be close to Sandra (even if she was dead?). She is very confused and sad. I think it is maybe 55% genuine but I'm not convinced so she has agreed to sit on it until Helen and I have a chance to discuss it with her. I think she may be okay but she may also be up to something and is probably bored with being in her room.

Staff: Ross F.

Tracy had a McDonald's (in her room), came down for a cigarette and then took herself back to her room. She is okay with me it seems.

Has been down a couple of times for a drink and cigarette. She seems okay and there is no bad look or feel to her. I saw a love bite on her shoulder and she said that Matthew gave it to her on Tuesday.

Staff: Pat S.

While I was tidying up, I just happened to look in Tracy's jean jacket pocket and found a letter.

At 4.20am, Ross and I heard a noise. Tracy was sitting up in bed sucking her thumb. She just looked around and then looked away. Ross and I came back downstairs and decided that Tracy would make the first move if she were going to move at all.

Checked upstairs at 5.10am. Tracy was still sitting up. I asked her if she had been out of bed as I had heard a noise. She said she hadn't. I asked her if she wanted anything but she didn't. She then lay down to go to sleep.

Staff: Sandra B.

At 5.45am, we have all been dozing on and off in very light intervals. Until now, I haven't been involved in checking the building. I heard the top door upstairs go. I woke Ross, however, Pat was automatically awake. I decided that I would check with both of them behind me. We checked all rooms but Tracy's last. I surprised her. I shone the torch straight in her face – she was half out of bed. I asked her if she had been to the loo. 'No!' angrily. I told her to lie down. I didn't go into the room, just stood in the doorway. Pat and Ross assured me that they had shut the door tight but it was open when we went up. We all feel that there is something but are not sure what. Maybe Tracy is just wandering around but she is fully awake. Now she knows that we are three on a shift.

***

I couldn't face school the next day. I feel sick to the bottom of my stomach just thinking about what I need to do. I am sure that killing someone is the only way I can stop this pain I am feeling so they will have to lock me away then and justice can be done. I bump into a couple of girls that are also running away and it is good to have some company with people in the same situation as me, so I feel I can relax a little.

We bump into two lads that are a couple of years older than I am, and that I have known for a while. One of them knows of a derelict house we can stay in and takes us further up the town. We go around the overgrown building and climb the fence into the garden where we can't be seen from the road. It is easy enough to pry off the wooden boarding although my heart is beating so fast, I am scared we will be caught and I will have to go back to Medvale. The house is dark and the floor is littered with newspapers, letters, books and other household items that have just been abandoned. Over the years, animals and maybe even other people have paid the house visits and now the dirty, worn belongings lay strewn, unwanted, unneeded and certainly unloved.

One book stands out above the rest; it is lying just inside the door, surrounded by rubbish. A very old book, with a thick, dark green, hardcover. Its title, *Murder and Madness*, makes me feel warm inside. I know it has been placed here for me and that inside I will find the help I need to succeed in my plan. I tuck it into my bag and continue exploring the house.

The stairs are rotten in places making the climb upstairs precarious, but we make it to the top and drag a heavy, old-fashioned sewing machine onto the edge of the landing so that we can push it on to the police if they dare to try to make us leave. Upstairs is not as littered and the master bedroom has a fireplace, so we pull over the mattress while the boys scout around for things to burn. One by one I burn my school books and then add my school uniform, confident that I won't be needing it anymore. The girls soon get bored and having got what they came for the boys decide to call it a day, leaving me back to wandering the streets on my own.

With no other distractions and feeling very low I make my way back to Medvale. I don't want to live like this anymore, I just want someone to understand how much I hurt. The staff are pleased to see me, although, send me to my room until Helen can see me. Once summoned to the staff room, Helen can sense something is wrong and insists that I empty my pockets. I have no idea what she is hoping to find but she seems shocked when I throw a condom – still in its shiny wrapper – onto the table.

Not wanting to digress from her initial line of questioning, I tell her briefly about the boys today. She didn't ask whether we used protection and I didn't tell her that I never have. She told me I wasn't old enough and we talked about looking for love from the wrong people and that she feels I am probably looking for a father figure, she really has no idea. She thought I had been taking drugs and that is what she was expecting to find, certainly not a condom.

I deny any involvement in drugs and don't feel that I am really lying. Sniffing glue and Tippex thinner are not the same as taking drugs. I can tell she doesn't believe me and fortunately it distracts her from questioning me further.

Being totally banned to my room gives me the time I need to plan how to end this. I spend a lot of time laying on my bed imagining the staff's faces as I squeeze the life from them, or watching their blood run in rivulets down their bodies as I stab them over and over again. I want them to hurt as much as I hurt inside; they will pay for not listening to me, for making me see my father. And as I thrust the knife into them they might just begin to realise that I am not mad or crazy, and that I really do hate him. I know they will care once I have killed someone, then they might sit up and take notice and realise that I am not doing this for attention. I am not playing games. I have tried so hard to stop myself, to be what they want me to be, but at the end of the day, I am a murderer and for that, I should be punished.

I am having sessions with Helen and/or Judy virtually every day and my mood seems to swing from feeling really positive and close to them both, to really negative and wanting to end it all.

***

Extract from Staff Communications Book
Date: 16/12/84
Staff: Pat S.

Up early in a good mood saying she had a dream last night – she had been sitting on a rock and all the kids and staff were all sitting around her looking. Very giggly. She went back to bed at 9.15am complaining of a sore throat.

Staff: Ross F.

I went up to see Tracy at 6.30pm, to see if she wanted a cigarette. She had been crying. She came down for a cigarette and I remarked that she looked sad. 'Yeah, it's nothing,' she said. I didn't pursue it.

Staff: Paul M.

Crying in her room. I held her and she sobbed real tears. Gradually I brought her out of it and then told her to stop wallowing in self-pity and look to the future. Much better later on. No weird looks. Settled well at bedtime.

Staff: Ross F.

I saw Tracy a while after Paul did. She was very much more settled – no looks for drama. We talked about school, future attitudes, etc. She came down for a cup of tea and a cigarette before bed. She remarked how happy Natasha was looking. I said that the whole group were happy tonight and asked 'How about you?'
'A bit better,' she replied, and she definitely seemed it. She said that she was looking forward to school tomorrow.

Pat, Paul and I had already agreed not to tell Tracy that she wasn't going to school until tomorrow (to avoid dramas, etc.). Lovely at bedtime, enjoyed the story, remarking with real softness, 'I haven't had one since Thursday.' Bottle, goody and settled well.

Extract from Staff Communications Book
Date: 17/12/84
Staff: Ross F.

I told Tracy that she would not be going to school today. This took her by surprise (ball not in her court). She protested but only mildly. I told her that Helen would be in at 9.00am and would be seeing her. She had a cup of tea and was okay.

Staff: Helen M.

I saw Tracy after I had read the book this morning. She looks dreadful. We went through what has been happening since I was last on duty. Tracy is saying that she wants things to work out e.g. foster parents etc. I explained to her the vibes she is putting round the building with her 'wanting to kill' feelings. Tracy does not think or understand that these feelings are not good for her or the rest of the group. However, after I made her view it as if though she was another child in the group witnessing Tracy Pain's behaviour, she understood better.

I have reintegrated Tracy into the group and she understands that she will be returned to her room instantly if she gives any rubbish to anyone. She is still on total restrictions unless Judy and I give other instructions. She is due to go to the cinema Tuesday evening. I have spoken to Peter Pain and explained where Tracy is at and that if she goes out with them tomorrow she could not be left unattended for any period of time at all. I will discuss with Judy and confirm with Peter Pain tomorrow whether she is in an okay state to go or not. As you are all aware, we do not normally penalise family visits.

I have spoken to Dr Balachander and he is making an urgent application for Tracy to see Dr Fishere. Not that for one moment, we think she is mad. She is very disturbed at the moment and needs to be seen, if only to reassure herself.

Staff: Rita W.

Seemed very okay this evening. Watched television for most of the evening and then helped Pat S to write her Christmas cards. Tracy had a sore throat and coughed quite a bit. Settled okay with a story, bottle and goodie.

***

The best thing about being here in Medvale is being given the chance to be myself. I don't feel any pressure to be or do things that I don't want to. I am surrounded by people that care about me, that worry when I am sad, who want me to get better. It gives me the opportunity to be real about the things I feel, even when I can't share everything with them, I have the chance to 'feel' angry, hurt, sad and I know they care. I know they will do everything they can to keep me safe.

Helen is keeping me off school for the last few days of the term; she is worried about me, and I think she is right. Helen asked Natasha to watch out for me; she has to sit outside the bathroom door while I am bathing and I'm not allowed to lock the door. I am not allowed to be on my own at all. I feel vulnerable and fragile and although I resent Natasha for supervising me, I like feeling safe. I know I won't do anything while I am being watched because I don't want to get caught. When I die I just want to slip away, I don't want to be stopped, I can't fight this anymore.

Helen involves me in decorating the house for Christmas and ensures I am kept in the thick of things. We go for drives to the beach and she holds me a lot, making sure I know she is there, that she won't abandon me. Helen keeps me alive at a time when I think without her I will die because I really have nothing to live for; these people here are the only people that care. But they are not my Mum and I miss her so much. The hurt I feel inside is physical, like a stone grinding inside my chest. It is heavy, painful and far too much for me to carry alone.

***

Extract from Staff Communications Book
Date: 18/12/84
Staff: Helen M.

I rang DCFP as suggested by the GP. I spoke to Marion Stapley and explained that I wanted a second opinion on Tracy (not Dr Blofeld). Eventually, after Marian telling me a million times what a great job we are doing with Tracy, and trying to convince me that she did not need to see anyone, I got the message through that we do not think Tracy is mad either. However, you can't have a child talking about her urge to kill and actually attempting this, without doing something about it, if only to convince Tracy that she is not insane. She will ring with an appointment for us to see someone, hopefully on Thursday.

Tracy is allowed to go to the cinema tonight with her Dad. It may be called off as cohabitee is ill, but Dad will ring about six o'clock. Tracy knows this. If it is cancelled, she will be going on Thursday. Dad is aware of the recent incidents and will not allow Tracy out of his sight.

Staff: Pat R.

Much better but you can feel the pain in her like a physical blow. She is so sad.

Helen and I had a session with Tracy regarding wanting to kill people. We went over all the things I had discussed with Tracy at the weekend. She took it all in but didn't really offer anything positive. She said that she wants to go the right way but couldn't guarantee attending school etc. I told her that was not good enough. Spoke about killing – still no reasons for last week's bits. She is angry that people in Medvale label her as mad. We told her that she has labelled herself. We left her to make the decision to go the right or wrong way, which she will probably do over the next few days. She is very much in limbo right now, and has given no indication of the way she will go. We will just have to wait and see.

The review went well – we discussed fostering and, along with Paddy, we want her to work through this killing bit and have a stable period (of probably one month) before we do anything e.g. Form E. to move towards being fostered. After our session, she went upstairs for a while and then came down with a photo of Mum tucked in her sleeve. She tried to be okay but was weird, dancing and singing to herself with false happiness. Settled at bedtime with chocolate, story and bottle and assured me that there would be no rubbish tonight.

She obviously needs very close watching until we see some positive moves from her.

Chapter 17

1984 – Aged 14

Medvale: Hanging On

Extract from Staff Communications Book
Date: 21/12/84
Staff: Helen M.

Tracy is asking for another sexuality session as soon as possible. I am giving it to her at 9.00am tomorrow. Fine all evening. She wants to tell me something in the session tomorrow that she says she should have told me a long time ago. Settled well.

Extract from Staff Communications Book
Date: 22/12/84
Staff: Helen M.

Had sexuality session. When she was around seven years old, she had a relationship with a school friend. The girl's mums were best friends so they saw a lot of each other. They (the girls) kissed and fondled each other and Tracy has felt guilty ever since. Soon after, Mum left home too. This is one reason that Tracy feels she could be homosexual. She talked about the sexuality group and how she felt people there were making her feel all of the old guilt, reinforcing her feelings about being gay.

We went through the whole bit again, who she feels sexual towards in Medvale and why. Tracy said that she woke up at 5.00am and felt that she wanted to kill Sandra. She says that she told herself that she was being stupid, turned over and went to sleep. I praised her for this and told her that this is the right way to handle it i.e.; feeling something, controlling it, and then talking about it. Tracy said that she really does want to go down the right path now. I felt that it was a good, genuine session with Tracy doing a lot of unprompted talking. Feeling close to Judy and grateful for our plain-talking of late. She says that it really has made her think about where she is going.

***

I have spoken to Helen and Judy at various points about my feelings for members of staff and have always fought against the suggestion that the feelings I have for female staff are sexual in nature. I care for and love Sandra so strongly but as I have said before this does not feel sexual to me; sex is what I let men do to me and I can't even imagine feeling like that towards someone I truly love.

This is not to say I haven't thought about girls sexually. I will always remember quite vividly the things I did with Maisie when we were both about seven years old. Maisie came with me to the shops and I hid a porno magazine, like the ones I had found in my Dad's bedroom, in a newspaper so that the lady in the shop wouldn't notice when she sold it to me. Then we went back to my house and copied some of the things the girls in the magazine were doing to each other. It was fun but at the same time I knew it was really wrong and that if we were caught I would be in so much trouble. I have always felt guilty and ashamed about this because I knew deep down that I had enjoyed it but, like everything I have done as a child, it is wrong and one day I will be punished for the sins I have committed.

I know I should tell Helen and Judy about this; it may help them to understand why I have found things so difficult since the sexuality meeting. It may help explain why I can't cope with people calling me homosexual when I know deep inside that I must be. Although, I have had sex with so many men, *what am I really?* The confusion I feel about this, mixed with the guilt and shame, causes me

155

so much pain. The only way I find that I can deal with it is to block it out and not let those feelings have a place in my life. Maybe this is why I will never accept that the feelings I have for Sandra are anything other than a need to be loved by someone who has gone through the pain that I know we share.

***

Extract from Staff Communications Book
Date: 3/1/85
Staff: Judy R.

Tracy had asked to speak to me yesterday so I saw her tonight. She said that we were distant and wanted to know what she could do about it. We ended up having an hour long, very positive session. We resolved what was outstanding between us since before Christmas. Talked through wanting to kill, playing games and learning not to overreact to circumstances, etc. Very good discussion. Tracy told me that she is going in the right direction and is wanting to work hard. I told her that she is proving it to me by talking to me in such an honest and mature way. She was very forthcoming and very real. She said that she still wants to punish Dad for all that has happened, but is learning to control those urges.

She wants fostering to work because it will bring her nearer to Mum i.e. she can visit more often, and then go and live with her. I told her that we would set up a session as soon as possible because although she knows it's not possible, she said that she needs to hear Mum say it. She told me that she promised Mum not to skive school and said that she won't as she has never broken a promise to Mum. She said that the day she tried to strangle Helen what she really wanted to do was be very, very angry but she couldn't. Also, a few days ago she was planning to run so that when she came back Helen and I would be very angry with her so she could then be very angry back. She

156

wants to learn to let he anger out as she feels that if she can do that she won't want to kill.

The bad dream last night was Mum trying to suffocate her and apparently, Matilda woke her up as she had her pillow over her head and was trying to suffocate herself. I treated it lightly, saying that we all have bad dreams and if it happens again to wake staff so that she can have a hot drink and settle herself.

This session with Tracy was the best I have ever had and I am now fairly sure that she is going in the right direction though she knows it's the last of her nine lives. Good vibes from her at present, and she is responding to all I say very maturely.

She is still not allowed out except with Paul tomorrow and to the NAYPIC disco (must be taken and collected), until Helen and I have discussed her restrictions. Up to bed early – 10.30pm. Goody and bottle and Tracy apologised to Matilda for making her worry.

***

This afternoon Judy came in and I had a good session with her. Afterwards, I felt glad about it because at last I felt close to Judy and I'd actually been able to talk openly about my 'killing' feelings. It wasn't to last though, Judy heard that I was planning to go out with Johnny and now she is furious with me again. Just because he is twenty-one, has just come out of prison for raping a ten-year-old, and getting her pregnant, then I should stay away. The irony of this is not lost on me; when the whole staff group make such a big thing about me moving on and not being blamed for the things I have done in my past, whereas others are not to be given the same courtesy.

***

Tracy came home from school with a face on. She had been involved in a row with her maths teacher. Matilda had asked to see me before Tracy came home. She said that Tracy had been asking her to 'do her in' while she slept for a week now. Matilda had agreed but chickened out each time (thank God). Matilda is worried about Tracy.

I saw Tracy after tea. She was hard faced and not okay. I told her plainly that she was asking to get herself labelled as a nut. If she were not careful, she would end up like the boy who cried wolf. I told her that she has been in Medvale over ten months now and how dared she involve someone (Matilda) who is new in Medvale and has enough problems of her own, in this sort of rubbish. I told her too that the ball is in her court and she had better start playing because if she continues with this kill-killing thing then Medvale has a duty to involve other professionals i.e. psychiatrists, which could mean that total responsibility for her welfare may not remain with us.

Tracy heard everything I said and for the first time ever she seemed scared of the consequences of her actions, which is exactly what I wanted her to feel. We went through all the other bits regarding this Johnny and it seems to me that thanks to that awful sexuality group, Tracy has now got to prove to herself that she is normal i.e. is not gay, so she will once again sleep/have sex with anyone. She has asked for more sexuality sessions with me and I will start them this week. Tracy put a lot into this session and says that she does want to work, and wants to live with Mum, but knows this is impossible. She was okay afterwards. Story, bottle, goody and settled well. Very close.

Chapter 18

1985 – Aged 15

Medvale: One Step Forward –
Two Steps Back

Extract from Staff Communications Book
Date: 9/1/85
Staff: Judy R.

Helen and I had a session with Tracy before tea. We went through where she was at with me, this being her very last chance, etc. She heard all that was said and then told us that she had thought and finally told herself after Helen's session that she wouldn't be going to live with Mum and it is beginning to sink in. She is hurting. We told her that she needs to talk to Mum and we will be setting up a session so that she can finally let go of that dream. She also wants to visit Dad on Sunday, which she can arrange herself and Peter can collect and return her please. It is fine with us, although I am slightly suspicious as to her reasons.

In the community meeting before I had to search the rooms, Tracy told me that she had a bag of glue hidden in her bedroom and that she had wanted to get rid of it before the community meeting, but hadn't had the chance to. I saw her afterwards (she asked to see me) and she handed me a penknife, blade and Tippex, and then told me that she had wanted to kill herself and this morning had gone to the art room and helped herself to a bag of glue.

She showed me tonight's entry in her diary, which confirmed that she wanted to let go of the dream of living with Mum, wanted to work and to move on in the right direction, etc. She told me that she had never put that in her diary before and really meant it. I told her it was the last time I wanted to hear her say it and now I wanted to see her actually do it, so we will wait and see. She is no longer suicidal or wanting to kill and felt much better afterwards. Bottle, story and goody from me. Settled and is okay.

Extract from Staff Communications Book
Date: 12/1/85
Staff: Helen M.

Had a sexuality session as requested by her so I left it to Tracy to open the session. Confusion again about sexual identity. She attributes the confusion to that sexuality group. She talked about how she was made to feel on that night and how the next morning she jumped school, met up with Matt and went with him to the lines where they tried to have sexual intercourse. They did not succeed, as Matt was a virgin. Tracy says that she did not have any sexual feelings for Matt, but was desperate to prove to herself that she was not homosexual. Because Tracy has had such a lot of input from Judy and I this week and she is in a very positive frame of mind where her work here is concerned i.e. foster parents etc. I was able to relate back to work done in the last lot of our sexuality sessions and reiterate to her how okay with sex and her sexual identity she had been then, and how we can get back to that point again.

Tracy seemed relaxed afterwards and has promised that should she feel not okay about her sexual identity before our next session, she will talk about it and not try to have sex with the first male she finds i.e. this Johnny. We will have another session next week.

Extract from Staff Communications Book
Date: 13/1/85
Staff: Helen M.

Tracy asked to see me as soon as I came in. She was not feeling good. It all started after she got back from Mum's yesterday but she did not really know why. After we had talked a bit, she said that it was to do with home visits, plus art exam, which she knows she will fail. I told her that it was great that she was able to talk so clearly about her feelings. She is doing what she promised Judy and me she would do and we were delighted. As to how to deal with both things I said we were seeing Mum on Tuesday at 7.00pm and I felt sure that Tracy will feel much better after she had discussed fostering etc., with Mum (Judy and I are hoping that Tracy will really cry then and let it go for once).

Regarding the art exam, I told Tracy that even if she does fail it is not the end of everything. The teachers will know that she has improved because she is working on it now and that will give her a better standing at school. She came on my lap and seemed much better, praised her highly.

Dad collected her at 7.00pm. On her return, she asked to see me again. She said that she had not enjoyed the visit to Dad's. She felt uncomfortable the whole time and was only at ease when she was with Dad outside the house. I told her that maybe the best thing would be to see Dad and family for outings in the future for a while anyway and see how she feels with that. Tracy is being very positive. She settled well with a story etc.

***

Helen and Judy keep telling me how well I am doing now. I think they are pleased that I keep telling them everything that is bothering me but I don't feel that I am doing well. It doesn't seem to matter how much they tell me how great I am doing, the bad thoughts are still there in my head. I wish more than anything that Helen and Judy would stop making me see my Dad, every time I go back into that house the fear I feel is crippling. There is a bad feeling oozing from the very foundations of the house and despite the staff's views that the bad feelings are just reflections of my own memories and the people that live in the house, I disagree.

I am not the only person to say this, the negative vibes do seem to be noticed by others although the burnt carpet upstairs and the cellar that is feared by cats and dogs alike, certainly do not encourage positive emotions. So much happened to me in that house, going back there is like digging a knife into an open wound and yet nobody sees me bleed or understands the hopeless desperation it leaves me feeling.

***

Betcha thought you had it all worked out,
Betcha thought you knew what I was about.
Betcha thought you solved all my problems,
Fuck you – all my problems!
Problems, got a problem?
The problems is you
What you gonna do?

On my face, not a trace, of reality.

(Twists of a Sex Pistols song)

The Sex Pistols are by far my favourite band, I love their music, can relate to their anger and find the message they give, totally invigorating. In addition, my father hates them and I can't deny that plays a part in my adoration of them. I recently read an article in a magazine, which explained how and why John Simon Ritchie – also known as Sid Vicious – died. He was the guitarist in the Sex Pistols and was gorgeous; however, on 2nd February, 1979, having previously been arrested for the suspected murder of his girlfriend, Nancy Spungen, he died of a heroin overdose. His mother loved him dearly; she had written an article claiming his innocence in Nancy's death, and how tragic it was for him to die when he was only twenty-one years old.

I find myself feeling sad at the loss of someone who I never had the opportunity to know but who I feel would have had an affinity with me. I keep feeling high and acting crazy in an attempt to blot the feelings from my mind, yet it doesn't work for long and I find his death weighing heavily on my mind. Saturday is the anniversary of his death and I have decided to go to Chatham and celebrate his memory. This puts me in a much better mood and I feel I have something to look forward to.

***

Extract from Staff Communications Book
Date: 2/2/85
Staff: Pat S.

Up early and cleaning Judy's car. Ready to go to Chatham.

Staff: Suzanne B.

Feeling ill and sick in the stomach. She can't drink the milk of magnesia. Lacey said that it might be because she had had something and that she was supposed to pick up some dope from a school mate today. I went up and tactfully questioned Tracy – had she taken anything or smoked or sniffed anything? Tracy, in a very adult way, said that she was going to pick some dope up today but chose not to and she will talk about it to Helen more fully tomorrow. I praised her for telling me and for her decision to take it to Helen.

Staff: Sandra B.

She did vomit once and looks genuinely ill. I checked her temperature but it is okay. Tracy thinks that it may be the result of her scoffing seven bags of crisps at lunchtime. She seems to be picking up.

Tracy is not okay. She has a bowl beside her bed and assures me that she won't sleep okay. I told her that she will if she lets herself.

Extract from Staff Communications Book
Date: 3/2/85
Staff: Sandra B.

Up at 9.00am and seems okay. She said that she had been up every hour on the hour being sick. All she is drinking is milk and she is not smoking. She seems a little better than she was last night. She asked me this morning not to let her out until Helen gets in, talking about herself too, and wanting things to be right in her life. I told her to work for it then.

Staff: Suzanne B.

Tracy still vomits every time she drinks anything but her temperature is normal. She is downstairs and smoking, so she can't be that bad.

Staff: Helen M.

Tracy was not okay when I came on duty. I saw her and she told me about pills etc. We had already arranged to go to the beach so I told her that we would have a session when we returned. Loads of anger – doesn't want to live, is not going to foster parents and was planning to burn Medvale down next Wednesday while the staff meeting was in progress and she can't say that she won't still do it. I tried to draw her anger out but no go, so I took her to bed at 9.45pm and told her that she was asking to be locked away somewhere. We can only enable her to help herself and she is not doing that at all at the moment. I told her that I know she is afraid to face the future. We will still do all we can but only if she is working too.

I will contact the doctor again tomorrow (twice last

*week) regarding the referral to Maudsley and hopefully
she will be seen as soon as possible given the above. Tracy
is still off restrictions but needs careful watching. At about
11.00pm, she said that she now wanted/could talk to me.
When I got back to her at 11.30pm, she was asleep, so I
will see her before school tomorrow.*

***

Saturday comes and after earning some money washing
cars, Lacey, Mia, Brittany and I go to Chatham. Brittany
goes home bored and we bumped into Leyla in the
Pentagon. Leyla has been going out with Lacey's
boyfriend Darius and she is fuming with her. We follow
her into the toilets and Lacey starts beating her. I grab
Lacey's bag off her because I know she's carrying a knife,
and I think she will probably use it. She leaves Leyla lying
on the toilet floor, cut and bruised. I thank my lucky stars
that it isn't me laying there; after all, I didn't just sleep
with Darius, I got him kicked out of Medvale and I still
can't believe that Lacey hasn't killed me because I deserve
it. You shouldn't do that to people you care about.

Lacey and Mia go off to find Darius and I go on my
own to buy some Tippex thinner and a bottle of
paracetamol. I make my way to the roof of the Pentagon
car park but it is far too busy to give me the peace I am
searching for, so I wander over to Victoria Gardens where
there is hardly anyone around and no one seems to notice
the little girl sitting on the grass.

Using my sleeve, I inhale the vapours of the thinner and
things begin to soften. I lose track of time and fall deeper
into a very dark place, my mood is sinking and I want to
be with Sid. I want to die; all I can think of is ending all
this. I don't want to feel like this anymore; at least if I
were dead, it would be over. With the Tippex all gone, I
decide to walk back into town to get a drink so I can take
the bottle of paracetamol.

A poster advertises that the Samaritans can help, that

they will understand how I am feeling. I know our local branch is in Rochester so I walk there, crying and thinking to myself of all the ways I could die and all the reactions people would have. Would they really care? Would they even notice? I hope my father feels bad that I've died, but I don't think he will. I see them all standing over my grave commenting on how shocked they are, and how they wished they had helped me.

I can't go in, I wouldn't know what to say, so I end up sitting on the wall of the Samaritans, drinking 'five alive' and swallowing the tablets one by one. I stop halfway through the bottle as I begin to feel sick and I can't stop crying. A lady walks past and asks if I am okay. I tell her to 'fuck off' and she scurries along with a disapproving scowl. I hope I have taken enough to do the job properly this time and start the walk home so I can go to bed for the last time.

I wake up and can't stop vomiting all evening. I keep crying and can't believe I have been so stupid again. I have messed things up completely this time. I tell Sandra but she dismisses my claims and is sure I haven't taken enough to kill me. I love her so much I would die for her, I really would, but I don't understand her coldness towards me tonight. I know that I could tell her everything if I was allowed; it makes me angry to think that they are stopping me from talking to her and I don't understand why. The vomiting continues throughout the night and keeps me awake but all I can think about is how much I want to be close to Sandra. How I want to feel her arms around me, holding me tight and keeping me safe, as I love her so much it hurts.

***

Extract from Staff Communications Book
Date: 4/2/85
Staff: Helen M.

I saw Tracy this morning. She admits that she is scared stiff of moving forward i.e. foster parents etc. She says that she will be okay until this evening. I will see her when she comes in from school, but she is still not okay. I told the school about Tracy's state today. I rang the Doctor and he has spoken to Dr Blofeld about Tracy, but is still waiting for a referral request letter from her (she has now left DCFP) I explained to DCFP this morning. Chris Cahill is on leave but they are trying to sort a letter out and will ring me back today. If this fails, I will take Tracy back to the doctor this week and demand a referral from him.

Tracy rang from the Pentagon at 11.30am. She sounded in a bad way. I went to pick her up and she was in a very depressed state. I took her into the staff room and she took good care from Peter while I had some lunch.

Later while sitting with me on the settee (still in the staffroom), she tried to get very angry and force me to restrain her, but I refused to let her. She was still down when we went to collect Darla and Brittany but started talking at least. Her anger is about being asked to tell us of her mood swings, which are then filed so that everyone knows everything. We then talked about how and when clients can read their own files, for her not for a long time yet. We talked about her relationship with me, love, anger, etc. She brightened up a lot afterwards and had a sandwich and drink.

***

I still feel ill the next morning and when I have a session with Helen, she is furious with me for yesterday. She says she is trying to stop me being admitted to a psychiatric hospital because she says I am not mad. I do wonder why people won't just accept it: I try to kill my family, I plan to

kill my friends, I try to kill myself – *and yet I am not mad?*
I get sent to my room and fall asleep before Helen has a
chance to talk to me again. I really want to die but I am
going to kill Medvale first!

Helen has a talk with me before school and says she's
not angry with me anymore, but I'm angry with her for not
seeing what is wrong with me. I skip school and go
straight to the Pentagon car park.

When I have calmed down, I call Helen and ask her to
come and get me; I know that she will be furious with me
but I am convinced that there is nothing else I can do. I
feel that I am sinking deeper into madness but I can't even
begin to explain it to anyone. Helen meets me in Chatham
and we do some shopping before going home. I don't
understand why she isn't angry with me; I am so angry I
could blow up tonight but she won't let me. I feel totally
crazy and I am worried about what I am going to do. I just
don't feel in control of myself at the moment.

***

I wish you were here to share the pain,
I've lost control, I've gone again.
I wish my actions would not be,
As hurtful as they seem to me.
I want to light another fire,
See the flames go higher and higher.
Watch the people burn inside,
While in my mind, I try to hide.
I know this is no way out,
But with suicide I have no doubt.
Maybe later on tonight,
I'll tell someone of my plight.
I just hope you'll understand,
When I'm not here to hold your hand.

Tracy Pain Aged 15

***

It's not all bad here, Saturdays are the best days when we get our pocket money and are allowed to the shops to buy our cigarettes, sweets and magazines. It's only a short walk to the paper shop and the road is so quiet it gives the impression of being in the country. There are only houses, set back from the road down one side; the other is overgrown with bushes and trees, which overhang the road in places. We are never asked for ID and I am sure this is because of the confident way I ask for twenty Red Band, making out I am older than I truly am.

I remember having my first puff of a cigarette when I was ten years old; one of the older girls that used to hang around with us was always smoking and one day managed to persuade me to try. I didn't like it much but I could see the admiration they had for me and for once I felt like part of the group. By the time I started secondary school I was regularly smoking, mainly stealing them from my Dad but sometimes getting the older kids to buy them for me.

One of the first things Helen asked me when I moved in was whether or not I smoke. I didn't deny it, although when she offered me a cigarette, I said no, it didn't seem right smoking in front of a grown up. We are only allowed to smoke in the dining room or office, which is probably why the dining room is my favourite room, I can relax, listen to music and smoke without feeling that I have to look over my shoulder.

The closeness of everyone within the home, between the staff and the children, the staff and staff and the children and children, seems so intense after such a very short time, and it is as if we are all clinging to each other for survival. This is certainly true for me, without this closeness, without feeling totally submerged in the love and affection that is abundant amongst the staff and children, I do not think I could survive.

I was asked if I could trim Peter and Ross's beards, a good example of that intimacy and trust. They trust me.

Tracy Pain, with scissors and a blade close enough to their jugular to be able to see it pulsing. It would have only taken seconds to stop that vein from pulsating, in and out, in and out, in perfect harmony with their heartbeat. To take away their life and show everyone just how powerful I really am.

I squash these thoughts and concentrate on the task in hand; I don't want to mess it up. I am being trusted with a very personal task and I get to stand close to each of them, leaning in and resting my body against theirs. The warmth I feel through the thin fabric of my T-shirt makes me feel special, wanted and needed. I don't want this feeling to end and to dig these scissors into that beating vein would end it all in an instant.

The staff are reaching the end of their tether and I know Helen and Peter are becoming more and more frustrated every time I slip back into my self-destruct mode. What they don't see and I suppose what they can't see, is the reason I keep doing this. The intensity in which I hate my very being is overwhelming. No amount of punching myself or beating myself with sticks, hammers, broom handles or even rocks can take away the feeling that there is something inside of me desperately trying to rip its way out. While the weight of a mountain is bearing down on me, stopping the thing exploding but in the process crushing the life from me.

***

They are talking now about sending me to the Maudsley Hospital, which has an inpatient facility for psychiatric patients. There seems to be some controversy over whether I should go or whether I should stay and at this point, I can't tell who is on my side or even which side that is. A big part of me thinks it's right to lock me up for what I have done and surely I must be mad to have committed such awful atrocities at such a young age. Part of me is scared to leave here; I have felt loved for the first time since my Mummy left.

***

Extract from Staff Communications Book
Date: 5/2/85
Staff: Sandra B.

At 2.00pm, Rochester Grammar School rang to say that Tracy did not register for the afternoon.

Tracy rang at 3.30pm asking for Helen. I asked her where she was and she said that she was just heading for the Pentagon car park. I told her to go down and wait by the fountain and that Helen would be back very soon. No answer – she was very slow in answering anything I said to her. She then put down the phone. I paged Helen as I thought it best as Tracy sounded very low.

Staff: Helen M.

When I was paged, I phoned security at the Pentagon and also the police and they will start checking now. Peter has gone to see if she is by the fountain in the Pentagon, which is where Sandra asked her to wait.

Staff: Sandra B.

Peter is on his way back. He can't find Tracy but the place is crawling with police and security, so if they find her so much the better.

Staff: Helen M.

Tracy rang in from the Delce at 4.45pm. I went to pick her up. She sounded as high as a kite and her hair has been shorn. She says that a school friend did it. I found some drug with a cigarette, which she had obviously been smoking. I emptied her bag when I got her back and found

*a new bottle of turps in it. I let her know how angry I was,
showing her how upset Natasha was, etc., etc. Peter got
her to cry and she really did sob and let go. All of her pain
is still around her Mum and she still needs help with this
but she will come through it. Tracy was okay afterwards,
very sad, though. She had refused to name the friend who
had cut her hair and given her drugs.*

Staff: Sandra B.

*Milo told me that he had overheard Lacey and Tracy
talking yesterday about Lacey cutting Tracy's hair.*

Staff: Helen M.

*I saw Lacey, Tracy and Matilda, Lacey first. She said she
had not cut Tracy's hair and was in school all day. I then
called Tracy in and she said that Lacey had not done it. I
called Matilda in and told Lacey that I knew that she had
done it. Tears and admitted that she did it at lunchtime. All
three were given a talking to and then went out to the
kitchen to make pancakes for the group.*

*Trying hard to be okay but still needs to cry more.
Story, bottle and settled okay.*

***

Another day and I can't stand being at school, so I decide
to go to Lacey's school and in her lunch hour she gives me
a skinhead; she doesn't manage to get a razor so she can
only cut it with school scissors, which really aren't very
sharp. It is more like sawing than shaving and the end
result is rather patchy and quite dramatic looking. I am
quite disappointed as a friend of mine has a lovely
skinhead and I really want to look the same. I smoke a
joint and then Lacey goes back to school while I walk to
Chatham.

I buy a bottle of turpentine because I am going to blow

up Medvale. I am so angry and it seems to be the only thing left to do.

I try calling Medvale but when Sandra answers and says, 'Helen isn't in yet,' I hang up. I can't talk to Sandra about this. I feel even worse now and cut myself a little more. Just seeing the blood makes me feel calmer somehow. I call back when I know Helen is there and she comes to pick me up. It is dark when I get into the back of her car so she has to look twice, but the look of shock on her face when she realises what I have done to my hair is a sight to behold. She is very angry and I guess my hair does look quite dramatic considering I usually have quite long hair. I can't tell her who cut it because that wouldn't be fair on Lacey, so when we get home Helen goes through my bag, hoping to find some evidence of where I have been.

If I thought she was angry over my hair what happens when she finds the turps and the dope is an apocalypse. She goes nuclear and makes me wait in the office while she calls Peter in. I sit on the settee and feel as if I am waiting for the world to end. I know it is bad for Peter to have to come in; I know that I am in serious trouble. As I sit here, I withdraw into my own world where no one can hurt me.

Curled up, surrounded by cushions, I let the noises in the house fade into the distance, the hum of the TV in the lounge, the jovial banter between staff and children, running footsteps and then, finally, the heavier thud of Peter's determined step. Sinking further into myself, fear forming a rock in my chest, I know there is no escape.

I believe that this is the angriest I have ever seen him; he is crazy. Peter pins me up against the wall shouting at me about how serious it is and how – if I carry on – I will end up being locked up in a psychiatric unit. I can see his spittle and feel its spray, as he seems to lose all control. I try to turn away but I'm resigned to whatever punishment they see fit to bestow. When I don't react, he pins me down across the chair with Helen's help until I think my lungs will explode. I try telling them that I can't breathe but they don't believe me and say that I am just exaggerating. They are both yelling at me. Do they not realise that I should be locked up? How can I possibly be sane and feel the way I do? How can anyone try killing their family and not be locked away for it? Things have really gone too far this time and I know it is only a matter of time before they move me to the Maudsley. I just want to be free of this pain that is consuming every waking hour, weighing me down and making it so hard to think clearly.

They are still shouting and restraining me. Peter yells at me that it will kill my Mum if I get locked up and Helen says she is really scared that I will be.

That hurts. The thought of my Mum having to go through the pain of seeing me in a place like that, picturing my little sisters having to visit me. Helen makes me picture it in my head and the images of their faces, questioning, wondering why their big sister is locked away, makes me cry a lot. I don't want to hurt her or anybody but I can't stop, not now.

They let me sit up once they can see I am crying, believing that they have got through to me. Helen holds me and I cry for a long time. I don't want to be like this anymore, I just want to be normal, but it is too late to take back all the things I have done. I need them to realise that I have to go through with this now; I am so confused.

I care a lot about everyone in Medvale and I don't want to hurt them. I smuggle some matches upstairs for later but I don't know if it will work without the turps. I dream tonight that my Dad takes me out of care, and is trying to kill me because of my hair. This dream distracts me enough to leave burning Medvale for tonight. Hopefully, I will be able to get some more turps when I am at school tomorrow.

***

Extract from Staff Communications Book
Date: 6/2/85
Staff: Helen M.

DCFP say that Dr Blofeld has written to Dr Balachander requesting him to refer Tracy to the Maudsley Hospital for EEG tests. I am chasing him once again.

Staff: Rita W.

Quiet and okay. She says that she is staying at school on her Mother's life.

Extract from Staff Communications Book
Date: 8/2/85
Staff: Sandra B.

Natasha told me that Tracy wants desperately to talk to Helen. I have told Tracy that Judy is in later. She said that she can't talk to Judy. I told her that whatever it was to be sensible and to hang on to it. She looks really awful.

Staff: Pat S.

I took Tracy to school and she does look awful. We kept her morning as normal as possible and let's hope that she stays in school.

Natasha told me that Tracy was talking to her about turps etc. this morning, and what she was going to do the other day (set light to Medvale or drink the turps). Tracy had told Natasha that she was going to get turps last night while at the pictures but didn't get round to it and if she had done what she had been going to do, then she would either be kicked out of Medvale or dead.

***

They're gonna regret messing with me,
They're gonna get hot like a burning tree.
Whether they live, or whether they die,
Either way I'll blow them sky high.
I've bought the turps, I've got the strike,
I think I'll try and do it tonight.
I hope this time it's gonna work,
It's the only way I get my perks.
You see I won't be satisfied,
Until I see, they all have died.
They have ruined my life and they're gonna pay,
And I will cause their dying day.

Tracy Pain Aged 15

***

I go to school the next day so that I can get some turps in my lunch hour. I have decided to bide my time and yet having the turps hidden in my room convinces me that I can smell it and I worry that everyone will be able to smell it too. I check every day that the turps and matches are still in my drawer; I am so scared that somebody will find them and then I won't be able to go through with my plan. I want them all to die; I want them all to hurt as much as I do. Maybe then, they will understand that I really am mad and need locking away.

***

Extract from Staff Communications Book
Date: 9/2/85
Staff: Helen M.

I had a long session with Tracy regarding her recent feelings. Tracy told me that she was going to set fire to Medvale on Thursday night (2.30am Friday). She had brought another bottle of turps on Wednesday. She had soaked a box of tissues with this and says that she had matches, but no strike. She could give no reason for wanting to do this. At this stage, I conferred with Peter and asked him to join the session: 1) Because of the seriousness of what Tracy was saying and 2) to see if, between us, we could discover the reason for her behaviour. We did not get a concrete reason but a pattern for prevention has been set up.

Tracy will at all times carry 30p with her for phone calls to Medvale (I will give her a purse for this tomorrow). If she rings in to say that she is wobbly and needs to talk to me I can be contacted and told; likewise, if she tells on duty staff while she is in Medvale.

Tracy may let her bad feelings out by writing them down (we will provide special paper etc.). It will be in the top drawer of Judy's and my desk. She can post these in a special pigeon hole.

It is all symbolic stuff but worth trying. Tracy has a real fear of leaving Medvale and Judy and I are working through this with her. Obviously, we will cover this incident very fully as part of the future sessions that we have planned for Tracy.

***

Blow dear Medvale to the sky
The only question asked is why?
I see no reason, but I have no hope
The only thing I want is dope
I can't cope with normal life
The whole worlds full of pain and strife
I don't want to live, I just want to die
Yet again they ask me why?
I can't explain it to myself
However hard I dig and delve.

Tracy Pain Aged 15

177

Things are getting bad here. Helen has been going on and on at me to tell her what I am thinking. She says she knows what I have been planning, although I can't see how. In the end, I give in and I show her my plans: my tin of turpentine, matches, and tissues…everything I need to burn Medvale to the ground, along with everyone in it.

Her expression says it all; this isn't what she was expecting and her shock quickly turns to anger. I want to ask her what she thought I was planning but she is shouting and I can't hear myself think. Her reaction scares me; she isn't meant to be shocked. I feel bad. I don't want to hurt people, especially everyone here, for these are my real family. These are the first people who have ever really cared about me, who have ever accepted me for who I am without wanting me to be someone different. I know I have let Helen down and I never wanted to do that, but inside I am hurting so much I just want to explode, to scream until someone really hears.

I go to my room, the weight of Helen's upset just adds to my already suffocating burden. I just want to die, to be free from all the hurt and pain that I feel, that I cause. I curl up on my bed and cry until there are no tears left and then I lay there hoping that if I wish hard enough my wishes will come true and I will just cease to be.

When Helen comes in her features seem softer somehow; the fear is there, but the anger has gone and I can feel how much she cares for me. This only makes me feel worse about what I had planned to do; she really cares and yet I was going to watch her burn. Hot tears well up and I feel them run down my cheeks, Helen scoops me up and holds me so tight. I want to be like this forever, to be safe, to be loved. I can't stop the tears now and they flow freely, while Helen just holds me close.

She takes me outside and Peter has built a bonfire, made up of an old chair, boxes, wood and paper. I don't understand but they want me to light it; they ask me to imagine whoever I want burning in that chair. The flames start small, licking up the cardboard and curling around the edges of the boxes. Blackening, and then turning orange, flames growing and spreading, devouring everything in their path. As the flames reach further, higher, trying to consume all that stands in its way, I can feel myself being drawn in, until I, too, am consumed by the flames. My mind is fixated on the possibilities my life could hold. Totally consumed by the power that such a tiny match can create, made to feel small by the energy I see before me. I don't need to imagine anyone in that fire; it is too beautiful, too powerful and in a way I guess I am in that fire being purged of the hatred I feel for the world around me.

I can feel Helen's arm around me and for now I feel safe, I know she will not let me make this journey alone.

***

Extract from Staff Communications Book
Date: 15/2/85
Staff: Judy R.

Helen and I had a good session with Tracy. She feels much better now after last week's session with Helen and Peter and feels quite certain that she won't ever feel like burning down Medvale again. She hadn't wanted to hurt people and hadn't thought it through to that conclusion, but did on Saturday while burning a chair and it hurt her. Her motives were simply to get her moved as it had twice before. We have threatened her with psychiatric lock-up so she thought she would do it herself. She admitted that it was attractive because it was sensational and a lot of what she does is for effect. Very open and honest session. Tracy is okay this morning and moving forward again.

***

I still have my sore throat but I go to school. I spend the afternoon in the sick room. I have a lovely session with Helen and Judy and tell them how positive I am feeling. I feel quite positive but I'm still unsure about what to do regarding the future, as I would love to light a fire in Medvale. I wish I didn't feel like this but I can't seem to stop.

***

Extract from Staff Communications Book
Date: 17/2/85
Staff: Helen M.

When I popped in after seeing Natasha, Tracy asked to see me. She asked when she could have a sexuality session as she needed one urgently. She started talking about Friday night's disco at Warren Wood. It seems that Matilda arranged for Tracy to meet a twenty-nine-year-old man outside the disco (he works with Devlin, Matilda's boyfriend). Matilda was outside the disco in his car with him and her boyfriend. She introduced him to Tracy, who got in the car. He took Matilda and her boyfriend home and then took Tracy to the Strand where she had full sexual intercourse with him. He then took her back to the disco.

I'm furious with Tracy, and I've blasted the hell out of her. I intend to contact the police regarding this man as soon as possible. I've put Tracy back on full restrictions. Judy and I will do a session as soon as possible but we will have a discussion first. Peter and Paul (on duty tonight) are fully aware of the situation. She will need watching tonight as she may run.

***

I go to the Warren Wood disco with Lacey and have a great time, catching up with my friend Harriet who has come back from Wales for her holiday. Matilda turns up with her boyfriend and his mate, Brent, and although I am enjoying myself, I get in the car and go with them. As soon as I'm in the car Matilda keeps telling me to kiss Brent. I don't, and I don't know what she thinks I am. Brent drops Matilda and her boyfriend off in Gillingham and then drives to a pub. I let him screw me before we have a drink and he drops me back at the disco.

***

Extract from Staff Communications Book
Date: 19/2/85
Staff: Helen M.

Tracy asked to see me. She said that nothing is working out and we might as well get her out of Medvale. I told her that she will be moving out of here eventually, but she will be going to foster parents. Tracy is unable to understand why she allowed Friday evening to happen. She says that she has no respect for herself so she expects that is why. She also said that she feels that Matilda had set her up for some reason, but blames herself for allowing her to do so. Tracy's biggest fear is that fostering will break down and rather than let that happen she would prefer not to try.

Once again, we went through how other kids were before they left Medvale for fostering, anxious, frightened, etc., etc. and I positively told Tracy that she would go to foster parents and it will work out. There was no drama attached to the session. Tracy was in a very calm mood and had given a lot of thought to what she wanted to say. Okay afterwards and settled well with story, bottle, etc.

***

My mood is still erratic, and it's affecting my relationships with other children in Medvale. I keep falling out with Matilda and even when we make up, I still use the knife she gave me to cut myself, I feel so low. I think I am more depressed when Sandra is on duty, as I just want to be close to her. It tears me apart seeing her and knowing that every time she is near me, I can't get close for fear of pouring my heart out to her.

Lacey is leaving soon to go to foster parents, we chat about our feelings for staff and children and she wants me to be okay before she leaves, but it's not possible. I don't know if I will ever be okay. I will miss Lacey. I love her so much.

I bunk off school often and each time end up having sessions with Helen. I try to tell her how I feel but I don't even understand myself why I am behaving like this, why I hate myself so much. I just miss my Mum and know that I would be happy if I could live with her. Everything would be okay, and then I could put aside all the things that have happened to me. I could be normal.

I start thinking that if I have a baby when I am sixteen life would be better. I would have someone to love and someone who would love me back. Making plans for this cheers me up and lifts my negative mood. Maybe there is hope for me yet; I think I would make a good Mum and I would never leave my children.

***

Extract from Staff Communications Book
Date: 21/2/85
Staff: Helen M.

Had an interview with WPC Best. Prior to this, I had a session with Tracy going over again what she was doing (regarding sex), and why. I feel hopeful that this may be sinking in at last. She has asked for more sexuality sessions. The police will not do anything with the statement until Matilda returns and gives us this Brent's name and workplace; even then he will only be cautioned

regarding Tracy's age, as she was a willing partner/
victim.

***

I know you think my love's a game
I know you think that I'm insane
But 'why?' is the only thing you ask
The reason I think I've found at last
You see to me you are a Mum
The hurt has caused the things I've done
Although you haven't hurt me yet
The past is something I won't forget
I can't risk my life to you
Yet breaking up is hard to do
You'll always stay here in my heart
But controlling feelings is my new start.

Tracy Pain Aged 15

***

Extract from Staff Communications Book
Date: 3/3/85
Staff: Helen M.

I saw Tracy this morning. She wanted to discuss her
restrictions (all to be okayed with Judy tonight). At the
moment, she only wants one evening outing and Saturday
for shopping. We did some sexuality work but Tracy was
very together about where she is at and reasons why she
gives herself to any bloke who comes along (she doesn't
know what else to do). We discussed learned behaviour
and how she can go about unlearning by 1) Try not to let
herself be tempted by making sure she is not alone with a
boy for a while. 2) Really think about why she is giving sex
to people she doesn't know. 3) Learn how to say no and
stick to it. 4) If she becomes sexually frustrated use

masturbation, which is perfectly healthy and normal. Tracy is very okay with this and is in a nice state of mind.

Extract from Staff Communications Book
Date: 7/3/85
Staff: Helen M.

When I left last night, Tracy asked if I would see her when I came in today. Tracy was still poorly but came into Pat's office to talk. She says that since her last outing with Dad (to the cinema) she has been feeling very sad. She says that she realises now how hard he has tried to keep her family together and how little she has done to help him to achieve this. She wished she was at home in her own room with the sun shining in. She does not want to go home as she says that she knows it wouldn't work. She realises that home would be – is – very different now. Carol is there, things – furniture, etc. – have been changed around. She is very positive about wanting foster parents. She has wanted to cry for over a week now.

I praised Tracy highly for bringing all of this to me. I told her that the amount and content of her feelings is a clear measure of how much she has grown and that Judy and I are delighted with her. I told her to accept her feelings for what they are (good, positive things) and if it is right for her, then she will cry eventually. We talked then about Tracy's sexuality and she says that she realises how stupid she has been where free sex is concerned. We talked again about all the diseases she could catch, let alone an unwanted pregnancy. All in all, it was one of the best sessions Tracy has ever given.

***

My cheerful mood doesn't last as I quickly become fed up again; talking to Helen doesn't seem to help, despite her assurances that I am progressing well. One minute I'm okay and the next I feel like committing suicide. I show her my poetry and she seems shocked as she thought I was further ahead than they say I am. I tell her that I wrote them ages ago (although last week wasn't that long ago) and I think this makes her feel better. I wish I weren't so honest and open with her sometimes, as it only ever gets me into trouble.

Chapter 19

1985 – Aged 15

Medvale: There is No Escape

Extract from Staff Communications Book
Date: 23/4/85
Staff: Judy R.

Tracy said that she had 'men problems' regarding Carl pestering her with phone calls etc., so she invited him round to tell him to his face not to bother her. She ended up inviting him for coffee and had a seemingly friendly chat. She seemed okay at bedtime but I think something is around with her.

Extract from Staff Communications Book
Date: 28/4/85
Staff: Judy R.

Helen and I had a long, difficult session with Peter Pain, who firmly believes all her problem behaviour is due to food allergies. He was unable to accept that it is purely emotional disturbance (because he can then disclaim responsibility), but has agreed not to discuss it with Tracy at this stage.

Tracy was very anxious and angry about his visit, as we had simply told her that it was to do with his bits on Form E. She asked me about it later and I told her that it was a problem that Dad had – to do with his past – and that he wanted help with and it was nothing to do with her. She is not to know anything about the allergy thing. Her behaviour is not directly connected to a food allergy and it would be very damaging to put her on a special diet, as it would automatically label her as 'not normal' and give her an excuse for any of her behaviour. Tracy was very okay after my discussion with her and apologised for being angry earlier.

***

I am finding it so difficult right now, that Judy doesn't trust me. I haven't lied to her any more than anyone else and yet she is suspicious of my every move, like everything I do has some hidden motive. It is really getting me down; I just wish she would leave me alone and stop with the sarcastic comments. Lacey is leaving as well, which isn't helping, as she doesn't want to live with foster parents, she wants to live with her Mum and I totally understand where she is coming from. This whole thing is so unfair; she is so unhappy but nobody seems to care.

Giving up smoking lasts a week. I am far too pissed off to last any longer. Apparently, Judy is having secret meetings with my sister, Debbie, and they are even going to have a meeting with my Mum! They won't tell me anything; seemingly, it is none of my business but I disagree, if someone is going to upset my Mum I have every right to know about it. Oh, and to top it all, Dad is getting married again, this time to Carole. I think my Mum is the only person who is honest with me and who tells me what is going on, and without her, I wouldn't know anything. I hate it here so much, I want to kill them all and I'm really scared that if I don't leave soon, then I will. Maybe I should just kill myself and be done with it.

***

Extract from Staff Communications Book
Date: 30/4/85
Staff: Rita W.

Not okay. Matilda told me that Tracy was having a little

*weep. She came down and started looking at the rota. I
commented that they were not on until Wednesday. Tracy
was very hard-faced and said, 'So?' I told her that she was
not okay. She said, 'No, but I'll be okay.' I gave her a
cuddle but got no response. She is blocking her emotions
out.*

Staff: Suzanne B.

*Reverse charge phone call was made at 12.30pm. It was
Tracy ringing from the Pentagon. She had walked out of
school one and a half hours ago. (The school didn't ring.)
Rita was in the building so she went to fetch her. I told
Tracy where to wait. She sounded drowsy on the phone.
When she came in, she had tea and a cigarette in the office
and cried a little. I took her up to her room and told her to
stay there. Rita asked her if she had taken anything and
Tracy said she hadn't. I paged Helen. I went up to see her
again. She was sitting on the bed crying. I told her that I
am glad to see her back, held her, and then asked if she
took anything. She knows we are trying to get in touch
with Helen. I rang the school to ask for the form tutor to
ring me back.*

*The form tutor rang. I told her that Tracy is with us and
is too distressed to return to school this afternoon. She
said that Tracy's history teacher told her that Tracy
doesn't attend history lessons (which start around
10.30am) and goes to Chatham until lunch time on
Tuesdays. She apologised for not telling us sooner (she
thinks this has been going on for a long time – some
weeks) and blames it on herself and her history teacher.
She also said that Tracy has picked up so well with her
work that it would be a shame if she went backwards now.
She also apologised for not ringing us earlier to say that
Tracy was not at school today. She thinks that Tracy left
school around 10 am.*

*Tracy talked to Helen on the phone. Helen will be in
this evening between 6–7.00pm to see Tracy. Tracy is not*

aggressive or anything like that, she just needs Helen to talk to. She looks very sad and depressed.

Staff: Sandra B.

Tracy had a horrid face on. She looked worried and upset but there was no anger. She is hanging on as best she knows for Helen.

Staff: Helen M.

I saw Tracy at 6.30pm. It was the first time ever that she sobbed and sobbed with real sorrow and sadness. She is scared stiff of fostering and wants to go to live with Mum, but knows she can't, so she is depressed. She was worrying that she would set fire to Medvale, feeling like committing suicide. We went through the whole bit again and she brightened a little, yet was still down. I told her that we want her at school tomorrow and it is very important that she stays there too.

***

I still can't face school and head off to Chatham as soon as I have taken some glue from the art room. Wandering through the Pentagon my heart sinks; the boy swaggering towards me with a leer on his face is someone I had hoped I would never have to see again. Carl walks with me telling me how much he has missed me, and although I try to tell him to go away, he tells me he can't. He says he wants me, and that if I don't go with him, he'll find someone to rape. The worst thing is, I know he will and I can't put anyone else through what I've been through at the hands of this boy.

He takes my hand and we walk over to Victoria Gardens and then through the gates onto the lines. I know if I go along with him it will be over quickly and then he will let me walk away. I feel dirty and cheap but at least it is over. I spend a while sitting at the top of the Pentagon car park, wishing I could just put an end to this for once and for all, losing myself in the dizzy haze of glue fumes, until the world seems like a slightly better place.

I wander around the town for a while before heading back to Medvale. I need to speak to Helen and I need her to make everything okay. Although I know I can never tell her what Carl and his friends did to me, just being close to her makes me feel safer.

***

The staff often question me about why I am scared of my Dad; what has he done to me to make me so scared of him? I don't know. I know he has hit me but I was scared of him long before that. They talk about people, who at times lock painful memories inside them, so that they don't hurt them anymore. Apparently, this is called repression, and they think it's important to remember these things so that we can begin to deal with them.

I listen to them talking and I know deep inside that they are right. I know there is something that I can't remember, something that explains why I hate my father so much and why I am so desperately unhappy.

I wonder if the hatred inside of me is because of how scared I am of him; how he manages to make me feel like a little girl, however old or mature I may become. I get angry and frustrated at myself for not having the courage to stand my ground and tell him how I feel, but I fear he will talk me down like he always has, he is always right and I am wrong.

I get the feeling that they are hinting at what he may have done to me, however, I will not allow myself to consider that. It scares me that I can't remember. When I can remember vividly what Carl and his friends did to me, when I can remember being abused from the age of nine by Bert, my Nan's next-door neighbour...it begs the question, how bad must it be for me to repress it?

Chapter 20

1984 – Aged 14 and 10 days

Home: Carl and his Friends

I don't think I will ever forget the day, Friday 3rd February 1984 – ten days after my fourteenth birthday. Only four weeks before I was admitted to Medvale – not that I ever saw a connection and by never telling, nobody else ever made the connection either. Only in later life did I realise that this day was probably the straw that broke the camel's back, so to speak.

I'm not sure why I stayed off school that day, not sure if it was to avoid someone or whether it was planned. I knew I wasn't ill as I had led my father to believe.

Carl turned up around 10.00am demanding to be let in. I had repeatedly tried finishing things with him, but he just wouldn't take no for an answer. I had initially only gone out with him because I wanted to defy my father, who thought he was bad news and had forbidden Debbie and me to have anything to do with him. I suppose I have to admit, just this once that he was right. But bad news was an understatement; Carl was manipulative, sleazy, threatening and dangerous. Yet part of me found him exciting and attractive and a means to get back at my family because I knew they would be horrified if I went out with him.

He pounded on the door, shouting that he knew I was home. When I wouldn't come to the door he tried breaking in through the cellar entrance and I could hear him kicking the wooden door and swearing. He must have found something to lever it up with as I heard a loud crack as something broke. I was scared of what my father would say when he came home, so I tentatively opened the door.

Carl came in with his friend Mark and demanded that I make them a cup of tea. He started kissing me, and rubbing himself against me. Thinking it was best to get it over with, I took him upstairs and he told me to undress. I lay on my bed and let him thrust himself into me, and when he was spent, he told me that he had some friends that wanted to screw me. He called to Mark and I heard the front door open; I can only imagine they had been waiting down the road because seven lads were queuing on the stairs within minutes.

They came in one at a time and Carl and Mark stayed to watch. One by one they had sex with me and I just lay there hoping it would be over quickly. My ability to detach my mind from my body came into its own and in a way it was as if I wasn't there at all. I remember Carl holding my arms above my head to stop me pushing against them. Mark was last and suggested that he had a threesome with Carl, who jumped at the chance, and I think seeing the others had turned him on more than ever.

I felt like a rag doll that was being pushed and pulled and contorted into whatever position suited them while they tried to fuck me every way they could. It seemed to last forever and when they were finished, they went into the bathroom while I just lay there.

I felt sore and numb, inside and out. I knew though, that by letting them, I had saved myself from being raped because there was no doubt in my mind that they would've raped me if I hadn't.

They left without speaking to me and I got dressed and went downstairs for a cup of tea. Before I had finished drinking it, the door knocked and a lad was standing there. He introduced himself as Martin and said that Carl had sent him for sex. I let him in and lay on the dining room floor; it was over quickly and he left.

I made another cup of tea and then Carl was thumping on the door again. He sounded angry and my stomach sank. I opened the door and he pushed his way in slamming it behind him. He grabbed me by the throat and held me against the wall, screaming at me that I was a whore because I had fucked Martin. I was terrified and desperately tried to explain that he had said Carl had sent him, but he just kept shouting that he didn't like Martin and I shouldn't have slept with him.

My head was whirring; I didn't know he didn't like Martin, how could I have done? I hadn't seen him before, I knew nothing about them. I said I was sorry, over and over again and told him I loved him, until he eventually calmed down. He told me to make him a cup of tea and then took forever to drink it. I asked him to go but he kept saying he hadn't finished, even though I had finished mine long before. He said he needed to remind me that I had to do what he said or he would rape me.

He eventually left and I curled up in bed letting my record player, play over and over again. Wishing that I could die to put an end to all of this, I knew my father would be furious when he came home because Carl had broken the cellar door; however, if he knew Carl had been over, then I would be in so much trouble. I had to keep quiet and prayed that he wouldn't find out. The fear I felt for him was a hundred times worse than anything Carl and his friends could do to me.

Chapter 21

1985 – Aged 15

Medvale: Goodbye, Bert

Extract from Staff Communications Book
Date: 4/6/85
Staff: Helen M.

Tracy had a letter from Nan – the first line told her that old Bert had died and his dog had to be put down. Tracy went white as a sheet and cried on my lap in the television room. Very obviously this was a shock to her.

I allowed her to stay up fifteen minutes later with Ross and me, talking very openly and in an okay way about Bert. She gave me some poems, which she assures me are just poems. Very mature and grown up tonight.

***

It is the beginning of June 1985, and as I sit at the dinner table with Ross and Helen, they give me a letter from my Nan in Somerset. It is exciting to get a letter but my excitement dies as I read the first line: 'Dear Tracy, Bert died on Sunday. He died in his sleep, and Peg had to be put to sleep because she pined for him.'

I burst into tears and flee from the table, racing up the stairs I throw myself on my bed crying. I can't believe I will never see him or Peg again. Helen comes in and tells me she has read the letter, and she is sorry that I found out like that. She seems confused as I explain that Bert was my Nan's next-door neighbour and she doesn't understand why I am so upset.

I can't even begin to explain, nobody will understand

how close we were or how much he meant to me. We shared a very special secret and now he is gone.

Eventually, she stops asking and leaves me crying in my room, listening to sad songs that match my mood, like Phil Collins' *Against All Odds*, Lionel Richie's *Hello*, and Randy Vanwarmer's *Just When I Needed You Most*. I cut my wrist, then go down, and talk to Helen and Ross about Bert dying. We talk about all the good times we had together; the stories he told me; playing with his dog, Peg, and the time I ruined his marble fireplace by drawing in it with a red hot poker. There are so many memories but I will never tell her the sex side of things, mainly because I don't think she will ever understand, but also because I don't want her to know how bad I am.

***

Extract from Staff Communications Book
Date: 5/6/85
Staff: Rita W.

Lying on her bed in tears – just a dose of good honest mourning. I told her that sadness when we lose people we care about is very normal and I just lay and comforted her. She says that she is cracking up about bits and pieces of everything. I told her that she isn't and she will be fine, and that all her feelings and fears are normal and okay.

Visibly, down but trying to help the other kids, later she came and sat by me and told me how everything that had happened had upset her. Sister's cat being put to sleep, Lacey going home, Bert dying and now problems with Mum. I said she must talk to Helen about it. She warned me that she had been having nightmares this week and she might be up in the night. I just sympathised and told her that she knew where to find me if she wanted me.

***

Bert was my paternal grandmother's next-door neighbour; he lived with his dog Peg on the ground floor of his house, as at seventy-six he wasn't fit enough to use the stairs anymore. I ventured up there once, always on the lookout for an adventure, but all I found was yellowing paintwork. The faded, patterned wallpaper brown with age and nicotine, thick dust, and the musty smell of rooms where time had stood still. It made me feel sad to think that once this man had a wife and this house was once a vibrant family home. He still ventured out into his back garden, which is where we first met him, leaning over the wall chatting to my Nan. Peg, he told us, was a whippet, which is like a greyhound only smaller. He said she would never get any bigger and she was delightful. She loved the attention we lavished on her; she enjoyed playing ball and racing up and down the garden and most of all she loved to be cuddled.

Over time, not content with just stroking Peg from the wall, I jumped at the chance of going over to his house. He let me help to feed Peg and showed me how. I used to curl up on the chair with Peg and cuddle her for ages; she was so warm and soft. I used to sit on Bert's lap at the table while he lit his pipe and told me many stories about his life, and how different things had been when he had been growing up. He showed me poems he had written when man first landed on the moon, his poetry was inspirational and I nagged him continually to have it published, yet he wasn't swayed.

I was forever fascinated rummaging through his belongings at the amazing things he had. I was particularly drawn to the tiny birds he had trapped in glass cases. He explained that they were real birds that had been preserved, which made me sad, as they looked so lonely, frozen in time. I could see how delicate they looked, how strangely alive their beady eyes were. He always impressed upon me the importance of not touching these, as they were very old and could easily turn to dust, so the cases had to remain sealed and in place on top of his bureau.

Sometimes Debbie came with me but she stopped coming after Tracey moved in and she was very critical of me for continuing to see him. I didn't understand then; I just thought it was her being stuck up, wanting to please Tracey by not getting her clothes dirty at Bert's. I didn't care. I liked getting dirty and I loved going to Bert's. It was the only place I could be myself, where I wasn't criticised and where I felt that someone cared about me.

When I told Bert that Tracey kept going mad about how dirty I was getting he suggested that if I took my clothes off when I got there, I wouldn't get dirty. This seemed like a great idea and I was happy to strip off the minute I went in the house, making sure I folded my clothes carefully by the door so that they didn't get dirty.

One time that I was sitting on his lap chatting about Tracey and how mean I thought she was, we got on to talking about keeping clean and Bert told me that he knew where the cleanest place on a woman's body was. He said it was the skin between my vagina and my bottom and to show me what he meant he touched me there. Then he slipped his finger inside me. I felt him shudder and he said he shouldn't be doing this, but he didn't stop and I didn't want him to. It felt good and I could see it was making him happy. I knew he was lonely and although I was only nine, I was old enough to realise that if I could make him happy then he would carry on letting me stay and would protect me from my family.

This became a regular event; every day during our holidays at Nan's I would go there, strip off my clothes and lay them neatly by the door, then climb on his lap so he could finger me. After a few times, he asked if I would touch him and I was shocked by how many layers of clothes he had on. I undid his flies, undid his thermals and then had to undo his underpants. Eventually, I managed to free him and he held my hand and rubbed my hand against him. I could feel him grow hard beneath my hand and

Bert's breathing quickened. He pushed me away saying that he was wrong and that he shouldn't do it. I told him I didn't mind as I was scared that he wouldn't let me come any more.

He did and I did everything I could to encourage these shows of affection between us; it felt good and made me feel wanted. Eventually, after a couple of years, I don't think he could hold back any longer, he told me to turn around so that my back was to him and my front was pressed against the table. He guided my bottom down and pushed himself into me. I didn't mind. I wanted to please him and make him happy, as he had given me so much happiness and shown me how special I could feel. I knew I couldn't tell anyone; I didn't want to because then I wouldn't be allowed to come anymore.

Bert was always letting me have money for sweets and often told me to help myself out of his money tins that he kept in the kitchen. One day I didn't bother asking and took a pound so that I could buy some sweets while I was out on a bike ride for the afternoon. When I got back to my Nan's house, Nan and Dad were furious. Bert had told them I had stolen from him and made out he was concerned that I may also have stolen from my Nan.

I felt so betrayed; he knew that now I would never be able to tell on him because he knew they thought I was vindictive and any recrimination would be seen as me being nasty, malicious and vengeful.

Our relationship was never the same after although I went there regularly and did whatever he wanted me to. Sometimes I fondled him, sometimes he fingered me and occasionally we had sex. I got to the point where I believed I was using him as much as he was using me. I enjoyed how he made me feel inside and although there were times I think he was deeply unhappy about what we had done, I pushed him time and time again in a desperate attempt to cling on to what I thought we once had.

The Easter of 1985 was just as the previous holidays although Bert was quite upset that he could no longer manage an erection, we still tried to have sex but it didn't happen so we had to make do with pleasing each other with our hands. He gave me a folder of all of his poems for me to keep, which I promised I would get published one day. He laughed not really believing that his work was that good, but I believed in him and that was what mattered.

I knew Helen and Judy would never understand our relationship and I was scared they would think badly of me, so it was a secret that I could never tell.

Chapter 22

1985 – Aged 15

Running Away to Wales

Extract from Staff Communications Book
Date: 10/6/85
Staff: Sandra B.

Rochester Grammar school rang at 11.30am to say that Tracy is missing from the prep lesson. They are going to check to see if she was in her French lesson. She is also supposed to have a detention tonight. They will ring if she returns and we will do the same.

Staff: Peter J.

Tracy was reported missing at 8.00pm to the police. Parents informed and the police given Lacey's address.

Extract from Staff Communications Book
Date: 11/6/85
Staff: Peter J.

No sign of Tracy during the night. On her return, I want to know where she has been, has she sniffed, etc., or had sex, where is the £3.30 dinner money and why. If it is early evening, for example, she is to stay in her room doing some kind of school work. She is then to resume back to school the next day and to be taken there. She is also to be on full restrictions. If she thinks that she's fed up with Medvale, then she ought to have a reason to be fed up.

Staff: Secretary

The school rang and wanted to know why she wasn't in. I told them that she is missing. They would like to know when she turns up. She did not pay in her dinner money yesterday.

At 9.30am, Peter Pain rang and I told him that there was no news. He wants to be informed if we hear anything and I told him that we would do that.

Mrs Simmonds rang and I told her that we had no news, but that we could contact her if we had any.

Staff: Sandra B.

Last night Angela's friend, whose daughter goes to Tracy's school, told me that her daughter said that Tracy Pain wasn't in school in the afternoon. Apparently, a crowd of girls were talking to Tracy in the school playground in the morning and she had a load of carrier bags with her clothes in. She was saying that she was fed up with Medvale and was going up to London.

Staff: Rita W.

Lacey rang and I asked her if she had seen Tracy. She said that she hadn't and I explained that Tracy was missing. Lacey assured me that she will phone me if she hears from Tracy.

Staff: Sandra B.

Tracy's Mum and Peter Pain both rang to see if there was any news.

Staff: Rita W.

I phoned at 4.30pm, to speak to the Women's Special Unit to ask if they had checked Lacey's home. No reply so I left a message.

I phoned Rochester Police after a phone call from Lacey and they are going to check that Tracy is not with Lacey.

***

Since Bert has died, I can't seem to shake myself out of my low mood, cutting myself and sniffing glue doesn't even make a dent on how I feel and I just seem to be sinking lower and lower. Helen and Judy are still talking about me leaving to go to foster parents even though I know I am far from ready, and there is still so much I need to work through. I can't even begin to tell them the things that have happened to me to bring me here because I am not clear myself about how it all fits together.

How can I ever tell them about what I have done with Bert when I am as much to blame? So much confusion, which just leaves me with the urge to run away, as far from here as I can get. To start a new life for myself and put all this behind me; if I don't do it now I think I will die, there are no other options for me now.

I leave the house with many layers of clothes on, nobody notices and when I get to the cemetery, I strip down to one layer, putting the extra clothes in bags. I go to school to say goodbye to my friends; I will miss them, for as much as I struggle with school the girls have always been there for me and put up with all the crap that I throw at them. I go straight from school to the bank and cash a cheque from the NAYPIC account. They should never have made me treasurer, the temptation is too great and I need this money now to make my escape.

At the train station, I get a one-way ticket to London, Victoria. Nobody questions me, nobody even gives me a second glance, and it is as if I really do not exist. I am lost in thought all the way to London, wondering where I should go. I remember a friend of mine from school saying how lovely her holiday was in the Brecon Beacons, so I decide to head there. Hopefully, I will be able to find work; either way, nobody will find me there.

I catch a train to Charing Cross, which costs two pounds and then a train to Abergavenny, which costs eight pounds. I get directions for the bus that takes me on my final leg of the journey to Brecon. The bus ride seems to take the longest, through country roads with me sitting on tender hooks, unsure of where I need to depart and not wanting to look too lost in case someone questions me travelling alone. The bus driver is helpful though and tells me when I need to get off, so I depart into the centre of the most picturesque village I think I have ever seen.

I wander around what appears to be the centre of Brecon for over an hour, taking in my surroundings and stopping for a time on the stone bridge, watching the river Usk flowing lazily beneath me. The whole town seems peaceful and calm, which gives me the space I need to gather my thoughts. I find a street with several bed and breakfasts advertising their vacancies and I'm lucky that the first lady I ask has a single room and is happy to rent it to me for seven pounds fifty, no questions asked. I provisionally book it for two nights as I only have a little money and need to find work before I can plan any further ahead.

I go to the shops to buy food and gas, which I take back to my room for me to use until the morning when I plan to visit the jobcentre and try to find work. As I sit alone in my room thoughts of Medvale push into my head making me sad, lonely and very angry. I cut away at my wrist wanting to bleed, wanting to feel something that is real and not just the numbness that I have created to protect me from the pain I feel inside. Even here, there is no escape from the guilt I am feeling. I can almost hear Helen's voice telling me to stop playing games, stop upsetting everybody, and stop hurting myself. I breathe in the gas to blot out the barrage of voices in my head, until eventually, I sleep and the blood clots.

In the morning, I head into town and buy two more

cans of gas as I used up the one I had yesterday. I find the jobcentre and even find a job I think I could do, working in an office as a trainee, which sounds easy enough. They give me some forms to fill out and seem to accept my story that I am sixteen years old; they give me the job details about who to contact and I leave feeling confident that I will be able to get myself a job. They ask me to return in the morning to finish the application, so for now I can relax.

I head into town and sit in the library doorway, inhaling gas and daydreaming about what will happen to me now. I buy another can and take this back to my room where I lay on my bed completely wrecked. Overall, today I have inhaled three cans and my life seems to be flashing along its own timeline in my head. I even see the test card girl with her chalkboard and clown doll from the television, that people used to say looked like me. It's funny the things you remember when your mind and body become separate entities. The rest of the day and night are a blur, but I feel that something very profound has happened to me.

***

Extract from Staff Communications Book
Date: 12/6/85
Staff: Secretary

Mrs Simmonds rang at 9.00am. She says that her Mum is away on holiday and the house will be empty. She is going to phone her brother who lives just down the road and ask him to check it out, and she will let us know the outcome.

Mrs Simmonds rang back. Brother has gone with Mum but his wife hasn't. She will probably be in about five o'clock. Rita rang the police with grandmother's address and they will check.

Staff: Helen M.

I found a note from Tracy (not in an obvious place). I rang the police and they will call up for a recent photo today. They are also checking the empty house in Chatham.

Staff: Secretary

A phone call at noon to say that Tracy has handed herself into the police in Wales. Helen and Judy have gone to collect her. Tracy is being taken to a Children's Home – Maes I Deri, Llanfaen, Brecon. I rang them and told them that Tracy will need careful watching.

Staff: Helen M.

Judy and I collected Tracy at 5.00pm from Brecon. She was very subdued. We made her write out why and how on the way back. She cashed a NAYPIC cheque for thirty-five pounds on Monday and put the chequebook in a post box. She said that she stayed in a bed and breakfast for two nights. She had been sniffing gas and had glue on her too, which she says she got from school. On return, she was sent to her room, and then Judy and I saw her. She is on total restrictions until she earns back what she has lost by this latest event.

She was crying when Judy said goodbye to her and crying when I said goodnight. She held me tight and was very sorry. She will prove she can make a go of things; she said she loved me and asked if I still loved her. I said that I did. Tracy was having a sexual relationship with this Bert (who was eighty-two), all logged in her diary. She is also to be taken into school and not to be given dinner money. Settled well with a drink and a goody.

Staff: Judy R.

Absolutely sobbed in my arms, said sorry and meant it.

205

I wake up feeling a little rough but soon perk up once I am outside in the fresh air. I head straight for the jobcentre keen to see if the woman will be able to get me a job. My earlier optimism is dashed when the woman insists that I need my national insurance number. I don't even know what this is and I can see doubt in the woman's eyes as my ignorance becomes known. She is adamant I can't get work without this number, and as the tears well up in my eyes, I flee the building before she has the chance to find out who I really am.

Crying, I make my way back to the town and sit outside the library where I am out of the way, and not noticed. I have used the last of my gas so I try to soften the edges of the pain that I feel with the glue I stole from school. I have no money left and no way to earn any. I don't know what I can do anymore. I don't want to go back to Medvale, but what choice do I have?

I make my way to the police station, as I am not sure what else to do. I tell them I have run away from home and come from Rochester, but they look very confused. Therefore, I tell them it is in Kent, which does not help the looks of despair they give me. Their eyes light up when I say I live in a children's home and they suddenly seem to know what they are doing.

They transfer me to a local children's home, where I am told I must wait to be collected by Helen and Judy. I know they will be angry and I feel bad about letting them down; however, for once I am not scared, as I know I am going back to somewhere where people really care about me. I resign myself to take whatever punishment they see fit and I know I deserve it. They are very angry but the only thing I really hear is Judy's threat. If I don't start behaving and acting in a positive way, then she will send me back to my Dad's!

Nothing else that they say matters to me. I can't believe she would do that to me when she said she cared. They have read my diary and know everything, and yet Judy would still send me back there, it doesn't make sense to me at all. I really thought she cared about me. It just goes to show you how wrong I can be. I know now that I must put all of this behind me and move on, go to foster parents and get my own place as soon as I can.

***

Extract from Staff Communications Book
Date: 13/5/85
Staff: Sandra B.

Down at 7.45am and looking sullen.

Staff: Helen M.

I thought she looked sad.
I took Tracy onto my lap after breakfast. Yesterday I could have murdered her, yet today she is a sad, small person who needs all the help we can give her. Tracy is to be taken into school until we review it next week. She owes us three pounds fifty and she will pay us out of her pocket money. She is on total restrictions. Watch all spray cans etc., as she is sniffing badly again. I will take her to school today and talk to staff as her last tube of glue came out of the art room. I saw Miss Trollope and then went to the upper school with Mrs Turner and Tracy. I saw the head of the art school and as usual, she was supportive and pleased to have Tracy back. I left Tracy, who appeared to be okay.

Staff: Judy R.

Sad and subdued on return from school, I saw her and she agreed that she is putting it all behind her and will be okay from now on. She also said that she won't sniff anymore and feels able to tell us if she is tempted. She told me that

207

she had some things to give me and brought down an assortment of Stanley knife, paraffin (from school), pills (collected over a period of months, some from us), blades, silicone crystals (small packet), all of which she has had for some months. I praised her for being positive and watched her flush the paraffin and pills etc. down the toilet.

Later she asked me about going back to Dad. She is worried that we meant it. I said that we did last night, but not today, but this is the very last chance so if she screws up again...

Feeling okay. She did a lot of school work, revision and had a typing lesson. Then she did some more school work for a while and had a bath. She went to bed at 10.00pm. She is trying very hard and doing well. I have told her that as soon as she starts proving herself we will start lifting restrictions i.e. if she is okay tomorrow, I will let her get herself to school. I feel positive about her today.

Extract from Staff Communications Book
Date: 14/6/85
Staff: Helen M.

Peter Pain rang and I had a long discussion with him about hair testing. He has had his hair tested and shows the same allergies as Tracy. I told him plainly that Tracy will not be started on any diet. Our main concern right now is to get her settled with foster parents. It has had a big effect on Debbie, who is sleeping naturally for the first time in years, but I pointed out to him that Debbie's level of disturbance was nothing like Tracy's. He was fine at the end of the conversation.

Tracy asked to talk to me when she came in from school. She asked if I had read her diary yet and I said no. She then told me all the bits Judy had earmarked, saying that she wanted to tell us herself (one was sex with Bert). I have not discussed this at length but will do so in a sexuality session as soon as possible. Tracy said that she *realised what a fool she has been and that it won't happen again. She spoke of foster parents and how she would not mind there being other teenagers there. This coincided with a phone call from Paddy, who said that there are serious problems regarding fostering i.e. no foster parents without teenagers and not likely to be for a long time.*

I told Paddy that Judy and I would discuss again and with Tracy too, but Paddy was wondering if foster parents at Newington might be a possibility. Tracy is now saying that she will know when she meets a family whether she will be able to live with them or not. Dad is coming around at 11.00am on Sunday. She had a short, okay conversation with him tonight. She was fine at bedtime and needs lots of care.

* * *

I knew I would have to talk to Helen at some point about Bert and me but she didn't dwell on our relationship. She knew that I already know I shouldn't be having sex with a man so old and gave me a mini-lecture about learning to say no and respecting myself more. Helen didn't seem overly concerned, only a little annoyed that I had let it happen, so I didn't go into detail and certainly didn't tell her when it had started. I don't want her to think that I am a total slag. It seems she wants us to have a sexuality session soon, so I guess that at some point, she will want to know it all. For now, she seems content with what I have told her.

* * *

Extract from Staff Communications Book
Date: 19/6/85
Staff: Judy R.

I have told Tracy that I am leaving and she is absolutely okay with it. We also had a long chat about where she is at

– back on top – so all restrictions are lifted and she is having the old sleeping-in room, which she is delighted about. We will be decorating the room together but Tracy can also do bits on her own if she wants to.

Extract from Staff Communications Book
Date: 30/6/85
Staff: Helen M.

Good visit to prospective foster parents. We only stayed for half an hour but that was long enough for Tracy, who is saying that she likes the family very much. Tracy will have her own bedroom if she goes there and she was shown the room before we left. Paddy Counsell will be talking to the foster parents tomorrow and I will talk to her later. If all is okay, I will arrange for Tracy to spend a day with the family next weekend.

Extract from Staff Communications Book
Date: 6/7/85
Staff: Helen M.

Down at 6.45am and anxious but okay. Foster parents will return her tonight between 7.00 and 8.00pm.

The whole child group was supportive of her this morning when we took her for her visit to her foster parents...so much so that she was really relaxed when I took her in (she had been really anxious before leaving the house). Very warm welcome from the foster family. I hope it all goes well. I will ring her later.

Staff: Peter J.

Tracy had a good day at the foster parents. She had been walking and she likes the dog they have. Bed at 10.30pm as she was tired.

Extract from Staff Communications Book
Date: 7/7/85
Staff: Helen M.

Tracy said that she felt all funny; when she is with her foster parents, she wants to stay there, then when she is here again, she feels scared and wants to stay here. I told her that that is all normal stuff and not to worry. Tracy was in a lovely mood and very close to me.

Extract from Staff Communications Book
Date: 8/7/85
Staff: Sandra B.

Tracy has been in a weird mood since coming in from school. She and Kirsty (Medvale child) came with me for a ride to the Regency – weird behaviour. Whether it is just a game or attention seeking, I don't know. She was trying to get close to me and I let her tickle me for a short while, but then had had enough of her silliness. Later, she asked for plasters and is now cutting her wrists, and has put a bloody tissue in the waste bin. I think she is waiting for my reaction.

Staff: Sandra B.

Tracy stayed outside for a while after Ross had had a word with her. Then, when I was reading to Kirsty, she came into say goodnight and asked if I would bring her a drink and goodie, which I did. She cried real tears when I said goodnight. I noticed that she was hiding her left arm and I also noticed blood coming through her pyjama sleeve. I asked to look but she wouldn't show me so I kissed her goodnight and left her to it. I think she needs watching tonight.

I went in to say goodnight to her and she was still crying a little. She let me cuddle her for a while and said that she would tell Judy and Helen about it tomorrow, and would be okay until then. She needs watching.

***

Sandra comes in to say goodnight and I hide my arm under my duvet. She sits on the edge of the bed and talks to me about why I am so sad. I'm sure she knows I have done something and although I try to reassure her that I am okay, she can see I have been crying. I guess my face is all swollen and blotchy. My arm is throbbing and I glance down and can see a flower of blood, blooming through my pyjamas. I try to cover it: 'Show me what you've done, Tracy. Trust me, I can help you.'

'It doesn't matter. Honestly, it's not that bad,' I reply, desperately trying to hide the slowly spreading pattern. Eventually, she leaves me; I wish I had shown her, I wish she had insisted so I would have someone to care about me. I put the glass back in my drawer for another day and turn off the light, I know by morning the blood will have clotted.

As usual, my baggy school jumper covers my arms and Sandra doesn't dwell on the night before. She gives me a hug and I just want to stay that way forever.

***

Extract from Staff Communications Book
Date: 9/7/85
Staff: Sandra B.

Still very odd this morning and has something on her mind. She said that she can wait for Helen and Judy when I asked her this morning if she will be okay. She was still clinging onto her wrist. All we have done, basically, is ignore it and keep her at a low caring profile. She has cut her arm with glass but allowed me to dress it and went off to school okay.

Staff: Helen M.

Tracy came in from school with a face, saying that she wanted to talk to me tonight. I told her that she would talk to me right now about all the rubbish that was going on. I literally roasted her non-stop – did she want foster parents? – If not, stop wasting everyone's time, etc., etc. She said that she did not want another mother and I said that she was not getting another Mum. She would be going to live with the Prior family i.e. Martina and Barry, not Mum and Dad, and they would care for her and her for them without needing to replace either one of her parents.

Tracy then came flying onto my lap and cried her eyes out. We then went through pre-foster placements and the sort of feelings they evoke in one. I told her that it was all natural but not to dare deal with it as she did last night. Tracy was okay afterwards.

I discussed with her the phone call I had from Martina this afternoon. She has been making calls all day to get Tracy included in their summer holiday: 3rd–17th August. The Prior's were hoping that Tracy could move in straight away, perhaps after next weekend. I said that she couldn't and we have agreed that after next weekend (Fri/Sat) Tracy will go the following weekend Friday after school (to be taken) and she will go to school from the Prior's on the Monday. She will come back to Medvale on Monday after school and will move out from here on Friday 26th July. I will come in to take her. Her leaving party is on Wednesday, 24th July.

Super all evening.

***

213

Helen is furious with me again, saying I am playing games as if I do this on purpose. I just wish they could see how much I am hurting and how much I am not ready to leave. There is so much left to tell and without them, I know I will have to keep this pain locked inside of me. But what choice do I have? If I refuse to go to foster parents they will send me back to my father, Judy told me as much. The security I had of knowing that they would lock me up in a psychiatric hospital has gone; this has not been mentioned again, as they have found a family that are prepared to take me instead. My only choice now is to bury what I am feeling and go along with their plans because to go back to my father's is a fate worse than death.

They are bringing forward my move because the Prior's want me to go on holiday with them. This is terrible news. I don't want to go but I know I have no choice. I really thought the staff here understood and really cared about me, but now I am not so sure. I am going to have to find a way to deal with this myself. I managed to lock away my feelings for so long I am sure I can do it again. I have come so close to being free from the pain that haunts me and there is no doubt that some of the pain I feel has eased with the love I have been shown here. I have been taught how to love and how to feel good about myself, and if I can hang on to that, then everything else can wait.

Chapter 23

1985 – Aged 15

Moving On to Foster Care

Extract from Staff Communications Book
Date: 15/9/85
Staff: Helen M.

I have seen Tracy six times since she moved in with the Prior's on the 24th July, 1985. Overall, everything is going very well, and there have only been two occasions causing concern since she left Medvale. First, Tracy had visited her Mum, who she had found in a very distressed state, having just discovered that she is pregnant again (fifth child all under six years old). Because of her emotional state, she was telling Tracy very personal details about her relationship with her husband. Consequently, when Tracy left there, she bought some gas and took it to the Regency with her, where she met up with two other children from Medvale and got high herself and gave them some too.

The foster mother contacted me the next morning and I went to see Tracy. She was soon in floods of tears and very ashamed of what she had done. I went through all the bits about Tracy being fifteen and having enough problems of her own without taking Mum's on board too. She was fine at the end of the session and wrote letters of apology to the two Medvale children concerned and to Peter J, whose opinion of her she values very much indeed.

Second, Tracy was on holiday on 2nd August, with foster parents in Devon. They only stayed one week instead of two because of illness of the whole family but, in particular, Tracy, who not only had the family bug, but was complaining of her knee too. I saw her on her return and she seemed fine. Her foster mother is taking her to the doctor about her knee.

Extract from Staff Communications Book
Date: 11/9/85
Staff: Helen M.

Two phone calls from the foster mother before I arrived at work. Tracy was in a very depressed mood and the foster parents were unable to get through to her at all. There was a phone call from school saying that Tracy was not in school today and they were worried if Tracy had a social worker now. They were reassured when I told them that Medvale is still involved and that I would see Tracy that night.

When I arrived at the foster parents, Tracy was in one of her hard-faced moods and all she would say was that she didn't want to be there and wanted to go to live with her Mum. I reminded her of the contract meeting. She did not have one complaint against the foster parents but would not give an inch. Eventually, I took her out to my car and within seconds she was sobbing her heart out.

It transpired that Tracy is missing the physical contact with people from Medvale. She feels that she needs to see me more than once a month. The foster parents are super but don't cuddle her and she needs that. I held her for a long time, let her cry herself out and then talked through the entire Mum bit again. Tracy was fine afterwards. Great with the foster parents when we went back in; she made drinks for everyone and the foster parents are now aware of what was wrong. I will see her weekly for a while. I am collecting her from school on the 16th September and taking her out for the evening.

***

Despite my fear of leaving Medvale, of losing the place I

call home and the people that to me are my family, leaving has made me focus on being independent. I have had to stop my self- destruction and had to bury my desire to kill those around me as much as I can. Helen keeps reassuring me I'll be fine and that I've come a long way, and I'm ready to live with a foster family. However much I trust her, I can't help but feel that I'm not ready for this and that burying the things I'm feeling will not last.

The staff at Medvale have shown me unconditional love and respect and in return have taught me how to love and respect those around me. The fear of losing them, of being rejected or abandoned by the staff at Medvale, help keep me contained and prevent me from spiralling out of control. I can't let them down, if I do, I'm sure they would disown me. This is not to say life is plain sailing.

My foster family are not what I was either expecting or hoping for. I've completed a Form E with Helen in which I stated the qualities and dynamics of the family I would like to live with. I want to be the oldest, with no children around my age. I've always been good with little ones and I know I would be happy in a family where there are younger children, but I don't get on with children my age and certainly don't want or need another big sister. In my foster family, I am the youngest and I have two older sisters. I must admit on meeting them I know straight away that we will get on; they are very kind and yet fun to be with, but it certainly isn't what I would call my ideal family. My foster dad seems fun but keeps his distance, which I really respect, as my history with men a dad that is too hands on would be a recipe for disaster. My foster mum is very straight talking and doesn't take any crap; a strong woman who is friendly, but very matter of fact.

I suppose my Form E is really a reflection of what I envisage life with my Mum to be like; life with the Prior's is very different. They have a boxer dog called Samson who is fantastic, and having always been passionate about animals it is good to live in a home that is equally enthusiastic about pets. I'm even allowed to walk Samson with my foster dad around the orchards in the evening, a special time that I really enjoy and appreciate.

I build a good relationship with the family and respect the fact that they have allowed me to live in their home and share their lives, knowing how bad I've been. It is for this reason that I never want to cause trouble and the emotional distance they keep from me stops me from feeling that I need to kill them.

The most shocking thing for me is the family's relaxed attitude to me drinking alcohol. Having come from a family that rarely drink and with Helen being teetotal and very anti-alcohol, I'm unprepared to be let loose in pubs and at parties. The first party I go to with the family I become friendly with a boy there, and although I've already had a fair bit to drink, they give me permission to go to the pub with this boy. I only have a sip of my cider in the pub before I'm throwing up in the doorway and with total disgust the boy takes me back to the party. My foster mum thinks it's funny and I'm not in trouble, so my taste for alcohol begins. Drinking is much more acceptable to other people than me glue or gas sniffing and the end result is pretty much the same – numbness and relaxation – so it makes sense to me to drink more and sniff less.

Friday nights become my nights to go out and get wrecked with or without my mates from school. I work out the best way to get served in the Prince of Wales, Chatham, is to go in there regularly at lunchtimes, acting confident when I order my brandy and coke, so by the time the weekend comes they can't refuse to serve me as they know me. Not that I often buy my own drinks on a Friday night. I usually buy one to get the evening started but then work my way round the bar, allowing men to chat me up and buy me drinks so that by the time I've circled the bar I'm often too drunk to stand.

I don't worry that I could get myself into trouble; at the end of the day if they want sex for all the drinks they have bought me, then I just oblige. I don't need to worry about getting raped because my theory is that if I let them do it then they can't rape me. My friends always ensure that I go to the train station in time to catch my train and often have to carry me down to the platform. The ticket inspectors get grumpy that I have my railcard clearly stating I am a child, when I am obviously completely drunk but they can't argue.

Helen is still very much involved and thankfully comes to see me regularly, and is still here to bail me out when I screw up, which I often do. I miss her, I miss Medvale, I miss being held and cuddled and being told everything will be okay. One thing my foster family can't give me is the intense affection that I have experienced at Medvale, and I physically crave that closeness. I have endured life with my father without any affection or human closeness and part of me feels that loss again. I continue to sleep with any man that will have me, as I need physical affection and I know that I can get it from them. Seeing Helen and being allowed ocasionally to visit the other staff and children at Medvale, also gives me a chance to soak up the love and affection that I miss so badly.

***

Extract from Staff Communications Book
Date: Staff Log: 2/10/85
Staff: Helen M.

Tracy arrived at Medvale after school unexpectedly looking pale and worried. She said that she didn't want to stay at the Prior's. When we discussed it further, Tracy could not make one complaint against them, except that she couldn't talk to them. Of course, when we looked at it, the problem is Tracy's, because the Prior's are certainly talking to her.

We looked at how long it took Tracy to form relationships when she came into Medvale and how, even today, when she gets depressed, she has to find a reason for it instead of just accepting it for what it is. This time, it is the foster placement. Tracy agreed with all of this but was still not right when she left. I said that I would ring her tomorrow and arrange to see her again as soon as possible.

Extract from Staff Communications Book
Date: 12/10/85
Staff: Helen M.

Tracy was in a much-improved mood at this session. She had a good discussion with the Prior's and her Dad on Thursday (her Dad had just popped in to return Tracy's purse). After seeing me on Wednesday, and saying that she was unable to tell the Prior's about her feelings of not wanting to live there, she then sat and talked it all through with them on Thursday.

Dad at one stage thought that she was saying that she wanted to return to live with him, but it seems that Tracy soon put that right. I was delighted that Tracy had been able to deal with it in the way she did and told her so when I was with her on Saturday. Tracy admits that there is nothing at all wrong with the Prior's; in fact, she is very fond of the whole family. She is able to see that much of her problems stem from her allowing herself to get as down as she does without discussing her feelings.

We talked at length about Tracy's future; independent living, and how she will achieve this eventually and one way she won't is by trying to hide things instead of facing up to them. Tracy was fine when I left her, very warm and close and her depression had lifted completely.

Extract from Staff Communications Book
Date: 9/10/85
Staff: Helen M.

I had a phone call from Peter Pain wanting to discuss last Thursday evening and saying that he didn't think things were working out for Tracy. He was hinting yet again about diet, hair testing, etc. I listened to all that he had to say and then told him that Thursday had been very positive for Tracy and far from things not working out, she was doing very well indeed.

Extract from Staff Communications Book
Date: 16/10/85
Staff: Helen M.

I spoke to Tracy twice on the phone. Her pet mouse had escaped and was run over? Tracy asked to see me and I am collecting her from school tomorrow. Her foster mum says that everything seems to be going really well.

***

My foster mum lets me buy a pet mouse of my very own. I'm allowed to keep him in my bedroom and I'm responsible for feeding, cleaning and playing with him. I have chosen a dark brown one and call him Ben, I know it's the same name as my last mouse but I loved him, and it's like having him back. This Ben is happy to be held and runs through my fingers with his little pink tail curling around my fingers for support. I love everything about him, the way he feels so silky smooth and the way he smells. I take him out every day and let him run as free as I can in my room, careful that he doesn't escape because I don't want him to come to any harm. I love him so much. He tickles my face with his whiskers when he comes up to sniff me; he is just the cutest little mouse in the whole world.

I can't explain why but after a few weeks I set him free out of the window. I watch him for a while running around and around on top of the porch roof, but then can't bear to watch as I don't want to see him fall. When I check later, he has vanished and what I have done hits me like a sledgehammer. How could I be so cruel?

I race downstairs and start scouring the garden; he must

be here, he can't have gone far. It is hard to see through the tears, the guilt tearing me up inside as I continue to search for him. Gina joins in and I appreciate her help. I just want him back. We search for what seems like hours, even joining Barry on Samson's walk around the orchard, hunting and calling Ben but he is nowhere to be seen. I feel dead inside when we return and see him squashed flat on the road. Gina picks him up and we take him home to bury him. I feel numb and I don't understand how I have done this again. What is wrong with me?

***

Extract from Staff Communications Book
Date: 23/10/85
Staff: Helen M.

I had contact with the head of Tracy's school saying that she and three other girls had absconded from school on Monday 21st October, 1985, and consequently they had missed a vital meeting finalising the last details for the Paris trip on 25th October, 1985. The school staff taking the children abroad had refused to take Tracy and the others. I saw Tracy and she accepted this. The school refunded the money and we refunded the twenty pounds, which her father had contributed.

***

I am so pissed off. Some bitches from school have told the teacher that I was smoking and selling dope at school, so I've been banned from going on the French trip. They reckon they can't trust me! I wouldn't mind but I wasn't even doing anything; they always think I'm on drugs even when I haven't taken anything. I'm so fed up with their attitude like I would be stupid enough to take stuff abroad with me. It's good to know they think so highly of me.

Anyway, I have bigger fish to fry. I'm sure my period

222

is late, and although I have thought many times before that I may be pregnant, this is different and I am sure I am. I know the baby's father won't want to know; he is just some soldier that got off screwing a kid. I won't get him in trouble for my own mistakes, and anyway, this baby may be a mistake but that doesn't mean that I won't love it with all my heart. I know I will be a good mum. I will never leave my children whatever happens. I'm not sure how I'll be able to keep it, especially as I can't get a job or anything at my age but other people do, so there must be a way. I have confided in a few friends but no one seems to have any answers.

I lay my hand on my tummy often, imaging my baby growing underneath my fingers. I know it is a girl. I can feel her. I just have to keep this secret for as long as I can.

***

Extract from Staff Communications Book
Date: 30/10/85
Staff: Helen M.

I saw Tracy and as already noted she confirmed in our session that she suspected that she was two months pregnant. She refused to name the father. We talked about her options and Tracy said that she wanted an abortion. I then returned her to her foster parents and brought them up-to-date on the current position. I arranged to collect a urine specimen the next morning to have it tested and to see Tracy to give her the results after school.

Extract from Staff Communications Book
Date: 31/10/85
Staff: Helen M.

I had a chat with the foster Mum when I collected the urine specimen. She seems to be very in tune with where Tracy is at and the sort of commitment needed to get her through this. The urine test was positive. I informed the foster mum. Tracy came in and was shattered by the confirmation of her pregnancy. She was very concerned as to whether Dad needs to know or not. I was unable to tell her, as the legal department had not confirmed it.

She stated once again that she wanted an abortion and was very depressed and young when I returned her to her foster home, constantly seeking my hand to hold. Her foster parents were very caring and supportive when I returned her there after the session. The foster Mum had made an appointment with the doctor for the next morning and, following this visit, an appointment was made at All Saints Hospital on Wednesday 6th November. The foster Mum and I will take Tracy.

Extract from Staff Communications Book
Date: 3/11/85
Staff: Helen M.

I informed Tracy of the advice from our Legal Department and arranged to take her to see Dad that evening. I had previously rang him and arranged the visit for 6.00pm.

Tracy was unable to tell Dad when we got there and I very briefly explained the reason for our visit. Dad was stunned but kept very calm and dealt with the whole business in a very caring way. At one stage, he was very near to tears and Tracy was weeping openly. He talked to Tracy at length about her future, unwanted pregnancy, etc. and we were able to tell him about the appointment at the hospital for the 6th November. Dad encouraged the abortion very strongly and in a very positive way. I told Mr Pain that I would keep him informed about the arrangements and that he would probably be needed to sign a medical consent for the abortion. He agreed to come to the hospital at short notice to do this.

***

224

I don't know who grassed on me but Helen knows that I think I am pregnant. She wants to know who the baby's Dad is but I won't tell her. It's not his fault, and he doesn't even know I am pregnant. She's my baby. Helen wants me to get rid of it; she says that if I have an abortion at the moment it will be just like a heavy period, just a bunch of blood and cells, not a baby at all. Part of me doesn't believe her, but I guess I just don't want to, I want to have a baby more than anything in the world.

Helen talks through how impossible it will be for me to support a baby, with no money and not being old enough to work and support myself. She tells me how awful mother and baby units are and even suggests we visit one so I can see just how difficult my life would be. She knows just how to wear me down and makes me agree with her and in the end, I agree to have an abortion. I really don't see that I have a choice.

I am still shocked when the pregnancy test comes back positive; part of me thought I must be wrong, but the wheels are in motion now so I roll along with them, doctors and hospitals, everyone so nice even though I am murdering my baby.

I am terrified that Helen will tell my Dad. I know he will be furious but again I have no choice, he is my Dad after all, and he has a right to know. He makes it very clear that abortion is the only way forward; as far as he is concerned I have broken the law by having sex under the age of sixteen, so I should not be allowed to have the baby. I hate him.

***

I'm an abortion, I live in a jar,
They gave my father a caution
My mother a scar
Abortion is murder
Murder's a crime
How could they abort me?

225

Did I have to die?
Accidents happen
They always will.
But please don't abort children
Unless they are ill.

Tracy Pain Aged 15

***

Extract from Staff Communications Book
Date: 6/11/85
Staff: Helen M.

I collected Tracy at 7.15am. She seemed very calm and was quite chatty on the way to the hospital. The staff were super towards her and allowed me to stay with her and walk to the theatre beside the trolley. She came round very quickly from the anaesthetic and was not in any pain or discomfort. She ate a light lunch and left hospital at approximately 3.30pm. Antibiotics were given.

Once again, she was fine on the journey back to her foster parents. She kept close to me, holding my hand and thanking me for being with her. I settled her back with her foster parents and she was fine when I left. I rang Mr Pain who was very relieved that everything had gone well and that it was all over now. Tracy is going to Somerset with him this weekend.

***

Martina and Barry are being very kind, no pressure, no judgement, just there looking after me. The night before we go to the hospital we go to the pub for a darts match as normal and that is just it, everything is normal, no fuss, and no atmosphere. It makes me feel safe and okay about what I am doing, not happy; in fact, deeply sad but I know it is the right thing. I know Helen is right and I am not capable of looking after my baby.

I am surprised at how little it hurts after the abortion; I don't even have a tummy ache. I wish it hurt. I deserve to hurt for what I have done, but by now I'm good at dealing out my own self-punishments and with a shard of glass, I let my baby know how sorry I am.

A trip to Somerset with Dad, Carole and Debbie is weird without Bert to run to. I don't fit in here, with this family. I can tell that they don't particularly like me. There is always a tension in the air where people are afraid to say what they think, where no one can relax and be themselves because everything is for show. A family full of falseness and hypocrites. I get treated like a slag although I am not the only one in my extended family to have an abortion, yet some other people can't do anything wrong. It's funny the things I learn about my family through my Mum, who knows first-hand how hypocritical they all are, how closed-minded they can be, and how certain family members are favoured. I always have a lot of respect for the honesty and respect my Mum shows me.

***

Extract from Staff Communications Book
Date: 19/11/85
Staff: Helen M.

I spoke to the foster mum this afternoon who said that Tracy is in a funny mood since she returned from Somerset on Sunday.

I saw Peter Pain and as I suspected, he wanted to talk about this diet for Tracy. I told him that it was entirely up to Tracy – if she wanted to go on it and he was prepared to provide all of the necessary foods, then that was fine. I had already discussed it with Tracy's foster Mum and she was in agreement with this too.

Peter had the wind taken out of his sails as he had expected to have a battle on his hands. I reminded him not to be surprised if 1) Tracy refused or 2) she agreed and then only stuck it for a short while. I spent about an hour with him discussing things in general. Tracy is spending Christmas day and sleeping over at his house this year. We spoke about the week in Somerset and Peter said that it had been a good visit with no problems at all.

***

Meanwhile life with the Prior's continues and in lots of ways, I feel I'm being given the chance to live the life of a 'normal' teenager. When the parents go out, Gina and I raid the drinks cabinet and Gina makes me hot toddy's, purely for medicinal purposes! We have fun and can relax and mess about, and most of the time get on how I imagine most sisters do. It makes me realise how damaged my relationship with Debbie is and makes me wish there was a way of repairing our relationship, so we can spend time relaxing and enjoying ourselves. My gripes with Martina are usually about rules that I think are pointless but to her seem like major issues. However, I guess this is probably true of most teenagers; I feel grown-up and resent being treated like a child.

***

Extract from Staff Communications Book
Date: 1/12/85
Staff: Helen M.

I had a meal with Tracy. She looked super, dressed in lovely clothes and make-up. She is a bit concerned that her father may be expecting her to go home to live with him eventually, and because their relationship has improved, she is worried that he will be hurt if she mentions to him that her feelings have not changed and that she does not want to return home to live. I asked her if she wanted me to have a word with him and she said no, she needed to be able to do that herself. Tracy was okay and behaved in a mature manner about the situation.

Chapter 24

1985–1986 – Aged 15–16.

A Change of Heart

Extract from Staff Communications Book
Date: 9/1/86
Staff: Helen M.

Tracy rang me on the 7th January and told me that she wanted to return home to live with her Dad. Because she had actually got to this point many times in the past and then changed her mind within the space of a few days, I asked her to come into Medvale on the 8th January so that we could discuss it in more detail.

On the 2nd January, I spoke to Tracy's foster mother and she said that Tracy had discussed it with her and seemed to be serious in what she was saying. I then rang and spoke to Mr Pain. He was understandably very pleased when Tracy had asked him on the previous Sunday if he would have her back to live at home.

I had told Tracy, foster mother and Mr Pain that the decision for Tracy to return home would be made at a statutory review. This will take place on the 21st February.

It would be a slow re-introduction to the family to enable everyone to be sure that the right decision was being made and that other than an occasional overnight stay from Saturday through to Sunday, longer stays would not commence until after the review. Everyone is in agreement with this.

Mr Pain was saying how mature and open Tracy has become. She now has a very good relationship with him and his cohabitee and gets on superbly with her sister, Debbie.

The family are going on holiday to Spain on the 27th June after Tracy completes her O level exams and all being well, we would hope to have Tracy living permanently at home a week or so before then.

I suspected some manipulation on Tracy's part. At the last contract meeting, she had fully expected to be told we would allow her to move into some form of independent living after her sixteenth birthday. In fact, she was told this would not even be considered until her seventeenth birthday was pending and she was none too pleased about this. However, when I saw her last night, Tracy was talking and acting in a very mature and sensible way of going home to live, and I was left feeling that she was indeed being genuine.

I have spoken to Dad and the foster Mum again today and told them the outcome of the discussion with Tracy.

Extract from Staff Communications Book
Date: 27/1/86
Staff: Helen M.

When I returned from leave on January 27th, there was written communication from Terry Barrett saying that he needed an urgent meeting on Tracy because there were problems in the foster family.

I spoke to Martina, and she was saying that she was finding that Tracy's father seemed to be wanting far more contact with Tracy than had been agreed. Martina was also feeling that every time Tracy had been home for the weekend, when she returned, Martina was picking up an awful lot of stick from her. She tackled Tracy about this and said to Tracy that she wasn't prepared to put up with it and she felt that this meeting was necessary too, urgently, so that the whole situation could be addressed.

I became concerned when it became apparent that the expectation of the meeting and K.F.P.S. was that Peter Pain should be involved in it. Peter Pain himself rang me that day asking me to confirm that he was expected at the *meeting and my reply to him was that I didn't anticipate his presence there because the problems were experienced between the foster parents and Tracy, and therefore should only involve K.F.P.S and myself.*

However, when I later spoke to Tracy she too felt that her father was going to be at the meeting and she was talking about things like Martina and Barry suggesting that Tracy should go home for a month to get the honeymoon period out of the way. I was very surprised about this and had another conversation with Martina. She was saying that she had said this to Tracy because Martina and Barry had become convinced that this move home would not be good for Tracy. They felt that if it were going to break down, it should break down sooner rather than later.

Later on that day, I spoke to Terry Barrett, K.F.P.S., and he suggested that we hold a contract meeting. I told Terry that I wasn't happy about this as Tracy's contract meeting was planned for the same day as the statutory review which is February 21st. I couldn't see that anything had happened to bring on this contract meeting sooner, and I wasn't prepared to discuss Tracy's future outside of a statutory review, which had already been agreed by all concerned at the last contract meeting. Eventually, Terry was able to see my point of view and the meeting was cancelled. I informed Peter Pain and left it that we would discuss Tracy's future at a statutory review.

Peter Pain is quite happy with this and we went on to talk about Tracy's stays at home. He feels that Tracy has matured in all areas and he is very pleased with the response he is getting from her towards himself, her natural sister, Debbie and his cohabitee, Carole. He is still in full agreement that this return home needs to be done slowly over a period of time. That as was agreed at Tracy's last contract meeting, the envisaged time of return home would be in June after Tracy's exams and just prior to when the family go on holiday to Spain together.

I had a session with Tracy and she seemed quite happy and bright. She openly admitted that she had had some problems with Martina and Barry, but Tracy put this down to the fact that she is studying hard for exams and is feeling very insecure about being capable of taking the exams and insisting that it was in no way to do with her return home.

She was honest about the fact that at one stage, she actually wanted to return home straight away but she now sees the sense in a long re-introduction and doesn't want to move quicker because she feels that this decision is very big and she wants to be absolutely sure that it is the right one for her. It was a good session with Tracy. I thought that she was very mature.

***

Christmas with my foster parents is a strange affair and very different from the Christmases that I have been used to. Father Christmas still comes as he has done since I was tiny but he doesn't deliver my presents to the foot of my bed. Instead, they are in Barry and Martina's bedroom. I have a present from my Mum to unwrap, which is the cosiest, most snuggly, striped, dressing gown. It means a lot, especially as I won't be seeing her until Boxing Day. Dad collects me and I stay the night at his house. The whole Christmas feels strange but not unpleasant and I can honestly say that I have a good time. My relationship with Dad, Carole and Debbie is better than it has been in a long while, and although I am not entirely relaxed, I am as comfortable as I ever remember being with them.

I know Dad thinks I should come home; he hasn't said anything directly but seems to hint at it and how much better things are – I am. Sitting in the back of the car after

233

another visit to his house, I watch the back of his head and his profile in the mirror. He seems sad and I want so much to please him. I blurt out that I want to come home, not sure what reaction I was expecting but not prepared for the cold, measured response I receive. He says he wants to be sure I mean it before he can be pleased about it. I try desperately to reassure him. I just want him to be pleased with me, to make him happy.

The news is just as cautiously received with Carole and Debbie, which makes me more adamant that this is what I want and that I am going to make it work. I can't deny that I was hoping everyone would be pleased and I was not expecting such a guarded response. The alarm bells that keep starting up in my head I squash before they have a chance to take shape, this isn't what I was expecting but to accept that I have made a monumental mistake is something I am not ready to consider.

My foster parents are not happy at all with the idea of me going home; they are convinced it won't work, and even Helen receives the news with caution, sure that given a few days I will change my mind. Their lack of support for my decision only makes me more determined to go through with it. I don't like to be wrong and I won't consider for one moment that they could all be right.

Eventually, I manage to convince them all that I am serious and that this is something I want to happen. It is only when this is done and the ball starts rolling towards the inevitable planned move that I give myself time to relax, and with that comes the time to reflect and ponder on the decision I have made.

***

Extract from Staff Communications Book
Date: 12/2/86
Staff: Helen M.

Tracy was talking quite unrealistically about staying on at school into the sixth form to take an A level in needlework and an extra O-level. She did understand, however, that the school, because of past problems, might not want to view that with much sympathy.

I had a conversation with Tracy's form tutor from Rochester Grammar school and she was saying her personal feelings about Tracy staying on to the sixth form to do an A level and she said that, just off the top of her head, she would prefer it very much if Tracy didn't. However, she understands the final decision will be with Miss Trollope.

***

As I am nearing the end of my time at school, I begin to realise just how much I like it here. They know me so well and I can do pretty much whatever I please, which I know I have taken advantage of over the years but it has given me the stability I needed to get me through the tough times that I have had. The thought of leaving fills me with dread and I am pleased when my Art teacher and my Needlework teacher, both say that based on my mock exams, I should be able to take A levels in their subjects. This means I could stay on at sixth form and I won't have to leave at all.

When I mention it to Helen, she doesn't seem to believe me and so I make a point of visiting my careers teacher, who blatantly tells me that there is no way I could take A levels as I am not clever enough. I am fuming; how dare she lie to me? I tell her as much and say that if it is because of my past behaviour then she should just admit it. That I can accept, I have been a bitch at school. I have disrupted lessons, been rude and disrespectful to teachers and even bullied other children, and that's when I bother to turn up, so I can totally understand why they wouldn't want me to stay on. But, to say I am not clever enough when I so clearly am, is totally out of order.

My careers teacher asks what I would like to do when I

leave school and I tell her that I want to get married and have children. She scoffs that this isn't a career and suggests I look at working in a bank or as a secretary. I give up with her narrow mindedness and grimly accept that I am going to have to leave school. Deep inside I know I want to be a mother more than anything else in the whole world, and this is a dream that I will strive to fulfil.

***

Extract from Staff Communications Book
Date: 3/3/86
Staff: Helen M.

Tracy rang and arranged to come in to see me at Medvale today. She said that she has decided that she doesn't want to return home to live. The only reason she gave was that her prospective stepmother was too friendly. Tracy says that she has been buying her loads of presents and her expectations of her are high in so much as she wants her to go shopping every weekend and Tracy is feeling quite peeved as she wanted to spend time with her own friends. She said that she just decided that she wasn't going to go home as it just wouldn't work out. I told Tracy that nothing was going to change for the next four weeks anyhow, and we would go along the same path that we decided at her review and she would be going home on a weekend basis.

***

As the plans for me to move home move forward, I begin to realise what a huge mistake I have made. Although a lot has changed and having Carole on the scene is much better than my father's first wife, Tracey, the house and the emotions are still the same. The carpet is still burnt from the first fire I set and is a constant reminder of the unhappiness that permeates the very fibre of the house.

Everyone in the house seems to live in their own little bubble. Debbie trying to stay out as much as she can; Dad working all hours so he too doesn't have to face the realities of life at home, and Carole, desperately wanting everything to work. Trying to smother the tentacles of despair as they ooze from the walls like a disease threatening to infect every occupant.

In an effort to show me that this can work, Carole showers me with gifts and takes me shopping, trying to build a relationship with me that I can only view with distrust. I'm not worthy of her attention and feel it is a reflection of the falseness so prevalent in our family.

I don't take the decision to not go home lightly. I spend many nights pondering on whether there is any chance of making this work if only to make my father happy again. But I can't reach a solution, so I decide to tell Helen, however, I'm unprepared for her negative response. I really thought she would understand; she was so unsure too when I first said about going home and now she is angry that I have changed my mind. She says that I can't keep doing this to people, that she won't let me keep doing this and that this time I've made my bed and I must lie in it.

I'm shocked and unsure how to proceed. I know this is not right and I know that I will never be truly happy living back with my father, but if Helen won't listen, then who else is there?

I continue with the plan as I have been told to, and eventually submerging myself in the practicalities of moving, help push the nagging doubts to the back of my mind.

***

Extract from Staff Communications Book
Date: 10/4/86
Staff: Helen M.

I have spoken to Tracy twice on the phone since my last visit and all seems to be going well, in terms of her still preparing to go home to live. I had also spoken to Tracy's Dad several times and he was quite pleased with the way things were going too.

Tracy said that since she stopped vacillating about what she was going to do, whether she was going home or not, she is much calmer in herself. She is enjoying her time at home and each week she goes she takes a bit more of her stuff and her gerbil is now residing at Dad's. She said that everything as far as she is concerned is going well with her foster parents and she couldn't really discuss any problems because there weren't any. In Tracy's opinion, the foster family are finding it difficult knowing that she is preparing to move out.

Extract from Staff Communications Book
Date: 7/5/86
Staff: Helen M.

I had a phone call today from Tracy unexpectedly asking me if she could come up to Medvale to see me. She arrived just after teatime and it was quite obvious that she had worked herself up into a fine old state before she came here. I hadn't actually seen Tracy in this sort of state for a good while before her leaving Medvale. Up until now, all of her visits home to her Dad had presumably been going very well. I had been in contact with her foster parents; I had been in contact with Tracy and I had been in contact with Tracy's Dad, and everybody was giving a very favourable response to what was going on there.

Consequently, I was very surprised when Tracy said that she didn't want to go home to live with her Dad; she wasn't going to go home to live with her Dad and that was the end of that story. All of this, as I say, was said in a very angry, dogmatic, abusive and aggressive way and Tracy was switched off, as she used to be in the old days, to anything that I was saying back to her in response to this. I asked Tracy to give me a reason why she wasn't going home and out of at least two dozen questions she couldn't give one positive answer as to there being any reason whatsoever.

Tracy was getting more and more out of control and eventually added in the fact that her boyfriend, Peter, whom she had been seeing quite seriously for some months now, had packed her in on Monday. As soon as I heard this, I was aware then that the breakup of this relationship was the instigating factor of her not wanting to go home. I actually mentioned this to Tracy and she denied it at first, but then admitted that this had caused her a great deal of upset.

As the session progressed, it became more and more obvious that Tracy wasn't hearing anything I was saying. She wasn't prepared to give an inch. She was becoming increasingly angry and in the end, there was no way I could put her right and she was ready to go. I checked that she had her fares and that she was going straight back to her foster placement, and then she left Medvale.

I felt pretty confident that Tracy wouldn't actually arrive back at her foster placement, so I rang her foster Mum, told her what had gone on in the session and told her to contact me as soon as Tracy arrived back home.

Martina rang at 8.20pm asking what time Tracy had left because she still hadn't arrived. I said that she should have arrived home long before now. We agreed that we would give it till 11.00pm and if Tracy hadn't arrived home by then, then I would report her missing to the Rochester Police.

At 9.40pm, I checked with Tracy's Dad and with her Mum to ask if she had called in there at all and she hadn't. At 11.00pm, I checked again with the foster parents and they hadn't had any contact with Tracy and she still hadn't arrived home. I then contacted Rochester Police and at midnight, we had two police officers from the missing persons to the house to take Tracy's details. I gave the police my home phone number and asked to be contacted as soon as they had any news.

I was contacted at 12.30am by Ross from Medvale, who said that Tracy had just rung in from Chatham Station. He told her to stay there until somebody went to collect her.

I went down to Chatham and collected Tracy and rang Medvale to tell them that I had got her and they cancelled the missing persons. Tracy was still looking as angry and as bitter and upset as when she had left Medvale. We did very little talking on the way back to her foster home. I had phoned the foster parents to say that I was collecting her from the station and that I was on my way back with her. Tracy claimed that she had visited her friend, Mandy, and that she had spent time walking around the Pentagon and sitting on the stairs in the Pentagon by the car park, which is one of Tracy's old haunts i.e. the Pentagon roof top.

Her foster Mum was waiting up for us when we got back with a cup of tea, and we sat in the lounge with Tracy and went over everything with Tracy again, and again, and again. Tracy was maintaining that she wasn't happy in her foster home either and it was a classic return, if you like, to the old Tracy tonight. Martina was hurt by what Tracy was saying but she coped very well indeed with it.

I told Tracy that the time had arrived when she actually had to be responsible for some of her own actions. That I wasn't just going to do what she was bidding me and that was, 'I don't want to go home – tell my father.' That the plans would go ahead as arranged and what Tracy should have been doing and what she needed to be doing was talking to people about any problems she was having. Of course, the reality of that is that Tracy wasn't having any problems until her boyfriend actually finished their relationship. I didn't leave the foster home until 2.45am and I told Martina to contact me if there were any more problems.

***

As my move home becomes imminent, the fear and panic

240

increase in intensity. I know that I only have myself to blame and that I should never have said I would go home but I don't know what to do. I'll never be able to get my father to love me or forgive me and when all I want is to be loved and cared for, going home feels like I'm sealing my own coffin. I'm upset that I have split up with my boyfriend, but all this has done is make me realise how alone I will be when I go home.

They don't care about me; they don't even know me really. I must make Helen realise that this is wrong before it is too late. But when I talk to her it falls on deaf ears and all she can do is say I am being silly, trying to justify my fears and ignoring the one burning fact – I tried to kill him. I didn't do it for fun or for attention; I did it because I hate him and I always will.

I can't go back to my foster home. I am too angry and inside I just want to explode, so I walk to Chatham and spend some time sitting on top of the Pentagon car park. I haven't been here for a while, but at least here I can be alone with my anger and there is always glass around to bring me back to reality. When I have finished punishing myself for the pain I am causing others, I ring Medvale and I'm told to wait for Helen to come and get me.

Helen is angry, I am angry and eventually she leaves me with my foster family who also seem angry. The fact that she came and got me in the middle of the night is not lost on me though and I spend a lot of the night contemplating how much she must really care about me to have done that. I don't want to let her down, and however much I don't want to go home, I don't want Helen to be disappointed in me. I never want to take the chance that she will give up and walk away from me, and I know I have pushed her to the limit. I owe her so much that the least I can do is to knuckle down and try my best to make this work.

***

Extract from Staff Communications Book
Date: 8/5/86
Staff: Helen M.

Tracy arrived at Medvale about 4.00 pm and she was very different again. She was soft, apologetic, very, very upset about the way she had behaved yesterday and the anxiety she had caused to everybody and admitting that the major problem was the boyfriend finishing their relationship. She was able to say that she did have fears about returning home to live but again was able to understand, when we talked them through, that it was acceptable and understandable. That after an absence of three years it was natural that she would have many fears and the only way to dispel them was to talk about them to me, to her foster parents and, in particular, to her father, his cohabitee and to her sister.

At the end of our session, Tracy was able to come on my lap and she cried very, very genuinely and took care in a very good way. She stayed and had tea at Medvale and for about half an hour afterwards and then she returned to her foster parents.

I told Tracy that I would see her at her Dad's tomorrow evening for a meeting between the whole family, where we would go through all these fears of hers.

***

I go back to see Helen the next day to apologise and hopefully to make her realise that I never meant to worry her. That I need her and that I will do everything I can to keep her from walking away from me and leaving me to face life with my father alone.

***

242

Very good family meeting at the Pain house. Tracy was able to be honest with her Dad about her fears regarding her return home to live. Dad, surprisingly, responded very well to Tracy. He himself pointed out that the last time Tracy was at home was when she was thirteen and a half years old, and he accordingly treated her as a thirteen-year-old, so it was unlikely that at sixteen, he was going to do the same sorts of things this time round. I pointed out that since Tracy's time at Medvale she wasn't the only one who had worked; her Dad had attended family sessions for a year, and he had done a lot of work in those sessions, too. Consequently, he was aware of the errors he had made in the past.

Carol, Dad's cohabitee, contributed quite a lot to the family meeting. It was quite apparent that she has a very good relationship with Tracy and she wants Tracy's return home to be successful. Debbie, Tracy's sister, on the other hand, was very ill at ease. It soon became clear to me that this had nothing to do with her relationship with Tracy; it was mainly because she does not have a good relationship with Dad's cohabitee, which was evident. Debbie was able to say that she and Tracy get on better now than they had ever done in their lives and she was looking forward to her returning home and hopes that that will go ahead as planned.

Tracy was feeling relieved at the end of the session. She had been open with everybody and I think that talking it through with her family, made her realise that the fears she was feeling were natural, as I had been telling her, and that everything would be okay but that what she had to do was trust herself as much as trust her family.

Her return home date continues to be 21st June.

243

Extract from Staff Communications Book
Date: 15/6/86
Staff: Helen M.

I had a telephone conversation with Tracy and she had already made it clear to me that she wanted me to move her when she returned home permanently on Saturday 21st June. She said her father was working but mainly she felt that her foster Mum and foster sisters were going to find it difficult for her leaving and she wanted some support from me. I agreed to collect Tracy from her foster parents at 10.00am on Saturday 21st June.

Chapter 25

1986 – Aged 16

Home, Holidays and Hurt

Extract from Staff Communications Book
Date: 21/6/86
Staff: Helen M.

I arrived at the Prior's at 10.00am today and found Tracy quite cheerful with all her stuff ready and waiting. Foster Mum was clearly distressed and emotional and she said that this was the worst parting from a foster child that she had had to date. We had a cup of coffee and a chat about different bits and pieces to try, and make the parting a bit easier. The foster Mum was absolutely delighted because Tracy's Dad had given Tracy the money to have a bouquet of flowers sent to the foster parents as a thank you through Interflora. Martina was clearly pleased and proud with this. Tracy had her usual number of boxes and bags, and her brand new suitcase, and it didn't take long to load the car and we were off.

Step-Mum was waiting at the door when we got there and was obviously delighted to see Tracy. It was a nice relaxed atmosphere around as we unpacked Tracy's stuff into the hall, and I left Tracy and step-Mum to arrange that in her bedroom. Tracy knows that if there are any problems at all she is to contact me here at Medvale and she may well be coming in to see me before she goes on holiday next week.

Overall today, Tracy has acted with maturity and appears to be happy and content. She seems to be quite positive that this is the right step for her now – returning home to live.

During the course of being on leave for a week Lacey, an ex-Medvale child, contacted Medvale and asked to talk to me regarding Tracy. She said that Tracy had told her that she was pregnant and Lacey was very worried about the outcome because her pregnancy was moving on. Tracy had told Lacey that she had stopped taking the pill a couple of months before and this was when she had become pregnant. The boy concerned was a twenty-year-old named Trevor.

I rang Tracy and arranged for her to come into Medvale to see me that same day. She said that she had not been feeling too well and that she had been having problems with the pill, for which she had been to the GP. She claimed that the doctor told her after she missed one period to leave it for another month, and if she missed a second period, to go back and see him again. She had done this and a urine specimen had been sent off. Tracy claimed that she had in fact never missed taking the pill, only one night when she had forgotten, but had taken it the next morning.

On the same day, I had had a conversation with her father, Peter Pain. They had just returned from their holiday in Spain and he said that Tracy spent a lot of her time in the hotel bedroom because it was too hot for her and the sun was making her feel sick. He did say that her behaviour had been superb and she seemed to enjoy the holiday, the evening bits, and she hadn't caused any problems at all.

I talked to Tracy about the Medvale holiday that's happening on the 8th August and which she was supposed to be coming on with us. She said that she was still looking forward to that providing the weather wasn't too hot etc. I told Tracy that I would ring her again when she had the urine result through and we would act accordingly.

During the whole session, Tracy remained positive that she was not pregnant. However, I felt positive that she was.

***

Now school is over and everyone at home is at work, I find myself with a lot of free time. Lonely time as I am not used to being all on my own so much. Luckily, Lacey lives close by and I spend a lot of my days and some evenings with her and her family. There is always lots going on and with lots of people around, I can lose myself in the hustle and bustle of family life, even if it isn't my family. They seem to accept me for who I am and always make me feel welcome whatever else may be happening.

I go on my first holiday abroad to Spain, with Dad, Carole, Debbie and her boyfriend, Martin. I get to share a room with Debbie and Martin, and with Dad and Carole on their honeymoon, I am definitely the holiday gooseberry. Fortunately, they are all preoccupied with their own lives to pay me much attention. I struggled with the heat as it makes me feel so sick but I know it's not just the heat.

I haven't had my period and I am sure I am pregnant again. Food is another problem as there is very little here that tastes like normal food, but I'm not sure if this is just another symptom of my pregnancy. I have a lot of freedom on holiday and I'm allowed to go to the nightclub in the evenings, but even my suspected pregnancy doesn't stop me getting involved with a local man. After that, I couldn't wait for the holiday to be over and used the heat and my sickness as excuses to stay in my room as much as I could.

After my holiday in Spain, I confide in Lacey that I have missed my period and we talk a lot about what I need to do to keep my baby this time. I am adamant that I want to keep her, and Lacey has been helpful in trying to find out what money I could get to help me look after the baby. She even spoke to the baby's Dad and gave him a right mouthful when he said he didn't want to know. I know she wants me to tell my family, but I don't want to take the chance that they will force me to get rid of it. I don't think I could go through that again.

***

Extract from Staff Communications Book
Date: 23/7/86
Staff: Helen M.

I rang the surgery again this morning and established that Tracy's urine specimen results were back and that in fact it was positive. I spoke to the doctor's receptionist about where we go from here in terms of Tracy, and without talking to Tracy and her parents, she would need to be seen by a doctor down there, if she is wanting an abortion.

I then managed to track Tracy down at Lacey's house, where I was met with aggressive interaction from her to me. Yes, she is pregnant, none of my business, she told her father last night, her father had called her a slut, whore, etc., etc. and made it quite clear that he didn't want her living at home and that she needed to be talking to her social worker.

Following my conversation with Tracy, I spoke to Lacey, who herself was very upset about some of the things that Tracy had told her that her father had said about Lacey's family and how Tracy's situation was because of the company she was keeping. Lacey was very, very upset by this.

I then spoke to Peter Pain very briefly about the current situation and made an appointment to see him at his home with Tracy tomorrow morning at 9.30am.

I rang Tracy back and told her the arrangements. Again, she switched right off about the whole situation. Needless to say that Tracy will now not be coming on the Medvale holiday to France, as there is no way we could be responsible for someone who may well be three months' pregnant.

Extract from Staff Communications Book
Date: 24/7/86
Staff: Helen M.

I got round to the Pains' house at about 9.10am. I purposely did this so I would have a chance to talk to Tracy on her own before her Dad came in for 9.30am. Tracy was hard-faced and very reserved when I got there and wasn't really wanting to talk about anything much. I merely pointed out the realities of the situation to her and told her that the choice would be hers this time round.

I did tell her that emotionally she was in no way ready to have a baby and her proposals for how she was going to finance the baby and herself were ludicrous to put it mildly. I suggested to her that she hadn't really given any serious thought to the fact that she would be living on her own with this baby. I also told Tracy that due to her past record, the time she was in Medvale and indeed her time prior to coming into Medvale, her attitude was to hurt everything she loved i.e. attempted to murder her father and family prior to being admitted here. She had killed her pet mouse which she loved very much, but when she was cornered and didn't think the mouse was getting a good deal, the easy way out for Tracy was to kill it.

It would be my fear that if Tracy actually produced a baby, then the very same thing would end up happening to the baby as happened to the mouse. I would have to put this in writing because, in my opinion, that would be one baby that would need a reception into care at birth.

Tracy's Dad arrived home and he was very calm and caring towards Tracy considering the circumstances. However, he made it very clear that he and Carole would be giving Tracy all the support they could, providing she wasn't actually wanting to dump a baby on top of them. Initially, Tracy was saying that she wanted to keep the baby but eventually she started crying and she said that she saw the futility of it all, that there was no way she could manage a baby, and that she would have an abortion. I told her father that this time round I very much wanted him and his wife to be involved in the organising and the caring for Tracy during and after the abortion.

Tracy actually seemed very relieved after she had cried and had taken care from me. She seemed relieved that she had made a decision. She still maintains that she took the pill regularly and I don't think she is going to deviate from that but the actual timing of pregnancy can't be set; she could be two months, she could be two and a half months, she could actually be less than two months pregnant. I have asked Peter Pain to ring me if there are any problems concerning the hospital appointment.

I have told Tracy that if the abortion happens early next week and she is feeling fit enough, there is no reason why she can't join us for the Medvale holiday as already planned. Hopefully, it would be beneficial for her too, as she would be surrounded by people from Medvale whom she knows and who care about her, and it would get her out of the environment for a little while anyhow. Hopefully, it would help her to get over the trauma of the abortion.

***

The positive result from the doctor doesn't bring with it the joy it was meant to, as now Helen knows and my father knows and the shit has really hit the fan. My father thinks that I am a slut and he doesn't even know the half of it. He has made it very clear that he wants nothing to do with me or the baby. So much for being sixteen…last time his excuse was that I had broken the law, and this time he is showing his true colours. He thinks I am a whore who deserves everything she gets.

Helen has said it is my choice, but then added that if I keep the baby, it will be taken away for its own safety as she knows that I will kill it once I realise I can't look after it properly. When she says this I know she is right; I try to kill everything close to me and as much as I tell myself that my baby will be different, I know it's not. Helen tries to say that it is my way of stopping things I care for from getting hurt, as they can't be hurt if they are dead. Either way they die at my hands. It's funny really that it's okay to murder my baby now when no one can see her, and yet if I have her, she will be taken away just in case I kill her.

The bottom line comes when Helen says that if my father says he is prepared to support the baby and me then I will be allowed to keep her. He refuses and says that there is no way he is prepared to support my baby and me. Let's not forget though, this is my choice!

So, another abortion is booked and this time Helen thinks my father should come with me; luckily, he is far too busy to stay at the hospital with me and just drops me off and picks me up afterwards. It saves us having to talk to each other and allows me time to grieve on my own for the second baby I have killed.

***

Extract from Staff Communications Book
Date: 31/7/86
Staff: Helen M.

I spoke to Tracy today; the abortion had taken place and she was feeling okay – a little bit uncomfortable with tummy pains but otherwise fine.

Extract from Staff Communications Book
Date: 7/8/86
Staff: Helen M.

Tracy's Dad brought her round to Medvale at 8.00pm tonight. She will be spending the night at Medvale prior to us leaving for the Medvale holiday to France very early in the morning.

Extract from Staff Communications Book

Date: 8-19/8/86
Staff: Helen M.

Over the first couple of days, Tracy seemed to be into one of her attention seeking 'I'm not well', 'I've had a hard time', acts. On the second day of the holiday, I had to take her to one side and actually tell her what she was doing. Explain to her, that the Medvale children were away on their holiday – some of them for the first time ever abroad, and that Tracy's mood was spreading around the group, and not in a very nice way. That I wanted for her to enjoy the holiday in a positive way, so literally to snap out of it.

Tracy heard what I said and for the rest of the holiday, without exception, she was absolutely superb. She was helpful, she joined in everything that was happening, she really did, in her own words, thoroughly enjoy the holiday.

We arrived back on Tuesday 19th August, and I had Tracy taken home by Sandra, one of our staff here. She seemed in a very okay mood when she left, and thanked everybody for the holiday.

***

Going away on the Medvale holiday to France is just what I need. Surrounded by so many people that care about me at a time when I am physically and emotionally very low. The first couple of days are difficult, although I know I am not to speak about the abortion because of the other children, I want everyone to know that I have been through such an awful time. Helen pulls me up and makes me realise that the others don't need to be brought down by my crap, so I pull myself together and have such a wonderful, relaxing time.

To be able to relax and be myself around the people I consider to be my family is fantastic. They always make me feel like their big sister, a role that I enjoy living up to. Being able to show them that we can all get through our tough times and be strong, kind and helpful like the staff that care so much for us. The staff also show me a lot of respect and considering the crap I have thrown their way over the years, it makes me love and respect them even more.

Sandra takes me home after the holiday, back to my empty house. A home devoid of any positive emotions. As I hug her goodbye, I don't want to ever let go.

Chapter 26

1986 – Aged 16

Full Circle: The Third Fire

I spend the next few days in limbo, the emptiness I feel after spending time engulfed in the love of people that genuinely care about me is unbearable. There is nothing here, no love, no compassion and no care. Just emptiness and falseness that comes with years of trying to pretend that everything is okay. I know I can't live like this anymore but I also know that they will never let me leave. The only way I can escape this living hell is to kill them. I guess I've known all along that it would come to this, that I need to finish what I started and kill them before they have a chance to kill me.

***

Extract from Staff Communications Book
Date: 27/8/86
Staff: Helen M.

I arrived at work today to be told by my principal, Peter Jaynes, that he had received a telephone call from Peter Pain at 7.00am that morning to say that Tracy had set a fire outside of their bedroom in the very same manner and sport as she had previously done and she had run away. He and his wife had woken up to their bedroom being thick with smoke and he was in quite a disturbed state. Peter J had quite a chat with him and explained bits and pieces about children's behaviour and the reasons they need to do the things that they do, and he told Peter Pain that I would be in touch with him at some stage during the day.

At 8.15am that morning, Tracy apparently arrived at Medvale with her bags. She was dealt with by Peter Jaynes, who told her that she was to go back and talk to her Dad, and then I would see her at her home later on that day. Peter had already advised Peter Pain to contact the police and to report Tracy as missing.

***

It doesn't really take much planning, it is not something that I want or need to dwell on, it is just something that has to happen. I wake early and soak some tissues in turpentine that I found in the cupboard. My whole body shakes as I lay them carefully outside their bedroom door, terrified that I'll be caught before I have a chance to finish this. Again, I light the match in my room, convinced that the scratch of the match on the box will be enough to wake them from their sleep. I light the tissue and hurry down the stairs, not stopping to look back, I gather my bags and shut the front door as quietly as possible behind me.

I hope this time it works and it will put an end to this forever. I know they will lock me up but anything is better than living in the emptiness of that house, that family.

After sitting on the top of the Pentagon car park trying to make sense of what I have done, I make my way to Medvale because I don't know where else to go. They will make sure I'm locked away for what I have done, but I need to say goodbye to them. To let them know that it wasn't their fault.

Peter J answers the door and I am shocked when he refuses to let me in and tells me to go and speak to my father. Surely, I haven't failed again. I stumble away in complete shock. If it hasn't worked, then I am in so much trouble. I know I have to hide and spend time on the Lines and Victoria Gardens where I can be invisible for a while.

The day goes past in a daze. I can't focus on anything; my anger has turned to numbness, and I don't even have the energy to try to end my life. I move around the town so that I don't get caught and sleep at the train station where it is a little warmer than out in the open. Nobody bothers me and I make no effort to interact with anyone. I just want to be left alone.

***

Extract from Staff Communications Book
Date: 27/8/86
Staff: Helen M.

In the event Tracy never managed to get herself home, I spoke to her Dad after lunch when I had finished my meeting and he said that he had reported her missing to the police, but he hadn't had any word from them.

I spoke to Peter Pain on at least four occasions during the day. He was saying initially that he didn't feel he could have Tracy back and where did he go from here? Had she been exhibiting any sort of naughty behaviour i.e. staying out late, drinking, whatever, he felt he could cope with that, but once again she was actually endangering the families lives and he didn't know if he could cope with that.

I said to Peter that when Tracy is picked up it is very much down to him to collect her from the police station and take her home. He wanted me to be involved when he saw Tracy and I said I was okay with that but I would do it in their own home and not in Medvale. I told Peter that I could understand his feelings of concern etc. but what Tracy needed to happen this time was to be treated as a very naughty girl who was attention seeking.

In my opinion there were several reasons for Tracy's act this morning, the main one being that Peter informed me that she had been back in touch with Lloyds, who had not only not taken any notice of her exam results, but had actually offered her the job nonetheless. In essence, Tracy is a very insecure girl who tries to give the impression of being secure. She would be terrified of starting this job

256

and she would try to get out of it. I also felt that Tracy's defiance was in some way a method of getting, she felt, back to Medvale, which is why she turned up here.

By the end of the evening and my last conversation with Peter Pain, he was definitely devastated by what had happened, but he felt that if the police picked Tracy up he would have her back home and then I would see her with all of them there or he would see Tracy with me there. He said that he had been through her bedroom and he had found, he said 'sick' poems – I would call them sad poems. He actually read two of them to me over the phone and they would have been written on Monday.

They were very much geared around Tracy's holiday with Medvale. How she had really enjoyed it and they were in the vein of what it was like being surrounded by people who loved and cared for people. How she felt filled up with the warmth, the care, that she got from the staff at Medvale and how she wished that that could continue. How sad it was that she had nothing to go back to except loneliness and depression. The other poem was literally identical and obviously her father felt very upset by this as he feels now that he has failed her in some way.

***

I have felt so very down,
Since the moment, I came home.
Now I have my results as well,
It feels as though I am in hell.
I find it so hard to cope,
I see why people start on dope.
I won't do that I'll just cry,
And carry on wondering why?
It scares me to think like this,
What happened to our family bliss?

Tracy Pain Aged 16

257

On holiday was lots of love,
And all the things that I dream of.
But now that I am back at home,
Yet again I am all alone.
It's hard to change so suddenly,
From love and laughter to being lonely.

Tracy Pain Aged 16

***

Extract from Staff Communications Book
Date: 27/8/86
Staff: Helen M.

I have told Peter Pain that the reality of Tracy returning home to live, which is what they all wanted, was that he does work long hours, as does his wife, who works full time. Tracy's sister also works full time and because Tracy is at this moment unemployed, that means that she is left in the house all day long. Tracy is sixteen years old now and when she gets a job, she will be in the same position as the rest of the family, so I've told Peter Pain not to feel guilty because he shouldn't literally have to wet-nurse a sixteen-year-old and I felt sorry for the man tonight.

During the course of the early afternoon, although Tracy had been reported missing to Chatham Police, I contacted our Special Women's Unit at Rochester and spoke to Jill Best. Jill is fully aware of Tracy and her behaviour patterns and her suicidal tendencies etc. and Jill said that she would go round to Lacey's to check out if Tracy was there. Jill also promised that she would keep an eye out for Tracy and that if she managed to pick her up would take her to Chatham Police Station, where the police would contact Tracy's Dad, who would go round to pick her up and take her home and then Peter Pain would ring me here.

  Tracy was not at Lacey or Natasha's.

Extract from Staff Communications Book
Date: 28/8/86
Staff: Helen M.

Peter Pain arrived into Medvale at 10.20am in a very irate mood. He wanted to know why he hadn't been contacted yesterday when Tracy arrived on the doorstep at Medvale. I explained to him that the course of action that was taken was the appropriate one for Tracy. At some stage in her life, she has got to be able to accept that she is responsible for her own actions. She clearly came back to Medvale seeking a haven here to escape from what she had actually done at home and it would have been very detrimental to Tracy if she had been welcomed into Medvale for a period of time.

  I also pointed out to Peter Pain that as he is very fully aware, we deal with quite severely emotionally disturbed youngsters here and it would have also had a very detrimental effect on them had Tracy been allowed to be present here with all her bags and baggage.

  Peter stayed at Medvale until about midday. He was obviously having a lot of guilt feelings about this recent incident at home, feelings that he failed Tracy, etc., etc. He was also pressured to some degree by his new wife, Carole, who had been quite understandably frightened by the instance of the fire setting at home by Tracy. She was clearly saying that she didn't feel that Tracy should go home and Peter Pain was saying things like, 'I feel that I should maybe report her to the police for a charge of arson and then she may get locked up in borstal for six months which would do her good.'

  I pointed out very clearly to him that this would not be good for Tracy to be locked away; it wouldn't be good at all. Ultimately, if we can work around it to some degree whereby he can see his way clear to having her back home, this is what Tracy would benefit from. If not, then we would probably have to look at independent living for her, which, in my opinion, she is no way ready to cope with.

I actually had a reversed charge call from Tracy, from the Medway towns. Tracy was very low and depressed and sounded quite devastated and the thing she wanted me to hear very clearly was that she was not going back home. She wouldn't give any reasons on the telephone and she said that she was moving around the Medway towns but she had slept rough last night and that if I sent anybody to look for her she would just keep moving and she would move out. I agreed to meet her at 2.45pm at C & A in Chatham and she has said that she will be there providing I am on my own.

I did contact Tracy's Dad, taking into account where he was at emotionally this morning with worry, etc. and told him that Tracy had made contact. I told him that I was meeting her outside C & A but that I would be bringing her home and requested that he left work to make sure that he was home at my expected time of arrival at his house, which he agreed to.

***

Tracy was duly waiting outside C & A when I arrived. She looked absolutely shocking. We went and had a cup of tea in Bowketts and she talked a little bit about why she did what she did. Unfortunately, she was back onto the same kick that she wanted to kill her father. Her reasons for this were that she thinks things weren't working out at home but that they were never going to work out, and she didn't know how to resolve it other than to get rid the lot of them. She seemed very much back to where she was at a long time ago in Medvale, and therefore I was very concerned about her.

I told Tracy that the person she needed to be talking to, was her father. She was clearly terrified about this but

260

nonetheless I told her that I had spoken to her father telling him that she had made contact and arranging that we would go round there for 2.45pm and he would be home and waiting for us.

When we arrived, Peter Pain was very angry indeed. He made it quite clear to Tracy that he couldn't understand why she had done what she did. He said that unlike other times he had had no indication that things were going wrong; she'd been a model child, and I quote, from the time she moved back in with him.

It was around this point that I suggested to Peter Pain that it might be a good idea if he called Carole home because I felt very much that she had been involved in the fire; she had been in the bedroom after all, and she should be involved in the discussion too. He was very happy about this and she arrived home within twenty minutes.

During the course of her arriving home, I actually went upstairs to look at the damage the fire had caused and I've got to admit that I was quite shocked at the extent of it. It was a very serious fire indeed and although we talked lightly about it initially, there was no way that it would not have actually set the whole house going had they not found it.

Tracy, by this time, had gone into one of her hard moods – 'couldn't care less' – and was really being very non-committal or downright rude to her father when he was talking to her about reasons. She said quite clearly that she intended to murder him. She didn't give any reasons apart from the fact that he didn't love her, had never loved her, has never been able to show any affection for her, etc., etc.

When her father pointed out to her that Carole had been nothing but kindness itself to Tracy and hadn't she considered the fact that Carole would have been hurt in the fire too, Tracy agreed that Yes, Carole had been good to her and, Yes, she had considered the fact that she could have been hurt in the fire, but that was just tough; she was in the same room as him and that was the way it was.

Peter Pain was saying that he couldn't have Tracy there because he couldn't put the rest of his family at risk. His wife was saying that she would go along if Peter said he wanted his daughter home – she would accept this but she told Tracy quite clearly that if she did return home to live that she, Carole, would never sleep again at night. It was quite clear that the woman was terrified by what had happened. She was puzzled too and was in a very nervous state throughout the whole interview.

***

The next day I make contact with Helen; she has got to understand that I can't go back there. I agree to meet her and we talk over a cup of tea. She is calm and kind and seems to understand, she says she cares but she still doesn't get it. She wants me to go home, to work this out. *What bit of me trying to kill them did she miss?* I hate them and I will never live there again.

She takes me home and I think the barrage of abuse thrown at me by my father shocks her. I can't do this, he hates me and has every reason to hate me. Carole comes home and makes it clear that she doesn't want me either, so Helen takes me away with her. The relief of not having to stay there is huge and, although I have no idea what will happen to me now, at least I have got out of there alive.

Helen is worried, I can see it on her face and I can hear it in her voice. She doesn't know what will happen to me now. Children are not allowed to go back to Medvale, I have always known that, but it upsets me that Helen is so concerned. Honestly, anywhere is better than going home, I just wish she understood that. I withdraw into myself, not sure what I am to do now.

***

Tracy clearly stated that she didn't want to stay there and the end result was that I rang Medvale and spoke to my Principal, Peter Jaynes. He presumably contacted someone in the Area Manager line i.e. Pat Donlan, who agreed that if all else failed, then for that night anyhow, Tracy would come home with me.

Tracy spent the night at my home and first thing next morning I spent a lot of time trying to secure her some sort of a place i.e. sheltered lodgings. It soon became very clear that there were no places available anywhere and the end result was going to be that Tracy would have to go to Glebelands. Before this decision was made, I had contact with my Principal, Peter Jaynes, who told me he had made the decision to re-admit Tracy to Medvale. I agreed with his decision because we actually had a new admission pending, so I wouldn't actually bring Tracy back into the building until as late as I possibly could that evening and I did this at 8 pm.

During the course of the day, Tracy was very nervous indeed, very tense, very anxious and very depressed. She was just with me – that's all I can say. She was with me but barely. I was relieved that she was coming back into Medvale. I wouldn't have wished her to be anywhere else because of Tracy's suicidal tendencies; I would have been extremely worried had she gone anywhere else in the state she was in at the time.

***

I am shocked when Helen takes me home with her and even though it is only for the night while they find me somewhere, I can't believe that she can still be so kind to me when I have let her down so badly. The fact that after everything I have done she trusts me in her house, with her family, I would never have imagined this could happen to me.

I remain withdrawn from events; for my own sanity I can't let myself be in the present, waiting for the inevitable trip to a secure unit. The only safe place I know is the place I go to in my mind. There I drift in and out of events and conversations, taking part but not engaging.

***

Extract from Staff Communications Book
Date: 28/8/86
Staff: Helen M.

Tracy was very touched. I suppose that's the word to use, when I told her that she would be coming back to Medvale. She was also concerned that it wouldn't upset the children in residence there and she was clearly aware that it is not one of our policies to re-admit ever, to Medvale.

When we arrived at Medvale she went upstairs straight away with Matilda and me, the girl she is sharing rooms with, and we got her bed-space ready. From that point, she settled quite well.

***

The day goes in a blur and I don't quite comprehend what Helen is saying to me at first.

They are going to let me go back to Medvale.

Helen is relieved. I am numb. I wasn't expecting this. I can't believe they are giving me this chance. I know now that I will never ever let them down again. I don't deserve this and I know Helen has put her neck on the line to make this happen. Coming back from this won't be easy, but if she can trust me to do the right thing, I will make sure that it is a decision she will never regret.

Chapter 27

1986 – Aged 16

A Place of Safety: A Home of My Own

Extract from Staff Communications Book
Date: 3/9/86
Staff: Helen M.

We held a statutory review on Wednesday 3rd September. It was a very short review, mainly because she was in no fit state to contribute anything and until some more work has been done with her, we didn't have a lot to offer to the review either. It was decided that as well as my working Tracy, Peter Jaynes would join me and it is his opinion that Tracy is stuck somewhere at the age of fourteen to fourteen and a half years old. We will be looking at reasons for what has happened and certainly Tracy will be with us until we review her again in November. Tracy has got a job in Lloyds and she will be starting there on 22nd September.

Her father rang Medvale once – this was the first contact that he made since I took Tracy from the home. Prior to that, he had no knowledge of where she was. Presumably, he thought she was with me somewhere; however, he didn't even ring to ask after Tracy's welfare. He rang to say that some clothes she had ordered from her sister's catalogue had arrived and she now owed her sister thirty-five pounds odd.

***

Being back at Medvale is like coming home. I feel relieved and although my mind is still in turmoil over recent events, being back here gives me space and safety to work through how I'm feeling. Luckily, there is no pressure for me to see my father and for that I'm grateful; at last I feel that they are listening to me about how he makes me feel. I feel I've grown up a lot since I left but because I've been allowed to stay in touch during my time away, coming home here seems so natural. I try hard to be a big sister to the others and not to involve them in the crap that has gone on in my life. I want them to know that there is a way forward and with Medvale's help they can get through their difficulties.

I am encouraged and supported to start work, with Helen and Peter J coming to my works welcome meeting, acting like my parents and making me feel like everyone else. They seem so proud of me and in return, I'm so grateful for what they have done for me.

***

Extract from Staff Communications Book
Date: 11/9/86
Staff: Helen M.

Tracy asked me if she could rescue her gerbils from home and bring them here, to which I have agreed.

Extract from Staff Communications Book
Date: 14/9/86
Staff: Rita W.

Peter Pain arrived at 7.30pm. He and Tracy were both very strained and he wasn't here more than five minutes. Apparently, he had cleaned the gerbils out and discovered they had been eating each other. Tracy looked them over with concern. She appeared very distant at times tonight.

Extract from Staff Communications Book
Date: 25/9/86
Staff: Mark C.

Tracy came down at 8.30am and seemed a bit depressed. She talked a lot about her family – all negative. Obviously, her father's visit yesterday unsettled her.

Staff: Andy R.

Tracy was very lethargic and white faced today, looking less together and in control of herself than when she first came in.

Extract from Staff Communications Book
Date: 20/10/86
Staff: Helen M.

Tracy was seen by Peter and me to discuss the fire incident and where we go from here.

Extract from Staff Communications Book
Date: 21/10/86
Staff: Helen M.

Peter and I sat down with Tracy. To date she'd settled very well into her job placement at Lloyds and is hoping that it will be made permanent sometime after Christmas. There had been no contact with her father at home until last week when Tracy had contact with her sister regarding going out socially with her. She actually had a brief word with her father. He wanted Tracy to go and visit the family in Somerset, an offer that Tracy declined.

I had to go round to Peter Pain's home to collect some of Tracy's clothing, as she had no winter clothing with her. I found him very, very angry and withdrawn from me in particular. He only assisted me with moving Tracy's multitude of stuff when I asked him to. His wife didn't

*show herself and Debbie, who did appear very briefly, was
very withdrawn. The atmosphere could have been about a
row within the family home, I don't know, but the
atmosphere was pretty dreadful.*

*Peter Pain didn't ask how Tracy was doing, didn't ask
to see her, he didn't ask anything – he merely got her stuff
together with me and I drove away.*

Extract from Staff Communications Book
Date: 24/10/86
Staff: Rita W.

*Tracy's sister Debbie is getting engaged and Tracy is
delighted, talking about how proud she is of her sister
because she has managed to cope at home although she
hates it, and how wonderful it will be when Debbie can get
out of that house. She talked about how they never talked
to each other at home and recounted how her sister and
step-Mum didn't know she was returning home to live till
three days after the review decision was taken. Dad just
wouldn't tell them. Debbie didn't even know it was in the
air.*

Extract from original Care File
Date: 17/3/87
Staff: Helen M.
Child Care Review: 17/3/87

*Prior to her last review on 3/9/86, she had been re-
admitted to Medvale due to her being made homeless by
her father after she had set fire to the family home again.
Tracy has now been back at Medvale for six months and
she has settled back in very well indeed. When seen by
Helen Mills and Peter Jaynes regarding the fire, Tracy
said that her reason for causing it was that she desperately
wanted to get out of the home. She claimed that she had
made a mistake in returning home to live and there was no
way it could work out. She felt she wouldn't be allowed to*

268

leave under normal circumstances, hence the fire.

Tracy's physical appearance since being back at Medvale has been very good indeed. She takes care of herself and of her clothes. Her behaviour has been very good. She is very much treated as an older member of the group here, for example, she has her own room and her own front door key.

Tracy's progress since she's been back in Medvale has been quite marked. She was in a mess when she came back in but since then has seemed to be able to move herself on her problems. It appears to be that Tracy is able to cope better away from her father's home.

During my discussion with Tracy recently she has made it quite clear that she would like to move into independent living at some stage. The review decided that Tracy would move out of Medvale by the end of May.

***

So I am allowed to move into my own place at last. I have waited for this day for so long, a chance to prove that I can look after myself, to be the grown up I have felt I have always been. I feel ready and although a little nervous I know this is the right decision for me. I have been collecting things for the past two years that I will need when I move, so I have my kettle, iron and other essentials. Helen takes me shopping to get food essentials and the last things that I will need. This really is the end of an era. I will never be returning to Medvale other than as a guest for tea, which Peter J assures me I am welcome to do. Medvale really is my family home and I love them with all my heart.

My new place is good. I have a large room to myself and I'm allowed to use the landlord and landlady's front room, kitchen and bathroom. It is a little bit of a weird set up with the landlady being very religious and the landlord being someone she met as a prison visitor. He tells me he has done fifteen years in a psychiatric prison. I don't ask what for but shun his lecherous advances as he seems to have no qualms about groping me when his wife is in the next room. On the whole, they let me live my life and I leave them to theirs.

My menagerie increases, and my two gerbils are joined by mice, hamsters and a rat called Richie. Apart from work, Richie comes everywhere with me, and is very popular in the pubs I drink in. He manages to get me barred a couple of times as he has a passion for vodka, and as I don't drink it, he visits other people's tables to get some, which doesn't always go down too well with the other patrons.

***

Extract from Staff Communications Book
Date: 2/5/87
Staff: Helen M.

Tracy moved into her bedsit on Friday 1st May at Cecil Road, Rochester. Being Tracy the usual 999 boxes and cases etc. had to be moved. All the children in the house helped to load the car, which took four journeys. Tracy was very excited but also sad, but I left her well settled, having made up her bed, etc., etc., and she was going to spend the evening unpacking more stuff and walking back to Medvale later that evening.

I came in early this morning and moved Tracy into her bedsit. Before we took the last of her belongings round, we went shopping at Safeway's and made sure that Tracy had enough food to last her, stocked her up with all the basic things, etc. Tracy was a bit down but managed to brighten up by the time I left her. She was trying to explain to me that she was ready to live independently but was sad to be leaving Medvale.

I reminded Tracy, as did Peter when she left the house, that we were only up the road and Peter was saying to her that he didn't expect to have to chase after her, but she can come up here when she wants to, quite literally. Tracy was saying to me in the car on the way that she thought it was very sweet of Peter, because it made her feel like this was still her home. That she could come back to it, without having to wait for an invite and she made the parallel of having to be invited to her father's house.

Extract from Staff Communications Book
Date: 9/5/87
Staff: Helen M.

Tracy visited tonight and had tea with the rest of the group and us. There was a lot of affection going on between her and the children. Quite clearly they see Tracy as an older sister who has moved on because she is older and they are all eager to hear how she is doing and anxious to hear that she is settling well etc. Tracy was very mature around the group and I was very pleased with her. She said that work is great and everything is going fine at the bedsit.

Extract from Staff Communications Book
Date: 5/9/87
Staff: Helen M.

Tracy visited for the barbeque and seemed very well indeed. In the preceding six weeks, I have had weekly contact with her by phone. All is going well with work and she has finally been offered a full-time job.

She has introduced me to Dean (her new boyfriend). He seems a pleasant nineteen-year old who has come from a stable family background. He clearly thinks the world of Tracy.

***

Helen keeps up regular visits and I'm allowed to visit Medvale and treat it as I would my family home. I'm always very careful not to bring my troubles to their door.

271

I need to do this on my own and I never want them to feel that I have let them down, which means showing no weakness.

After a few months I meet a lad called Dean at my friend's house. I give him all my diaries to read, as I know he will need to know everything about me if we are ever to make a commitment to each other. It doesn't faze him and within a week we move in together. A whirlwind romance, but one that is to change my world forever.

***

Extract from Staff Communications Book
Date: 9/9/87
Staff: Helen M.

I visited Tracy at her new address, in Strood. She moved there on the 22nd August. She is sharing a house with Dean and two other girls at a much cheaper rent than her bedsit. She had a full consultation with me before the move was made. Tracy has her own room, the two girls share a room and Dean has his own room.

It is a lovely house, very clean and in a good state of repair. Tracy and her housemates made me feel very welcome.

Tracy has a good relationship with Dean's parents, who live in Gravesend. Dean wants Tracy to get engaged. He has already bought her a ring but she will not make it official for a while yet and says she does not want to get married for at least another two years. She seemed in a very good state of mind and there are no problems.

Extract from Staff Communications Book
Date: 19/11/87
Staff: Helen M.

When Tracy arrived with Dean, we had tried to make an engagement tea for her. The children had baked a cake, we bought a bottle of bubbly, and she had a few presents to open. I find Tracy in a very mature coping frame of mind these days. She has now got a full-time job in Lloyds Insurance. She keeps regular contact with her mother, who seems to approve of her relationship and engagement to Dean. She sees her father periodically, who wasn't too pleased with the fact of Dean being on the scene, but seems to be more accepting now. Dean himself is a very nice lad. He quite clearly idolises Tracy and looks after her very well indeed. I found no problems with Tracy, and will actually be looking to closing her case in January.

***

Extract from original Care File
Date: 25/1/88
Staff: Peter J.

CLOSING SUMMARY

TRACY PAIN

Tracy now resides at 18 Cedar Road, Strood, with her boyfriend, Dean.

She appears to be a normal, well-adjusted eighteen-year-old girl, holding down a steady job with Lloyds Insurance.

There seems to be little need to continue any social work support beyond normal contact between Tracy and Medvale. Great credit has to be given to Tracy for the way she has used her care episode following all the problems she has had with her family and the seemingly impossible task suggested by previous social work agencies prior to her contact with Medvale, that she is today a competent member of society. The work done by Medvale and

Tracy's social worker, Mrs Helen Mills, also deserves credit.

CASE CLOSED

Epilogue

So this has been my story of how a staff team's total commitment and one woman's unconditional love for me took a psychopathic child and kept her alive, taught her to love and respect others by showing her love and care which helped her become a confident and successful young woman. I could never have achieved everything I have without them; I am under no illusion that without Medvale I would be dead or locked up.

Today I am a forty-six-year-old mother of seven, with four birth children and three adopted children. I have been a foster carer for over twenty years and have recently completed a BSc Psychology honours degree. I married Dean back in 1990 and we have now been married for twenty-five years.

Life, since my time in Medvale, hasn't been easy, our journeys never are. The strength that Medvale gave me has carried me through the toughest of times; through the losses I have suffered and the challenge to live as an acceptable member of society. To put behind me the sex, drugs and need to hurt those close to me and focus on being the best mum and wife that I can be, has been a challenge that I will share another day. I am still in touch with members of staff from Medvale now, their love still gives me the strength I need to continue my journey through life.

For every person out there that works with children I have a message and that message is simple. Don't ever underestimate how important it is to really care for a child, to totally commit to a child as you would your own. Your love can make the difference between life and death, between surviving and living.

As a foster carer I have heard many carers write off children as being too old to help. I was 14 years old when Helen saw through everything to reach the little girl inside of me, grabbed her and held on to her through the darkest of times. Refusing to let go whatever was thrown at her.

Helen kept that little girl alive, gave her strength and helped her to grow. I don't think I will ever understand how or why, but I will always be indebted to her and to all the staff at Medvale that helped to make it happen.

Interestingly when I went on my own personal journey of self-discovery as part of my studies I found that little girl inside of me, the little girl that cries so loud but only I can hear her. Without making a connection I called her 'Helen' as Helen is my middle name and the name my Mum chose for me. Finding 'Helen' helped me realise that at that point in my life I had lost touch with Helen from Medvale although she had always been there in the background and was very much a major part of life in my head. The power of the subconscious at work, I needed Helen at that time so much so that my subconscious led me to the little girl she saved so long ago. It wasn't until I met back up with Helen that I realised, by trying to prove how strong I was, how distant I had become. A mistake that I hope I never make again. Finding Helen was and always will be the best thing that ever happened to me.